China's Stealth Fighter

China's Stealth Fighter

The J-20 'Mighty Dragon' and
the Growing Challenge to
Western Air Dominance

Abraham Abrams

AIR WORLD

First published in Great Britain in 2024 by
Pen & Sword Military
An imprint of
Pen & Sword Books Ltd
Yorkshire - Philadelphia

ISBN 978 1 03610 550 1

Typeset in INDIA by IMPEC eSolutions
Printed and bound in the England by CPI Group (UK) Ltd, Croydon, CR0 4YY

Pen & Sword Books Ltd. incorporates the Imprints of Pen & Sword Archaeology,
Atlas, Aviation, Battleground, Discovery, Family History, History, Maritime,
Military, Naval, Politics, Railways, Select, Transport, True Crime, Fiction,
Frontline Books, Leo Cooper, Praetorian Press, Seaforth Publishing,
Wharncliffe, White Owl and After the Battle.

For a complete list of Pen & Sword titles please contact

PEN & SWORD BOOKS LIMITED
47 Church Street, Barnsley, South Yorkshire, S70 2AS, England
E-mail: enquiries@pen-and-sword.co.uk
Website: www.pen-and-sword.co.uk

or

PEN AND SWORD BOOKS
1950 Lawrence Rd, Havertown, PA 19083, USA
E-mail: uspen-and-sword@casematepublishers.com
Website: www.penandswordbooks.com

Contents

Abbreviations

AESA	active electronically scanned array
AEW	airborne early warning
AEW&C	airborne early warning and control
AI	artificial intelligence
CCTV	China Central Television
CMC	Central Military Commission
EOTS	Electro-Optical Targeting System
HMD	helmet mounted display
IISS	International Institute for Strategic Studies
IRST	infra-red search and track
ML	machine learning
NATO	North Atlantic Treaty Organization
NDIA	National Defence Industrial Association
NGAD	Next Generation Air Dominance
PACAF	Pacific Air Forces (United States)
PESA	passive electronically scanned array
PLA	People's Liberation Army
PLAAF	People's Liberation Army Air Force
R&D	research and development
RDA	research, development and acquisition
RoC	Republic of China
RoCAF	Republic of China Air Force
UAV	unmanned aerial vehicle
U.S.	United States
USAF	United States Air Force
USSR	Union of Soviet and Socialist Republics

Chapter One

Origins: The Cold War and China's Historic Need for Air Superiority

Air War Over Korea

The crucible that first forged Chinese combat aviation into a jet age power, and the struggle that shaped its focus on air superiority and formed the core of its historical memory, the Korean War's legacy has deeply influenced China's twenty-first century military modernisation efforts and in particular its J-20 fighter program. The key importance attributed to air power and particularly defensive air superiority today by the armed forces of the People's Republic of China, the People's Liberation Army (PLA), is partly a legacy of its pivotal role in Korea where the new republic fought what is to date its only protracted war against state adversaries. The conflict forced the young People's Liberation Army Air Force (PLAAF), which had barely begun training its first jet fighter pilots, to meet the challenge of American and Western air power, and would significantly influence the service's strategic and doctrinal thinking, structure, performance, and capabilities.

On 25 June 1950, the Chinese leadership had been startled upon hearing that war had broken out between North and South Korea,[1] with Beijing having at that time been in the process of downsizing its armed forces.[2] When a U.S.-led coalition fighting under the banner of the United Nations intervened days later to repel North Korean advances into the Western-aligned South, and proceeded in September to launch a full-scale invasion of North Korea, the Chinese PLAAF fielded just a single operational fighter unit. The infant 4th Mixed Air Brigade deployed just thirty-eight modern MiG-15 jets, and had been established just three months prior in June. Training for the brigade's 126 pilots had only begun in July, the month after the war began, and by the end of September, as Chinese intervention in Korea appeared increasingly inevitable, thirty-one of them had only just had their first solo flights in the MiG-15. Ten weeks of operational training commenced with support from the Soviet 106th Fighter Aviation Division on 1 October, just a day after U.S. National Security Council policy paper NSC 68 received White House approval facilitating a more than tripling of the Pentagon budget, initiation of covert operations against, and opening of dozens of airbases surrounding China and the USSR. By that time Western forces in Korea numbered in the hundreds of thousands, and fought alongside South Korean forces under direct American command.

The controversial decision to invade North Korea, rather than restoring the pre-war division between the two Korean states, was seen to considerably raise the risk of China being forced into the war, and as coalition forces rapidly approached Chinese borders Beijing perceived an imminent threat. The U.S. had contributed tens of thousands of personnel and billions of dollars in aid to fighting the PLA in the Chinese Civil War that had ended just eight months before war in Korea began,[3] and the coalition's Supreme Commander General Douglas MacArthur, alongside many in the Pentagon and State Department, strongly advocated using the momentum from the Korean conflict to take offensive action against China.[4] As China deployed ground units to create a buffer zone protecting key border infrastructure on the Sino-Korean border, the first clash between Chinese personnel and advancing coalition forces on North Korean soil occurred on 21 October. Within a month hostilities had escalated into large scale battles involving tens of thousands of personnel from both sides, with all fighting contained to Korean territory.[5]

From the outset the lack of a viable air force had been a central factor in Beijing's reluctance to deploy forces to Korea despite the perceived imminent threat posed by advancing Western forces under General MacArthur's Command.[6] The devastation which American air power had wrought on North Korean forces in the three months before Chinese intervention, targeting logistics to starve frontline units of supplies as well as attacking army formations themselves, was overwhelmingly evident. It was a leading factor preventing the North from securing a rapid victory, and quickly proved a serious hindrance to Chinese ground forces' operations as well.

American air superiority left Chinese units vulnerable to attack and demoralized by the tension of 'living and hiding like hunted animals,' as some on the front described it, in constant fear of air strikes.[7] North Korean personnel too, despite their fearless reputation, were traumatised with 'aircraft fright' according to their officers due to the toll American jets took strafing, bombing and drenching them with napalm.[8] With Chinese forces relying on superior night fighting skills to compensate for their vast disadvantages in firepower, and often in numbers, American aircraft took to flying back and forth through the night dropping parachute flares exposing their units for minutes at a time – enough to cause tremendous casualties.[9] Control of the air allowed American casualties to further be reduced with rapid evacuation of the wounded to Japan,[10] where the Chinese could mount no similar extraction operations for their own personnel.

Beyond direct attacks on the frontlines, by early 1951 thirty to forty per cent of Chinese supplies were being destroyed in transit by American air interdiction.[11] Approximately 190,000 bombs were dropped on North Korea's railways alone – one bomb for every seven meters of rail line – with the air campaign paralysing both combat and logistics efforts in the daytime.[12] Failing supply lines on multiple occasions cut Chinese and North Korean momentum, with frontline units running out of food and ammunition when on the verge of overwhelming coalition forces and thus forced to suspend their advances.[13] Near the end of the conflict on 10 June 1953, for example, as a last minute Chinese offensive took hill after hill on the frontlines striking South Korean units from all sides, coalition forces were able to respond with massive air strikes – a record 2,143 sorties on one day – to completely halt the advance.[14]

Where war in Korea demonstrated the tremendous costs which enemy air superiority could impose, it also spurred the rise of the Chinese PLAAF, which expanded during the conflict from a negligible fighting strength into the world's third largest air service – and one which proved highly capable against incredible odds. By the time the PLAAF began to conduct significant combat operations in Korea in November 1951 the service had formed three combat-ready MiG-15 Fighter Air Divisions, with four more becoming operational in early 1952. By the end of May all divisions had been cycled through Korea providing invaluable combat experience, and in August the service began to receive new enhanced MiG-15bis fighters.

The MiG-15 was the PLAAF's first fighter widely deployed for combat operations, and the vast majority of the service's most formative experiences in fighter aviation in its first two decades would be gained flying the aircraft and its close derivative the MiG-17. The fighter had become operational in the Soviet Union in June 1949, less than two years after its first flight and just twelve months before the Korean War began. As the first Soviet combat jet considered a world leader in its performance it remains one of the greatest achievements in Russian military aviation history. Having witnessed Western nuclear and incendiary bombings levelling sixty-nine Japanese cities in 1945, which in larger strikes could kill over 100,000 residents within hours, the USSR's new fighter was developed primarily for defence against such attacks to prevent population centres across the Soviet Union from enduring similar fates. The perceived imminence of this threat made the MiG-15 a priority program. As columnist Alfred Friendly observed in 1952: 'The MIG-15 is an interceptor with a short range, 160 miles (260km), and is not an offensive fighter,' with deployments reflecting this.[15] In Eastern Germany, on the tensest frontline between Soviet and Western forces, airfields were built with runways that 'could handle fighters, but were not strong enough to take bombers,' forming 'a network of defensive airstrips ... to make a fighter screen against either atom bombers or conventional bombers.'[16]

U.S. Director of Central Intelligence and Second Air Force Chief of Staff General Hoyt Vandenburg conceded after the first air-to-air engagements with MiG-15s in Korea: 'Soviet technicians have mastered the design and production problems of extremely high-speed aircraft to a degree which equals and in some respects excels all that we are able to demonstrate in warfare at the present time.'[17] United States Air Force (USAF) Lieutenant Colonel Earl J. McGill, an expert and author on the air war in Korea, concluded: 'The aircraft proved reliable, easily maintained, and more than capable of beating the best the West put up against it.'[18] Regarding its ability to tackle the Western world's top fighter the American F-86 Sabre, he added that 'the MiG's superior performance left the 86s far behind' and that 'the MiG-15 was a machine well ahead of its day.'[19]

Upon being deployed for operations over Korea the MiG-15 left all Western fighters entirely obsolete other than the F-86 – an aircraft which formed only a very small portion of American units. The Sabre had a similar swept wing design to the MiG-15, and was rushed into production on a larger scale when it became apparent that the MiG's performance had left it the only viable fighter class in the Western world. Even the F-86, however, faced a steep performance disadvantage. The MiG-15bis' 0.60:1 thrust/weight ratio was some thirty per cent better than the Sabre's, while its more powerful VK-1A engine allowed it to sustain a turn longer and losing less altitude and to quickly climb back to heights at which it was immune to any Western fighter's attacks. The MiG's service ceiling was around 1,000m higher, and on early variants in particular lighter wing loadings provided a tighter and faster turn rate. MiG pilots frequently waited at high 'perch' altitudes beyond reach before Western fighters reached the area, and used their altitude advantage to dictate the time, place and approach angle at which engagements were initiated. MiGs often made diving firing passes before climbing fast to return to high altitude and repeating this, with Western fighters' much slower climb rates meaning they could not keep up. The MiG-15's superior climb rate on many occasions saved its pilots.[20]

Where Chinese personnel were far less well armed on the ground, but considered hardier and more skilful fighters,[21] in the air much the opposite was true with the MiG-15 providing superiority which America's vast pool of more skilled and experienced Second World War veteran pilots did much to compensate for. F-86 pilots included not only Americans but also Canadian and British exchange pilots, with their access to anti-gravity suits helping them to endure extreme manoeuvres to further balance against the MiG-15's performance advantages. The Chinese PLAAF by contrast had few trained pilots, and those rushed into combat had often experienced just eighty hours in the air and as little as twenty in jet aircraft. General Wang Hai, who had flown under PLAAF 3rd Fighter Aviation Division in Korea, stated in his memoirs that the average PLA pilot had had under fifty-seven flying hours when sent into combat.[22] Had they not been sent into battle in fighters near unanimously considered the world's finest, this extreme lack of experience would have made the PLAAF almost totally ineffective, particularly in its first months of engagements.

The memoirs of Li Han, a Chinese pilot who fought in Korea, highlighted the discrepancies in experience with the adversary: 'We had a strong spirit even though our fighting experience was weak. We tried to engage them in combat but we knew that if we couldn't keep fighting, then we should just crash into them.' Another Air Force veteran recalled: 'Almost all of the Chinese pilots in the Korean war were "dare to die"... their spirits were so strong they were ready to die.'[23] Although the PLAAF was accompanied by North Korean and Soviet MiG-15 units, the former's scant numbers and the latter's prioritisation of guarding airfields in China itself, and thus their more limited flights over Korea, meant a heavy burden fell on the Chinese. Indeed, Soviet pilots' reluctance to operate in Korea led the military leadership to send pilots to Pyongyang and other Korean population centres to witness the massive civilian casualties from Western bombings in an effort to provide more motivation.[24]

Chinese air units began to play a significant role in the war from the second half of 1951, although due to their small numbers, operations were restricted to guarding the north-west corner of North Korea between the Chongchon and the Yalu rivers – an area key to ground units' logistical efforts. Limiting Western air operations by getting more fighters in the air and strengthening air defences had increasingly been seen as key to ensuring the ground campaign took a more favourable turn after the stalled Sino-Korean Spring Offensive in April–June 1951, as Chinese logistics had suffered tremendously from U.S.-led air attacks.[25]

New PLAAF pilots rushed through emergency months-long seven-day-a-week training courses began to become available for combat operations from mid-1951, leading to fast mounting successes. One of the most notable victories was won on 23 October 1951 at the Battle of Namsi when of nine B-29 strategic bombers deployed, MiG-15s shot down three and badly damaged five others – two of which would never fly again. Targeting bombers was the primary role of MiG-15 units over Korea, and this and other victories were sufficient to force B-29s and smaller B-26s to operate only at night from then on[26] – a feat it was noted German and Japanese air power had never come close to achieving.[27] American journalist I.F. Stone was among those to highlight that 'the Battle of Namsi and its aftermath represented a military, technological, and strategic setback of the first magnitude.'[28] By then coalition Supreme Commander General Matthew Ridgway noted that Chinese anti-aircraft artillery was also enjoying growing successes in downing B-29s in particular.[29] The bomber was a prime symbol of American power, and had gained a fierce reputation after conducting mass incendiary raids against dozens of Japanese cities and nuclear strikes on Hiroshima and Nagasaki.

Amid ongoing losses in the air, on 21 November the U.S. Director of Central Intelligence and Second Air Force Chief of Staff General Vandenburg stated: 'A significant and, by some standards, even sinister change has occurred ... Almost overnight China has become one of the major air powers of the world ... the air supremacy upon which we have relied in the past is now faced with a serious challenge.'[30] From September to December U.S.-led coalition forces lost 423 aircraft over North Korea compared to just 336 by their adversaries.[31] By the end of 1951 some American fliers in Korea considered enemy pilots to be as good as their peers.[32] As one F-86 pilot from the 4th Fighter Interceptor Group stated to this effect regarding who was piloting the MiGs and how well they were flown, 'for all we know there may be some ex-American World War Two fighter jockeys up there.'[33] The vast discrepancy in experience made this difficult to explain, other than that it was compensated for by superiority of the MiG-15 over Western aircraft.

Chinese and allied successes in the air continued into 1952, and in February America's greatest ace, F-86 pilot George A. Davis Jr., was shot down and killed by a Chinese-flown MiG. This had a serious impact on morale – as if the top pilot flying, by far the West's most capable fighter, could be lost in air-to-air combat then anyone could. Despite having downed fourteen enemy aircraft, Davis had written to his wife lamenting very high losses among pilots, stressing that 'things can't go on like they are' and that Soviet-built MiGs 'are so much better than the Sabres.'[34] In Tokyo on 2 February the U.S. Far East Air Forces reported the loss of fifty-two American aircraft in January which was the greatest one-month loss of the war, with a large portion of these shot down by MiG-15s and even larger numbers lost to increasingly capable air defences on the ground.[35]

As Americans introduced faster and more capable variants of the F-86 – the F-86E and F-86F – new and improved MiG-15bis* jets began to be fielded against them.[36] As *Associated Press* reporter Charles Hanley noted: 'More than ever it becomes a duel of technological advance and production capacity, as much as a test of pilot skills.'[37] The Chinese fleet was nevertheless overwhelmingly outnumbered, with Western fleets flying well over 1,000 sorties daily while Chinese and allied fighters flew little over 100.[38]

Although it outperformed the F-86 in fighter-on-fighter engagements, the MiG-15 had been primarily designed to neutralise enemy bombers with defence of key transportation lines and other ground targets being its main mission in Korea. The McGraw-Hill correspondent observed regarding its performance in such a role:

'The MiGs take off ... climb into the sun to high altitudes. There they are picked up by other radar-tracking equipment and vectored into attacking positions. They then press the attack home against our B-29 medium bombers in a high-speed downhill pass that is virtually impossible to stop ... MiGs coming downhill can't be headed off even if the Sabre pilots see them at maximum visibility. By the time the Sabres turn ninety degrees to meet the attack the MiGs pass and are on the bombers.'[39]

MiGs could target B-29s from well outside the bomber's defensive range, which was made possible by their cannons' greater range and impact power.

---

* In October 1952 the MiG-15 was surpassed by the MiG-17, which joined the Soviet Air Force after having been ordered into production at five factories 13 months prior. These were not deployed for operations in Korea.

Despite its very limited theatre of operations just 120km across the border, the successes of Chinese air power over Korea not only played a critical role in keeping supply lines open to support ground forces, but also had significant strategic implications far beyond the peninsula. As the *New York Times*' esteemed military editor Hanson Baldwin wrote in December 1951, the MiG-15 had 'forced some of our most ardent advocates of strategic bombing to take another good hard look at our prospects.' He stressed that the fact Soviet-built fighters could devastate American bomber units left the viability of Western bombing raids on major cities in serious question.[40]

Award winning journalist and expert on the Korean conflict, I.F. Stone, wrote regarding the consequences of the MiG's performance:

'It showed that the subsonic bombers on which the American military had depended for delivery of the atom bomb in a future war against Russia were indefensible against jet interceptors flying at or above the speed of sound ... America's famous atomic strategy had become obsolete ... The subsonic bomber proved obsolete over Korea and with it the foreign policy based upon the subsonic bomber. The atom bomb was still a "deterrent to aggression" from either side. It was no longer a threat with which either side could hope to dictate terms.'[41]

Writing for the *Washington Post*, Walter Lippmann was among those to reach the same conclusion.[42]

Western scholars would years later increasingly acknowledge that there was no 'walkover' in the skies of Korea, and that American pilots 'probably highly inflated' their victories.[43] While Western sources initially claimed kill ratios as high as 7:1 (enemies: friendlies), this was later revised to 2:1 – a close fight considering the vast discrepancy in experience and the nature of the MiG's primary targets, which were heavy bombers rather than fighters.[44] The Chinese claimed a victory ratio of 1:1.42 in air-to-air combat over Korea,[45] with other sources pointing to a 1:1.46 ratio in the eight months from September 1951 and a 1:1.42 ratio only after May 1952.[46]

In 1952, Chinese pilots reportedly engaged F-86s eighty-five times, winning twenty-four and losing twenty-seven with thirty-four engagements being stalemates. They downed at least one enemy and took no losses in nine engagements, shot down more enemies than they lost in fifteen engagements, and lost more than they killed in twenty-seven engagements.[47] Against other fighter classes than the F-86, Chinese MiG-15s that year won thirty and lost just two engagements with eight being tied, which was credible when considering the very limited capabilities of straight wing jets like the F-84.[48]

After Korea: China's Pressing Need for Air Superiority

During the Korean War the senior Chinese leadership deeply involved itself with the air force's development and personally took part in related negotiations with the Soviet Union. Throughout the war and through the first half of 1954 the PLAAF received sufficient Soviet equipment to outfit twenty-two air divisions – ten divisions' worth in 1951 and then one-and-one-half divisions' worth per month until mid-1954.[49] As the newest and by far the most technologically advanced branch of the PLA, with a state of the art and world-class inventory contrasting sharply with those of the ground forces or navy, the Air Force gained considerable prestige and was seen to symbolise the new People's Republic's aspirations to strength and modernisation. Where the performance of Chinese ground units against overwhelming disadvantages in firepower had been described by leading British military historians as 'triumph not merely for the prestige of Communism, but for that of an Asian army,'[50] the PLAAF's performance demonstrated that a country for a century derided as backward could now fight at a world-class level with highly complex weaponry.

The discrepancy between the state-of-the-art fighter fleet and the remainder of the military came in part because the PLAAF started from a clean slate in 1950, was relatively small, had great importance attached to it, and because the USSR was willing to provide its very latest weaponry. For the Soviets not only were fighters flying over northern Korea far more difficult for an enemy to capture for study, but demonstrating the MiG's prowess did much to ensure Soviet security as well as that of China. This was particularly vital since the Pentagon had been planning for possible nuclear strikes against Soviet cities from as early as 1945, with plans drafted that year involving dropping 204 nuclear bombs on sixty-six cities.[51] FBI archives revealed that Britain had persistently lobbied Washington to consider such attacks.[52] With the B-29 and similarly vulnerable B-36 responsible for delivering nuclear strikes, demonstrating the former's high vulnerability had significant strategic benefits.

The importance of air defence was also far from lost on the Chinese leadership, not only because enemy control of the skies had heavily shaped the course of the war against Beijing's favour, but also because of the sheer damage done across Korea by Western strategic bombing – for which China itself could be the target in the next war. Bombers targeted 'every means of communication, every installation, factory, city and village' in North Korea,[53] with journalist Robert Jackson reporting that B-29s were fully loaded 'to burn the selected cities from end to end.'[54] Assistant State Secretary Dean Rusk later elaborated that bombers would attack 'everything that moved in North Korea, every brick standing on top of another.'[55] European journalists observed that there were simply 'no more cities in North Korea ... my impression was that I am travelling on the moon, because there was only devastation.'[56] U.S. Air Force General Curtis LeMay reported regarding the air campaign: 'We burned down just about every city in North Korea and South Korea both ... we killed off over a million civilian Koreans and drove several million more from their homes.'[57] This was far from unprecedented, with the firebombing of sixty-seven

Japanese cities in 1945 having caused considerably more damage. One night of incendiary bombings on Tokyo alone killed around 120,000 people with some estimates being several times higher.[58] The lesson was not to be forgotten, with Chinese leader Chairman Mao Zedong's own son Mao Anying having himself been killed in a napalm attack by American aircraft in Korea.

Against this threat, which could be made even more potent with nuclear warheads, fielding of the most capable anti-aircraft capabilities possible became a priority for the PLA. During the Korean War the U.S. had on multiple occasions strongly considered using nuclear weapons against Chinese forces or population centers in China,[59] with Supreme Commander MacArthur persistently calling for nuclear strikes, including over a dozen on Chinese industrial centres,[60] while the Joint Chiefs of Staff repeatedly recommended nuclear attacks.[61] This led to authorisation being given to commanders to use nuclear weapons, deployments of nuclear-configured bombers to East Asia, and initiation of reconnaissance flights over airfields in north-east China to obtain targeting data for potential attacks.[62] Beijing was notified repeatedly that nuclear attacks remained an option, with the threat of nuclear war widely seen, including by the White House, to have been key to gaining multiple Chinese concessions during armistice negotiations.[63]

The Chinese leadership's interest in building a strong air arm was prominently addressed in the 1953 First Five-year Plan for the country's military development, which called for expanding the air force to 150 aviation regiments fielding more than 6,000 aircraft and the construction of 153 new airfields. Although this plan was revised to a more realistic schedule after the war, the PLAAF continued to be prioritised for funding throughout the 1950s.[64] China's air doctrine was closely based on that of the USSR with an overwhelming focus on air defence.

Another motivating factor for investment in the PLAAF was conflict with remnants of the forces of China's former ruling party the Guomindang, which from 1949 based themselves on Taiwan and surrounding islands. Guomindang forces were a first priority client for deliveries of the latest American hardware, including AIM-9 air-to-air missiles, F-101 supersonic fighters and multiple classes of surveillance aircraft such as the RF-84, RF-101, RB-57 and U-2, which frequently flew over mainland Chinese airspace as did U.S. operated aircraft.[65] Taiwan was further used as a base for U.S. operations against the mainland, including airdropping of paramilitary units for 'promoting domestic anti-government guerrilla operations' and operations to 'collect intelligence and possibly engage in sabotage and psychological warfare,' according to CIA reports.[66] This threat made the need for modern air defences all the more apparent, and the well-equipped PLAAF, armed with new Soviet S-75 air defence systems and MiG-17 and MiG-19 fighters, downed multiple Guomindang and American aircraft.[67] As U.S. intelligence reports concluded: 'What the penetration flights [over China] did accomplish was to motivate the PRC leadership to more quickly build an air force and create an effective air defence system.'[68] This was largely successful with the PLA according to U.S. reports fielding 'an air force that today ranks as one of the toughest to defeat,' as part of a highly potent multi-layered air defence network that left American aircraft highly vulnerable over Chinese airspace.[69]

Chinese and American fighters further clashed after 1965, when U.S. violations of southern Chinese airspace during offensive operations against North Vietnam increased significantly, leading Beijing to abandon its prior policy of only monitoring such violations. Within a year the PLAAF had reportedly shot down twelve and damaged four manned U.S. aircraft as well as downing twenty drones.[70] By then, however, the loss of Soviet support following the Sino-Soviet split had slowed PLAAF modernisation considerably. This would only worsen over the next twenty-five years, leaving China's fighter inventory entirely obsolete and two full generations behind the Soviets and Americans by the time the Cold War ended.

Chinese Military Aviation in the Cold War

Following the end of the Korean War the modernisation and expansion of the PLAAF tactical combat fleet centred around large acquisitions of Soviet aircraft, and following 750 regular MiG-15s delivered from early 1950, 1,500 MiG-15bis fighters were delivered from August 1952 into 1954. Some of these were assembled in China under the designation J-2. Amid massive transfers of technologies and industrial support to China, the Soviet Union also supported the production of jet fighters in the country with 1,250 MiG-17 fighters produced under license from 1955-1960 under the designation J-5. Fifty of the newer MiG-15UTI twin seat trainers delivered during the Korean War were supplemented by 125 more built under license from 1956 under the designation JJ-2. These were followed by the more capable MiG-19, which was produced in China as the J-6 from 1958 after the USSR supported the establishment of production lines and transferred associated technologies. The lack of access to more capable aircraft meant the class would remain in production until 1984, and continued to equip the large majority of PLAAF fighter units for years afterwards.

Fighter jets were only one of several areas where the Soviet Union comprehensively transferred technologies and full production lines to China, with others ranging from An-2 transports produced as the Y-5, Mi-4A helicopters produced as the Z-5, T-54 tanks produced as the Type 59, and S-75 air defence systems produced as the HQ-1. This came as part of what leading China scholars referred to as 'the largest planned transfer of technology in world history,' and allowed China's negligible technological and industrial bases to make tremendous and rapid advances in the 1950s in both the civilian and military sectors.[71] The technology transfers were so comprehensive that after the Sino-Soviet split in 1960 China was able to continue production and later improve on advanced Soviet aircraft and weapons designs domestically.

Where the new Soviet administration of Chairman Nikita Khrushchev oversaw the Sino-Soviet split, a second major setback to both Moscow and Beijing was a result of the former's strong de-emphasis on tactical assets, and particularly fighter aircraft, in the belief that they were largely irrelevant in the era of nuclear and missile warfare.[72] Top Soviet fighters retained their advantages over their Western counterparts into the 1960s, largely due to momentum from programs initiated before Khrushchev-era reforms, with U.S. analysts summarising the performances of the F-86's successors the F-100 and F-104's against their Soviet rivals: 'Both were thrashed ... over the Taiwan Straits and Vietnam.'[73] Indian Air Force MiG-21s similarly won overwhelming victories over Pakistani-flown F-104s in 1971 – their direct American counterparts.[74] Moving into the third generation of jet fighters from the mid-late 1960s, however, the Soviets began to lag behind in bringing new technologies to the field. The clearest example was the MiG-21, which entered service in 1959 but had no viable successor for over a decade until improved variants of the MiG-23 began to enter service in the mid-1970s. During this time clients ranging from North Korea and North Vietnam to Egypt and Syria suffered consequences of being unable to match the top American fighter of the third generation F-4D/E Phantom.[75]

While the Soviet tactical aviation industry was reinvigorated following Chairman Khrushchev's deposition in 1964, it took until the early 1980s and the introduction of fourth generation fighters for the advantage in the air to be regained. The MiG-31 interceptor commissioned in 1981 introduced the world's first, and for two decades the only, phased array radar built for air-to-air combat, as well as unmatched top and cruising speeds, an unmatched payload, and formidable space warfare capabilities allowing it to use a range of missiles well above the Armstrong Limit. The MiG-29 medium weight fighter commissioned from 1982, meanwhile, set the trend for widespread use of infrared search and tracking systems and introduced unrivalled manoeuvrability, the world's first high off boresight air-to-air missile attack capability enabled by helmet mounted sights, and an unmatched austere airfield capability optimising it for deployments near frontlines.[76]

It was the Su-27 Flanker heavyweight fighter, however, developed as a higher end counterpart to the MiG-29 and commissioned from 1984, which would epitomise Soviet leadership in tactical combat aviation in the superpower's final decade. A key requirement during development was for the Flanker to outperform the heavyweight F-15 Eagle, which had succeeded the F-4D/E and was by a significant margin the most capable fighter in any Western air force.[77] The Flanker's relative fuselage cross-section was twenty to twenty-five per cent less than on the F-15C and its lighter counterparts the F-16A and F/A-18,[78] while its blended body-fuselage layout generated greater lift with a smaller wing area and thereby reduced the total wetted area – saving structural weight and generating less drag.[79] It had a higher thrust/weight ratio than any Western fighter,[80] with its AL-31F engines putting out more thrust than those of any other fighter. Its integrated statically unstable configuration provided outstanding manoeuvrability allowing altitude changes unavailable to other fighters.[81] The resulting very significant discrepancy between what the Su-27 and Western fighters could do at low speeds, as demonstrated at multiple airshows,[†] raised widespread doubts about the ability of the F-15 and others to compete.[82]

Where the Soviet Union and the United States were competing neck-to-neck in a league of their own to field the top fourth generation fleets, and by 1980 both had fifth generation aircraft well

---

[†]   It was highlighted by a number of analysts that the Su-27 performed well at airshows with a full complement of air-to-air missiles while Western fighters, despite not performing with their missiles, still had much more modest flight performances. If they had it was expected that the flight performance discrepancy would have been far greater. (Gordon, Yefim, *Sukhoi Su-27*, Hinckley, Midland Publishing, 2007, p. 522.)

under development, China was still producing MiG-19 derived J-6 fighters that dated back to the mid-1950s and attempting to produce an indigenous derivative of the MiG-21. By the time the Cold War ended approximately seventy-five per cent of its fighter fleet was still comprised of J-6s, with the remainder split between older J-5s based on the MiG-17 that had first flown before the Korean War, and a small number of MiG-21 derived J-7 fighters. Although limited technologies acquired from Israel, France and the United States in the 1980s had provided some improvements in areas such as avionics and missiles, China's domestic R&D, combat aviation industry and the PLAAF's training and inventories were all decades behind the cutting edge.

China's position in tactical aviation began to recover only after the end of the Cold War when improving ties with the Soviet Union saw the beginnings of renewed cooperation and the first sale of combat assets in decades – a contract for twenty-four Su-27 fighters signed in December 1990 with an option for twenty-four more. While the USSR had not offered the Flanker abroad, instead pressing the PLA to accept the MiG-29, the need to gain export revenues and improve ties with Beijing, and the low possibility of the PLA compromising the technology with transfers to the West, led it to agree to the sale. China was the only country to ever receive Su-27s from the Soviet Union, with three delivered before the superpower disintegrated in December 1991, after which deliveries were completed by Russia within a year.

Upon receiving its first Su-27s, China became by far the lowest income country to field heavyweight fighters from the latest generation. While it could not afford a large fleet of such aircraft, a qualitative edge over the fleets of potential adversaries was highly prized and favoured over modernising more squadrons with cheaper fourth generation fighters like MiG-29s. The Flanker's unrivalled 4,000km endurance, designed for escort missions deep into British airspace from bases in Poland with a high degree of independence from ground control, combined with a powerful sensor suite and long range missiles allowed each unit to patrol large areas of Chinese airspace.[83] The proportion of the Su-27's internal capacity allocated to fuel carriage was greater than any other fighter, fifty per cent more than the F-15, and it had an unprecedentedly high mileage per gallon at all altitudes.[84] Specific fuel consumption, the ratio of the mass fuel consumption to the break power, was far lower than any Western rival – twenty-five per cent lower than the F-15 and forty per cent lower than the F-16.[85]

The Flanker was the world's first fighter with load-bearing airframe components made of high-strength titanium automatically arc-welded in a liquid medium; with structural components made of high-strength titanium sheets manufactured by automated dual-arc welding; and with welded titanium structural components advocated using new fixed-temperature annealing technology.[86] Tailslide manoeuvre showed a high level of tolerance to engine intake disturbances, and the fighter could achieve angles of attack far beyond any Western fighter and exceeding ninety degrees.[87] Between 1986 and 1988 the Su-27 had claimed a total of twenty-seven time-to-height and sustained altitude records.[88] Technologically, the Flanker was three decades ahead of anything the PLAAF had previously fielded, with nothing in its fleet being remotely comparable in endurance, situational awareness, manoeuvrability, weaponry, or any other metric of combat performance. Integration of the Flanker into the fleet thus provided critical experience in operating modern fighters, including major advances in beyond visual range combat capabilities and a much reduced reliance on ground control. For the PLAAF and its personnel, adapting to the entirely new way the Flanker allowed them to fight in the air, to the multi-generational leap which its new capabilities represented, and to operating a much more maintenance intensive aircraft three times the size of their former top fighter the J-7, was a daunting task.

When the Cold War ended the Su-27 was widely considered by both Russian and U.S. sources to be the most capable fighter operated by any air force in the world in terms of its air-to-air performance.[89] In 1995, head of the USAF Tactical Air Command General Joseph Rallston informed Congress regarding the deficiencies of the U.S. fleet in the face of the Flanker: 'We do not need an intelligence effort to realise the Su-27s ascendancy over the F-15 in agility and power.'[90] USAF Chief of Staff General Michael Ryan observed in 2002 that if pilot quality were equal Flanker could reliably outperform the F-15.[91] Project personnel working on the F-22 fifth generation fighter similarly stated: 'The Russians are hot fighter jocks and the MiG-29 and Su-27 are hotter than anything we have in our inventory,' referring to the latter as 'the top gun at the moment.'[92]

Perceptions of the Flanker's primacy were strengthened by the results of simulated air battles pitting it against Western fighters, with the Su-27 in 1992 proving capable of tackling multiple F-15s simultaneously at the home of the USAF First Tactical Fighter Wing at Langley Air Force Base. The Flanker did so even when starting a mock fight at a disadvantage with the Eagles on its tail.[93] Prominent Lithuanian aviation expert Yefim Gordon noted regarding the U.S. response to the results of multiple similar exercises: 'Trying to avoid the adverse publicity for U.S. aircraft, Western media have been tight as a clam about the fact that the Flanker had won in mock combat against the F-15C as witnessed by USAF specialists.'[94] 'As for the Flanker air combat training sessions – both simulated and otherwise – have long since shown that the F-15C loses out in a dogfight even to the baseline Su-27, never mind the Su-30,' he noted, with the latter being an improved variant of the Su-27 that had first flown in 1989.[95] Mock engagements with Indian Air Force Flankers in 2004 and 2005 similarly showed an overwhelming disadvantage for the F-15, as did USAF simulated F-15 sorties against Flankers in a complex of 360° simulation games at the Boeing facilities in St Louis in which the Flanker reportedly emerged victorious almost every time.[96]

China's investment in the Su-27 was a result of the PLAAF's strong emphasis on fielding the most capable air superiority fighters possible, in part influenced by the historical memory of the Korean War where, even lacking trained pilots, the new service had had a strong strategic impact, facilitated largely by the MiG-15's performance advantages. The view that the Flanker as a top end heavyweight air superiority fighter was vital to China's security was strengthened in 1991 in the final weeks of the Gulf War, which pitted a large U.S.-led coalition force against the Ba'athist Iraqi Republic. The coalition's very high emphasis on air power and ability to use air superiority and precision strikes to devastate a large ground force demonstrated that a mass mobilisation army alone would have only a very limited ability to defend Chinese territory. As had been the case in Korea the cost Iraq paid for losing control of the air was extreme, with an estimated 100,000-200,000 personnel and thousands of civilians killed in forty-four days of hostilities, and well over half a million more dying throughout the decade as the fallout from the bombing of infrastructure exacerbated the impacts of economic sanctions.[97] America's extreme reliance on air dominance, perceived as a precondition for almost all other aspects of a military campaign, made the ability to blunt or neutralise American air power a key Chinese priority for years to come with even greater perceived importance than in the Korean War.[98]

U.S. National Security Policy expert Professor Daryl G. Press noted in a prominent paper for *International Security* in 2001: 'For U.S. foreign policy, the Gulf War seems to show – and the 1999 Kosovo conflict appears to confirm – that air power is now so lethal, and American air power so dominant, that the United States can win nearly cost-free military victories against its foes. For U.S. military procurement debates, the lessons are equally clear. The United States should significantly alter its military procurement priorities to favour air power over ground forces; in the future, decisive battles will be won from the air.'[99] This was a trend widely observed in papers by leading think tanks.[100] Where U.S. tactical air power had proven more limited in the Korean War, the Gulf War demonstrated that much had changed. Chinese analysts particularly highlighted that new sensors on U.S. aircraft allowed them to operate with full efficiency at night – contrasting with the Korean War where Chinese forces' emphasis on night fighting limited American aviation's ability to provide close air support.[101] Combined with advances in precision weaponry, this was widely seen to have constituted a Revolution in Military Affairs – an irrecoverable change in the conduct of warfare caused by technological advances.[102] The PLA's modernisation drive from 1991, most notably its renewed emphasis on advanced air defence capabilities, represented a response to this.

Regarding the impacts of the U.S.-led coalition victory over Iraq in 1991, a prominent Brookings Institute paper concluded: 'The Persian Gulf War marked a new era in American power projection … Operation Desert Storm showed that U.S. forces could quickly amass at an adversary's doorstep and project power into adversary territory.'[103] This left significant grounds for Beijing to see itself as vulnerable, and the possibility that China, which in 1992 was one of very few remaining powers outside the Western sphere of influence, could similarly be targeted for a U.S.-led attack, remained highly significant. Prominent figures in both the ruling Communist Party and the PLA increasingly predicted that China, or its treaty ally North Korea, could be subsequent targets for U.S. attacks,[104] with the perceived threat only growing as Washington came very close to authorising an air assault on North Korea in June 1994.[105] Concerns were further heightened by the U.S.-led military interventions targeting Yugoslavia that decade, which included a highly precise satellite guided strike on the Chinese embassy in Belgrade in 1999 by a CIA-operated B-2 stealth bomber.[106]

On 11 January 1991, Central Military Commission (CMC) President Yang Shangkun, who was also the commission's vice chairman and secretary-general, emphasized that the Gulf War had ushered in an era where wars, rather than diplomacy, would increasingly settle international disputes. He stressed that new conflicts would be three dimensional – requiring modern air, land and sea elements – and urged the PLA to accelerate R&D efforts accordingly.[107] Similar calls from among the military leadership were made for cuts to ground forces and increases to overall defence spending with the PLAAF to be the greatest beneficiary.[108] The Gulf War not only strengthened the perceived need for a modern air force, but the need for the PLA and China's defence industries to raise their technology levels more broadly. The CMC held further major meetings in February and March and decided to increase defence spending with the bulk of the increase allocated to R&D. Finance Minister Wang Bingqian explained increases as follows: 'That the PLA's budget needed more funds to modernize defence in order to handle unexpected changes in the increasingly complicated international arena.'[109] Manpower was cut by 500,000 over the next five years, which would be followed by multiple further reductions to ground forces in subsequent decades.[110] Military industries and particularly defence-related R&D were given priority over the civilian economy – unheard of in two decades – with military research prioritised with respect to funding in the expectation that it would spin off benefits to the civilian sector – rather than vice versa as before.[111]

Echoing President Yang's conclusions Defence Minister Qin Jiwei warned the National People's Congress that PLA equipment was twenty years behind that used by U.S. forces against Iraq, and that under the new international environment a larger budget and more R&D spending was vital.[112] Commission for Science, Technology, and Industry for National Defence Vice Minister Shen Rongjun similarly stressed the importance of increased spending on high-end technologies, stating that it would be impossible to apply modern tactics without sophisticated equipment.[113] The *Christian Science Monitor* would conclude later that year regarding the shift in PLA priorities that 'the enthusiasm over high technology apparently stems from the decisive role of "smart" weapons in the Gulf War,' with similar assessments made by other major publications.[114] The new emphasis on R&D would have disproportionately significant implications for the Navy and particularly the Air Force.

After becoming the Su-27's first overseas client, the PLA would become the largest client for Flanker aircraft by a considerable margin, far surpassing orders by the Russian Defence Ministry itself, with two Su-27UBK trainers ordered and delivered in 1992 followed by twenty-four more Su-27s in 1995 and twenty-eight more in 1998. Under a contract signed in 1996 105 more Su-27s were built in China under license between 1998 and 2007 under the J-11 designation, of which approximately sixty produced from 2001-2007 were enhanced with local technologies as the J-11A variant. An advanced Su-27 twin-seat derivative with an extended range and improved avionics, the Su-30MKK, was ordered in 1999 and again in 2001, with thirty-eight purchased each time, before twenty-four of the more advanced Su-30MK2 were ordered for the Navy in 2003. China's Su-30s were considered the most capable fighters in the world when first received in 2000, and were far more sophisticated than anything the Russian Defence Ministry was willing to finance for its own forces.

By the time China received its last Su-30s in 2004 it had become increasingly evident that Russian fighters had lost their strong and hard-won performance edge which the Soviet Union had established in the 1980s, with sharp post-Soviet decline in the defence sector and broader economy preventing all the most ambitious new combat jet programs from being realised. A prominent indicator of this was America's operationalising of the world's first fifth generation fighter, the F-22, in December 2005, where Russia's own initially promising rival program had by then long since been terminated (see Chapter 2). Advances in China's own defence sector, meanwhile, had placed it on the cusp of producing fighters on par with the latest Russian models. This could be most clearly observed at the Su-27 production line in Shenyang, where production quality exceeded that seen in Russia due to China's superior machinery for manufacturing and assembly. Chinese industry was also able to improve the Flanker design to develop a variant broadly on par with the top models in Russia itself, designated the J-11B. This first flew in 2004, with notable improvements including use of China's indigenous multimode pulse Doppler radar the Type 1493, a stronger but 700kg lighter airframe resulting from a modified structure, and much greater use of composite materials.[115] Signs of Chinese leadership in fighter aviation would emerge increasingly clearly the following decade.

Flanker acquisitions from Russia were hardly made in isolation, with modernisation of the PLAAF being fully comprehensive. While Russian pilots were often flying just twenty hours per year in the 1990s, Chinese pilots enjoyed a steadily rising number of flying hours, which increased by around fifty per cent over a decade for Su-27 and Su-30 pilots to approximately 180 hours per year by 2003.[116] These trends continued over the next two decades, and by the mid-2010s American officials were lamenting that Chinese pilots were often getting twice as many flight hours per year as their USAF counterparts – among the very highest levels in the world.[117] Chinese advances in satellite communications and navigation, semiconductors, composite materials, air missile engines, display screens and a wide range of other areas all did a great deal to press the country's defence sector forward systematically. As a result, the aircraft it could produce improved noticeably and at a rapid rate.

China's fast-growing economy and even faster growing defence budget and scale of R&D facilitated its emergence as a leading power in combat aviation by the mid-2000s. Unlike in the 1950s, when this had previously been achieved, however, the country was not reliant on Russian technologies but rather on doing the research and development work and pioneering technological advances itself. Where a cutting off of Soviet support had quickly ended China's status as a near peer air power to the USSR and U.S. in the 1960s, in the 2000s and more so the 2010s, China's need for foreign technology inputs was fast diminishing as it emerged as a technological and economic leader in its own right.

Where the Su-27 and Su-30 had been acquired from 1991-2004 to ensure a performance advantage over the U.S. Air Force's F-15s, as the F-15's successor the F-22 was introduced the Soviet Flanker's continued ability to provide defensive air superiority was brought into serious question. With Soviet fifth generation fighter programs having floundered after the state's disintegration, an independent Chinese fifth generation fighter would need to be developed if top PLAAF fighter units were to see their advantage restored. It was thus fortunate for Chinese interests that rather than relying on Russia to develop a next generation fighter for it to purchase, the PLA had independently initiated development of its own successor to the Flanker. The fighter was intended to effectively provide a superior counter to the F-22 just as the Su-27 had for the F-15 – and as the MiG-15 had years before done for the F-86.

Chapter Two

The Fifth Generation of Fighter Aviation

What is a Fifth Generation Fighter?

Fifteen years after the world's first fifth generation fighter the American F-22 became operational in December 2005, by the early 2020s just three other fighter classes of the same generation had entered service worldwide – the American F-35, the Chinese J-20 and the Russian Su-57. Of these only the F-35 and J-20 were both in production and operating in full strength squadrons, with F-22 production having long since ended while the first full Su-57 regiment was expected to be fielded only in 2024. The immense technological requirements to develop such fighters meant that, despite their distinct performance advantages, very few further programs were expected to produce aircraft capable of operating on a comparable level.

United States government sources defined the following eight features as prerequisites for a combat aircraft to be considered fifth generation: use of a stealth airframe with internal carriage of missiles and significant reductions to both radar cross section (RCS) to infrared signature; active electronically scanned array (AESA) radars;* sensor fusion; advanced data links and network-centric

---

* While AESA radars had superior situational awareness and electronic warfare capabilities compared to older radar types, one of their most important benefits for stealth fighters in particular was their significantly reduced radar signatures, which meant when operational it was considerably more difficult for potential adversaries to use their radar emissions to home in on the aircraft they belonged to. Integrating sensor suites with reduced radar signatures was

warfare capabilities; sophisticated electronic warfare suits with advanced Digital Radio Frequency Memory jammers and electro-optical (EO) defensive systems; long range multiband EO targeting systems; advanced glass cockpits; the ability to reach supersonic speeds without using engine afterburners otherwise known as a super cruise capability.[†]

Where many of these features can be seen on newer fourth generation fighters, and were often introduced gradually as Cold War era designs were modernised, the key feature that distinguishes fifth generation aircraft is the degree to which their radar cross sections can be reduced. The radar cross section refers to how much radar energy a body reflects back to its source, with a lower cross section making it more difficult for radars to detect, track or lock onto. While stealth fighters are very far from invisible to radars, particularly those with longer wavelengths, they are detectable at shorter ranges and, most importantly, difficult for radars, and particularly the small high frequency radars on anti-aircraft missiles, to lock on to. The advantages this can provide in all manner of missions, whether for air-to-air combat, air defence suppression, anti-shipping, or even bombing runs with gravity weapons, are tremendous – with even those radar-guided weapons systems specifically designed to target stealth aircraft still doing so with far more difficulty than they would be able to against a high RCS target.

RCS reductions can be achieved through changes to the airframe shape, as well as through altering structures of airframe elements, particularly contacts between covering, hatches, and moving and

---

vital to an aircraft's overall stealth capabilities and highly complementary to reductions in airframe radar cross section.

[†] Soviet definitions were broadly similar, although use of advanced passive electronically scanned array (PESA) radars was considered sufficient and very high levels of manoeuvrability were seen as a requirement and emphasized far more than they were in the United States.

fixed parts of the airframe. Use of radar absorbing materials and coatings are a third major means of reducing RCS. Conservative reductions to the radar cross sections of modernised fourth generation fighters have notably been made in a number of cases, an example being the Russian Su-35S, which due to modifications to its airframe has under a third of the frontal RCS of the Su-27S from which it is derived. Multiple fourth generation fighters also make use of stealth coatings and radar absorbent materials, with notable examples including China's own advanced Su-27 derivative the J-16 and the American F-16C/D and F-18E/F fighters. Nevertheless, even with such enhancements, these aircraft still have radar cross sections several orders of magnitude greater than genuine stealth fighters of the fifth generation.

Stealth fighters nevertheless have a number of shortcomings compared to their fourth generation equivalents, and have often required more maintenance and been more difficult to keep at high levels of operational readiness. Stealth coatings in particular, especially in the technology's early years, were time consuming to maintain. The need to carry weapons internally to preserve a low RCS also means stealth fighters often have less firepower than their non-stealth counterparts. The F-22, for example, carries up to eight air-to-air missiles, while enhanced variants of its fourth generation predecessor, the F-15, carry up to twenty-two – although this is a more extreme case.

While use of an RCS-reducing stealth airframe has been consistent to all definitions, the other defining features of fifth generation fighters have not always been agreed upon. A notable example is the lack of super cruise on the American F-35, and possibly the Russian Su-57 as well, which seriously limits their supersonic ranges. Under a strict reading of requirements this would disqualify them as fully fifth generation fighters. This was also an issue for early variants of the Chinese J-20 produced before 2019. Access to high off-boresight air-to-air missiles and paired helmet mounted sights, allowing a pilot to engage enemy aircraft at extreme angles, has also often been considered a requirement, and was standard even in the fourth generation for Soviet fighters from the mid-1980s and for Western ones from the mid-2000s. This and modern sensor fusion and network centric warfare capabilities are nevertheless absent on the F-22.

A number of factors have meant that there are far fewer successful fifth generation fighter programs than there were in the preceding fourth generation. One is their sheer complexity and the wide range of technologies that all need to be brought to very advanced levels to produce such aircraft. Much as the number of countries that could independently produce successful fourth generation fighters was significantly lower than those which could produce second or first generation ones, so too were many countries excluded from the fifth generation fighter race despite having been able to compete in the fourth. Only the United States and China, tailed a way behind by Russia, are expected to have defence sectors capable of supporting truly fifth generation fighter aircraft relatively independently before the first sixth generation fighters begin to be introduced. Even Russia, however, is heavily dependent on overseas inputs, particularly electronics, while the United States also relies on electronics and other key components such as panel displays and circuit boards sourced from East Asia and Europe for the F-22 and more so the F-35 (see Chapter 4). Indeed, the F-35 was pursued as part of a joint program with eight other countries that contributed to R&D and manufacturing. The unrivalled concentration of high-tech manufacturing in China, however, and its far larger scale of research and development (see Chapter 4), has made its defence sector less reliant on foreign inputs and its fifth generation fighters very likely the most fully indigenous as a percentage of components used. As the standing of Chinese industry continues to rise relative to leading rivals, in areas as diverse as semiconductors and machine tooling, this position is only expected to further improve.

Paving the Way to the J-20 Program: Chengdu's Fourth Generation Fighter the J-10

As Chinese industry and high tech advanced rapidly in the 1990s and 2000s, poising the country to contend for global leadership in growing numbers of key manufacturing and technology areas in the 2010s and 2020s, its military aviation sector also transformed significantly. The process was accelerated by work on the country's first successful jet fighter not derived from a prior Soviet design – the fourth generation J-10. The program marked a transition from the third world level defence sector of the Cold War era to one reflecting China's twenty-first century scale of defence spending, high tech industry and cutting edge R&D. Developing the J-10 played a key role in paving the way for the subsequent development of the world's first non-American fifth generation fighter, the J-20, which would enter service just thirteen years after it.

The J-10 program was described as having 'a transitional role in catalysing development of China's modern military aviation RDA [research, development and acquisition] process.'[1] Development challenged traditional risk aversion, introduced design competition and linked user needs more closely to existing design and manufacturing capabilities. The third change marked an end to the requirements creep that had seriously impeded progress on the preceding failed J-9 program in the 1960s and 1970s, for which the raising of technical requirements by political leaders' at times unrealistic demands had caused serious setbacks. Among the important developments in the J-10 program which paved the way to the J-20's success were application of a top-down decision-making process and vertical management hierarchy throughout the RDA process and introduction of competitive mechanisms between design institutes into the military aircraft design system which did much to stimulate design improvements.

The request to develop the J-10 originated with PLAAF Commander Zhang Tingfa in 1981, with China's three main combat aircraft design institutes proposing competing designs signifying a marked change from the past. The No. 601 Institute at Shenyang proposed an F-16-like strake-wing jet, the 320 Factory at Hongdu a variable swept wing design resembling the MiG-23, and the No. 611 Institute at Chengdu an unconventional double-canard layout based on the J-9 it had previously worked on. The Chengdu Aircraft Design Institute's experience with the J-9, and its ability to incorporate significant aspects of the older design, which had already received considerable investment, into the new program, is thought to have been an important factor helping its proposal to prevail after plan evaluations and engine proposals had been implemented. Chengdu maintained that the superior operational parameters of its non-traditional design, and the limitations of conservative design from Shenyang, were key to its success. The Shenyang Aircraft Design Institute's difficulties developing the J-8 interceptor was seen as another factor that led to Chengdu's design being favoured.

Joining the PLAAF as a basic fourth generation lightweight fighter in 2004, the baseline J-10A's capabilities were 'considered roughly on par technologically with America's mainstay F-15s, F-16s, and Navy F-18s,' according to a range of Western assessments.[2] Considerable investment in its modernisation saw the fighter evolve significantly as China's defence sector advanced, culminating in 2018 in the service entry of the J-10C with fifth generation level avionics and armaments. The J-10 program catalysed Chengdu's rise to prominence in Chinese military aviation where Shenyang had previously held undisputed dominance, which was furthered from the 1990s by Shenyang's focus on license producing and later developing new derivatives of the Soviet Su-27 Flanker. This led Chengdu to be more closely associated with fully indigenous fighters. Experience developing the J-10 was key to allowing Chengdu to serve as the prime contractor for the J-20.

Fifth Generation Fighters Outside China: American and Russian Programs

Lockheed Martin F-22 Raptor

Developed under the Advanced Tactical Fighter (ATF) program from 1981, the F-22 Raptor was intended to serve as a successor to the F-15 Eagle to restore the American air superiority advantage against challenges from the Soviet Su-27 and MiG-31. The fighter was largely developed with combat against the Flanker in mind, and like the F-15 it was a heavyweight twin engine aircraft with a large radar, high endurance and high degree of manoeuvrability at all ranges. Among its most significant advances over older fighters was its introduction of F119 engines, which put out twenty-five per cent more thrust than the F-15's F100s, compensating for the much greater weight of the aircraft's stealth airframe and facilitating superior manoeuvrability and super cruise.

The first fifth generation fighter technology demonstrators, the Northrop Grumman YF-23 and Lockheed Martin YF-22, flew in August and September 1990,[3] with the latter selected to form the basis for developing the ATF program further. The lack of near peer competition after the USSR's disintegration, however, combined with deep budget cuts and a sharp contraction in industry in the 1990s, meant the aircraft had its capabilities seriously watered down with several key systems removed.[4] Although initially intended to boast twice the F-15's combat radius, double its sortie rate and half the maintenance requirements, the F-22 turned out to be far inferior to its predecessor in all these key respects.[5] The fighter had a shorter range, much poorer availability rates, lower reliability, much lower versatility, much greater difficulty incorporating upgrades, and many more performance issues. The Raptor failed to deliver improved performance in those areas in which the Air Force assessed the F-15 as most deficient,[6] and cost 276 per cent as much per airframe as initially planned – at \$412 million up from just \$149 million.[7]

With pre-production costs reaching more than double the initial estimates, the Raptor's development time, initially estimated at nine years, took nineteen.[8] Severe delays in development meant an initial operating capability was only achieved in December 2005,[9] and while the F-22's engines and stealth features were revolutionary the aircraft overall proved highly problematic.

A key requirement for the Advanced Tactical Fighter program was that it would be easier and cheaper to maintain than the F-15, which the Air Force was assured as late as 1999 would be the case.[10] The fighter's actual maintenance needs were in fact far higher with annual operational costs over five times those of the F-15 – at $3,190,454 vs. $607,072.[11] More conservative estimates still placed the F-22's hourly operational costs at well over double the F-15's – over $68,000 vs. $29-32,000.[12] The man-hours needed to service the fighter for every hour in the air were similarly far higher for the F-22, with the discrepancy making it not only economically unviable to succeed the F-15, but also ensuring that a far lower proportion of a Raptor fleet would be available at any time compared to an F-15 fleet of the same size.

Excessive operational costs and maintenance needs resulted in very poor mission capable rates, well below those of either Cold War era fighters or twenty-first century foreign competitors, and were a major factor in the decision to cancel over seventy-five per cent of planned production aircraft.[13] One Air Force report highlighted 'maintenance troubles' and 'unexpected shortcomings' with serviceability,[14] while the very large suite of ground support equipment needed limited where and how the fighter could operate. Issues with breakdowns, poisonous effects on pilots' lungs known as 'Raptor Cough' caused by 'a "mosaic" of interrelated cockpit equipment issues,'[15] and problematic avionics and computer architecture,[16] among several others, sharpened the contrast to the F-22's famously successful Cold War era predecessors the F-15 and F-4. As Lockheed Martin's F-22 program chief Sherman Mullin noted after his retirement regarding the procurement system which produced a fighter that proved so problematic: 'The system is totally broken and everybody knows it.'[17] The fighter, alongside the B-2 bomber and subsequently the F-35, were seen to symbolise broader trends towards industry being unable after the Cold War to provide reliable clean sheet combat jet designs particularly at the higher end – or to remain anywhere near within budgets.

With the fighter program failing to provide a viable successor to the F-15, the decision to terminate Raptor production was finalised and approved by Congress in 2009, with the production line in Marietta, Georgia closing in 2011 less than six years after the first unit entered service. The F-15, by contrast, would remain in production and on order by the USAF into the latter half of the 2020s, over fifty years after it entered service in 1975, with greater perceived cost effectiveness facilitating continuous orders which in turn allowed the aircraft to be modernised continuously over time. The result was that F-15s produced in the 2020s had far more advanced avionics and sensors than the F-22. Only 177 production F-22s were ever built, alongside eighteen test and development airframes, where 750 Raptors were initially planned to be built for the Air Force with further orders from the Navy previously expected.[18] Compared to the F-15, which would see a production run of over 1,800 aircraft, the new fighter developed at far greater cost to replace it saw less than ten per cent of the production airframes completed.

In May 2021 longstanding suspicions that the Air Force would condemn the F-22 to an early retirement were confirmed, with the fighter set to be outlasted in service by several decades by the F-15 and other Cold War-era fighter designs which had proven much less troublesome.[19] Deputy chief of staff for Air Force futures Lieutenant General Samuel Clinton Hinote explained at the time that the fighter suffered from 'limitations' that 'we can't modernize our way out of,' referring to the Raptor as a '1990s – and even late 1980s – design', an age often masked by the fact that it only became fully operational close to 2010 due to development delays. Hinote singled out growing parts obsolescence as a particular issue – one which was harder to address due to production lines being closed for over a decade.[20] The first Raptors to be retired would be less than one third of the way through their airframe service lives, even without counting the possibility of life extensions through refurbishment, meaning the USAF was ridding itself of the aircraft decades earlier than necessary. The F-22's mission capable rates of around fifty per cent, which were by far the lowest in the American fighter fleet, were expected to begin to improve slightly as airframes began to be retired, allowing the decommissioned Raptors to be cannibalised for much needed spare parts.[21] While F-22s were being retired the Air Force simultaneously continued to purchase new F-15s at over $100 million per airframe, indicating a strong preference for the older aircraft and serving as perhaps the clearest indicator of the newer fighter's failings.

Lockheed Martin F-35 Lightning II

The F-35 was developed to provide a lighter, cheaper, more numerous counterpart to the F-22 in much the same way as the USAF had commissioned the F-16 in the 1970s to form the backbone of its fleet due to the unaffordability of large numbers of F-15s. Unlike the Soviet Union, which had begun developing both its heavy and light fighters in parallel, the F-35 was developed after the F-22 with the first demonstrator airframe making its first flight in 2000 – ten years after the F-22's own first demonstrator flight. Like the F-16, the F-35 used only a single rather than twin engines, had much lower maintenance needs and operational costs than its heavier counterpart, and was restricted to much lower speeds, altitudes and levels of manoeuvrability and to carrying a much smaller weapons payload and a smaller radar. Its flight performance limitations significantly reduced its maximum engagement ranges compared to heavier aircraft like the F-22, which could fire missiles from much higher altitudes, imparting far more energy upon launch.[22]

Unlike the F-16, which was developed during the Cold War at a time when Soviet and Warsaw Pact air power posed a real threat of gaining air superiority, the F-35 was developed at a time when the Air Force was increasingly focused on air-to-ground missions and air defence suppression.[‡] As indicated by the name of the program – Joint Strike Fighter – the aircraft was designed with advanced electronic attack, network centric warfare and strike capabilities, but was much more limited in the air-to-air domain. With the fighter entering service a decade later than the F-22, and expected to remain in production for decades longer, it boasted an increasingly distinct edge in its avionics. These ranged from sensor fusion and the use of distributed aperture systems to boost situational awareness, to integration of infrared sensors and helmet mounted sights optimised for closer range air-to-air engagements. The F-22's 1990s avionics by contrast have received only relatively conservative updates.

The F-35 program's primary goal could be summarised as making fifth generation fighters affordable, with over 3,000 of the aircraft initially expected to be produced for the U.S. Armed Forces and for clients across the world. Although its operational costs have remained far higher than intended, leading the possibility of deep cuts to planned orders being widely raised,[23] the F-35A's flyaway cost has nevertheless led it to be widely considered the most cost effective fighter in the Western world with its price falling below those of the F-15 and European fourth generation aircraft.[24] Its much lighter weight than the F-15, single engine configuration, and much

---

[‡]   As early as 1999 the F-35 was referred to by experts at the *Brookings Institute* as 'both more affordable and more important for the United States than the F-22,' reflecting the consensus view that resulted from the USAF's reduced focus on air superiority after the Cold War. The collapse of the Russian MiG 1.42 program in the 1990s, and failure of its successor the Su-57 to materialise in the 2010s, meant it would take China's J-20 program to revive a perceived need to refocus on air superiority capabilities and F-22-like aircraft. (O'Hanion, Michael, 'The Plane Truth: Fewer F-22s Mean a Stronger National Defense,' *Brookings*, 1 September 1999.)

larger more efficient production lines than those seen in Europe, were primary causes. The program by the mid-2020s had succeeded in turning fifth generation aircraft from a niche asset fielded in a very small number of units to a widely available one that formed the backbone not only of the American fleet, but also of several of its major military allies. The intention for a large-scale program to equip vast fleets was reflected by how it was pursued, namely as part of a joint development effort with the United Kingdom, Australia, Canada, Italy, Norway, Denmark, the Netherlands and Turkey as eight junior partners in development and manufacturing.

Alongside the standard F-35A developed for the U.S. Air Force, and representing close to seventy-five per cent of airframes planned, the F-35B and F-35C variants were developed for the Marines and Navy respectively, the former with short take-off and vertical landing capabilities and the latter with folding wings, an arrestor hook and other features needed to operate from the Navy's supercarriers. This was intended to maximise commonality between the services' next generation aircraft, although as the program evolved this largely failed to be realised, resulting in only twenty to twenty-five per cent commonality primarily in avionics. It left the very different airframes 'almost like three separate production lines,' as multiple assessments concluded.[25]

Even before the F-35's entry into service the program was already $163 billion over budget and seven years behind schedule,[26] with hundreds of design defects meaning it would be several more years before the fighter would be ready for medium or high intensity combat.[27] The number of flaws was counted at 873 in January 2020[28] and shown in March to still be increasing as more continued to be discovered, while efforts to fix existing ones remained stagnant.[29] Although the program's development phase officially concluded in 2018, the Pentagon Office of the Director, Operational Test and Evaluation, confirmed five years later that 'the overall number of open deficiencies has not significantly decreased', indicating a very slow rate of progress in making the aircraft operationally viable.[30] Despite benefitting considerably from prior R&D into the F-117 and the F-22 stealth fighter programs which pioneered many of its technologies, the fighter's development cost before entering service was estimated at $55.5 billion[31] compared to just $26.3 billion for the F-22[32] and an estimated $4.4 billion§ for the Chinese J-20.[33] The F-35 program was by the early 2020s expected to cost over $1.7 trillion, making it by far the most expensive weapons program in world history.[34] In particular, the fighter's major overruns in operational costs seem increasingly certain to make acquisitions in the originally planned quantities unfeasible.

Following the F-35's entry into service the Pentagon would for years decline to grant approval for full-scale production on the basis of shortfalls in capabilities.[35] In early 2022, after again withholding certification for expanded production, it cut orders for the following year by thirty-five per cent.[36] Where the Air Force was initially expected to acquire 110 F-35s per year, this was gradually scaled down to eighty, then sixty, and finally just forty-eight aircraft.[37] The fighter's underperformance was attested to by a number of sources from military think tanks such as NSN[38] and RAND,[39] to organizations such as the Project on Government Oversight,[40] and individuals such as the Pentagon's chief weapons tester Michael Gilmore[41] and Marine Captain Dan Grazier.[42] Senate Armed Services Committee Chairman John McCain referred to the F-35 as 'a textbook example' of the country's 'broken defence acquisition system,' and as 'both a scandal and a tragedy with respect to cost, schedule and performance.'[43] More bluntly, Defence Secretary Christopher C. Miller stated in 2020 that 'the F-35 is a piece of ****,' while his predecessor Patrick Shanahan referred to the troubled

---

§   As China's first ever stealth fighter, the burden on the J-20 for research and development was considerably higher, which made its much lower development cost all the more outstanding. While few figures are available for the J-20's R&D costs before service entry estimates all place them at around one tenth those of the F-35.

fighter in 2019 as 'f—ed up.'[44] An inquiry by the Pentagon's Office of the Inspector General found that Shanahan's criticisms of the F-35 'were consistent with other comments about problems in the F-35 program made by other senior DoD officials.'[45]

The F-35's F135 engine proved particularly troublesome, and by 2022 was causing fighter unavailability at 600 per cent the rates that engines of other American fighter classes did.[46] This was a leading cause for calls to develop an entirely new engine for the fighter. Following the latest in a series of reports by the Government Accountability Office reflecting very poorly on the fighter program's performance, House Armed Service Subcommittee on Readiness Chairman Congressman John Garamendi stressed that prevailing trends in the defence sector meant a new engine probably wouldn't work either. 'You give us an engine and it doesn't work, well it worked for a little while until it gets some dust around and then it doesn't work. What the hell? What's going on here? ... For the contractors out there what in the hell are you doing? Why can't you give us a piece of equipment that actually works?' he stated. F-35 Joint Program Office Lieutenant General Eric Fick notably concurred – lamenting serious issues with logistics and maintenance. The hearing raised that 'maintenance is taking twice as long as originally intended' for existing F-35 units, a full twenty-two years after the fighter's first flight, and was far from isolated in the kinds of criticisms it saw the fighter program receive.[47] A report from auditors from the Government Accountability Office found in June 2023 that the F135 engine alone had cost the Pentagon $38 billion dollars in unexpected maintenance costs, largely because its cooling capacity was wholly insufficient to meet the power demands of the F-35's sensors and electronics. Lockheed Martin had notably discovered the issue in 2008, but the Pentagon declined to address it in order to avoid further program delays.[48] This was far from an exceptional case among the multitude of issues affecting the program.

Signs that the Pentagon would begin to reduce investment in the F-35 program began to emerge in the late 2010s, with officials and experts consistently highlighting that, much like the F-22, the fighter's operational costs had too far exceeded original requirements and made a larger fleet unaffordable.[49] The F-35A's annual sustainment cost in the early 2020s was still 190 per cent as high as budgeted, meaning the planned fleet size could need to be cut by close to half to remain within the Air Force's means.[50] As the program further matured the possibility for meaningful reductions to operational costs and maintenance needs appeared increasingly slim. This was very likely a major factor influencing the USAF in 2022 to cut its long-held goal of building its fleet to 386 squadrons,[51] with the Joint Strike Fighter program's failure to provide a fighter with comparable lifetime costs to the inexpensive F-16 seriously limiting options to even sustain existing fleet numbers. The program's cost overruns, and particularly the much higher lifetime costs a large F-35 fleet would have, were seen to potentially seriously threaten the Air Force's ability to fund other important weapons programs.

Under one proposed plan for cuts in the early 2020s, a portion of F-35 acquisitions would be replaced by an enhanced derivative of the F-16 or something similar – a design which would have been flying for over fifty years when the first new variants were delivered and would be over eighty years old by the time they were retired.[52] The fact that a return to something resembling F-16 acquisitions was even considered underlined the extent and severity of ongoing problems, and mirrored how the Air Force cut F-22 production and moved to retire existing airframes while resuming acquisitions of the F-15. It became increasingly apparent that even if performance and reliability issues were resolved, the F-35's excessive maintenance needs and operational costs were prohibitive to allowing it to serve as a primary fighter and day-to-day workhorse of the fleet for the bulk of its missions as the F-16 had, and that it would instead need to be deployed in more limited numbers and for a more select few missions.[53] This meant fourth generation fighters were likely to continue to form the backbone of the American fleet for the foreseeable future.

Despite its shortcomings, the fact that the F-35 was still far more widely used and affordable than the F-22 gave it the potential to revolutionise American and allied strike capabilities once operational issues were overcome by providing a genuinely fifth generation aircraft that could be fielded in medium numbers. Its unique status as the only Western post-fourth generation fighter in production allowed it to consistently defeat competition from both rival American fighters and European rivals to win contracts across countries that needed NATO-compatible hardware, and facilitated a scale of production greater than all other Western fighter classes combined at close to 150 airframes per year. While the program was already 'too big to fail' in the hundreds of billions of dollars, the fact that there were no NATO-compatible alternatives from the same generation whatsoever was a further major factor in the F-35's favour that gave its clients little choice but to overlook its many shortcomings. The F-35's long projected production run will allow the fighter to be incrementally modernised into the era of sixth generation avionics, materials, coatings and weaponry, meaning the aircraft has the potential to stay relevant and close to the cutting edge for considerably longer than the F-22. The tremendous discrepancies in avionics between the latest variants of both fighters meant the F-35 was overall a much more capable fighter by the mid-2020s despite its inherent limitations in areas such as flight performance as a far smaller single engine aircraft.

Sukhoi Su-57 Felon

Envisioned as a direct successor to the Su-27 Flanker, the Su-57 Felon fifth generation fighter began development in early 2002, with a 2004 timetable stipulating a maiden flight in 2006 and serial production from 2010. The new twin engine heavyweight aircraft made its first flight four years behind schedule in January 2010,[54] with a revised schedule at the time stipulating a conclusion of initial flight testing in 2013 and service entry in 2015-16.[55] The Defence Ministry intended at the time for fifty fighters to be operational by 2020 and 200 by 2025. By the time of the fighter's first flight, however, it was clear that factors such as Russia's shortage of technical specialists and of suitable production facilities would make putting it into production highly challenging.[56] The Su-57 only entered very low-rate serial production in June 2018, and only began production on a significant scale in 2023, with the first fighter entering service in December 2020 over a decade behind schedule. These delays occurred despite the Su-57's development benefitting significantly from the extensive R&D work done for Soviet fifth generation programs.[57] Further delays to engine development meant Su-57s built before 2025 would use a derivative of the Su-27's AL-31 engine as a stopgap which seriously limited their flight performances.

Due to Russia's post-Soviet economic and industrial decline the Russian Air Force by the early 2010s had received almost no new tactical combat jets for two decades, with the Su-57 being the first and for thirty years the only major clean sheet Russian fighter or interceptor developed.[58] The Air Force and aviation industry were accordingly unanimous in asserting that the program was essential to prevent technical expertise and manufacturing from falling further behind competitors. Where the USSR had developed and serially produced four entirely different fourth generation fighter/ interceptor classes simultaneously, Russia's sole fifth generation fighter would be relied on to replace multiple older classes in its much smaller less diverse fleet.

While the USSR's international standing in tactical combat aviation had been highly favourable in the 1980s, with the Su-27's unrivalled performance being a notable example, post-Soviet decline meant Russia's position was significantly poorer by the turn of the century.[59] As Russia had abandoned the ambitious Soviet program for developing a successor to the Su-27, the MiG 1.42, the Su-57 which replaced it represented a more conservative program better suited to the country's post-Soviet technological and budgetary limitations. Where the Soviets had sought to field a top end fighter with clear performance advantages over foreign rivals, as they had with the Su-27, which would be capable of deep penetration flights into enemy territory, the Su-57 was designed to work with ground-based air defences in a defensive counter air role for which performance requirements would be much less demanding. Russia's GDP and R&D were very far below Soviet era levels, with only a fraction of the USSR's defence budget, and as a result it relied much more heavily on cost effective ground-based missile assets such as S-400 air defence systems, which were supported by much smaller numbers of less cutting edge combat jets.¶ The Su-57 was accordingly far less costly than the MiG 1.42 was expected to have been.[60]

Many of the Su-57's features set it apart from the two other heavyweights of its generation the F-22 and J-20, and while designed to be able to launch precision strikes deep behind enemy lines it relied on stealthy long-range missiles to do so – avoiding the need for deep penetration flights. It accordingly had deep internal weapons bays to carry high diameter weapons such as cruise missiles. The Su-57 was the only fighter that used defensive laser turrets, which fired small modulated beams to neutralise infrared guided missiles' seekers on approach. Alongside slat L-band radars in its wing flaps, cheek-mounted side-facing X-band AESA radars provided a very wide sensor field of view, and allowed fighters to perform 'beaming' tactics to evade detection while maintaining situational awareness. Such radars had previously been planned for but removed from the F-22 to reduce costs.[61] The Su-57's five radars allowed for the tracking of up to sixty targets and engagement of up to sixteen simultaneously, making the fighter comfortably the world leader in this area.[62]

¶   The focus on a cheaper more conservative fighter mirrored similar changes in the United States, where the Cold War's end was also thought to have influenced the decision to invest in the much more conservative F-22 over the more ambitious and costly proposed F-23 design.

The Su-57's range far surpassed all Western rivals, much as the Su-27's had, and it similarly strongly emphasized manoeuvrability with an impressive flight performance and from three-dimensional thrust vectoring engines. The fighter otherwise strongly emphasized electronic warfare, and could deploy a wider array of very long ranged missiles for both air-to-air and strike missions, which partly compensated for its more limited stealth capabilities. The Su-57 had the advantage of being deployed for intensive combat testing against a major state adversary from early 2022, due to the escalation of Russian-Ukrainian hostilities, and was reportedly employed in strike, air-to-air and air defence suppression roles among others.[63] No other fifth generation fighter had a remotely comparable degree of combat usage.

The Su-57's procurement timeline appeared particularly unremarkable considering that the Soviet Union had begun work on developing fifth generation fighters in the late 1970s, and had been expected to field multiple squadrons' worth of the aircraft in the early 2000s. This placed the Russian program around a quarter century behind, with the first fifth generation regiment fielded forty-five years after development of such aircraft had begun. With both Russia and the U.S. facing contractions to their defence sectors, procurement budgets, and wider industrial bases after the Cold War's end, resulting in declining conditions in many areas of their defence sectors (See Chapter 4), both showed signs of struggling to move into the next generation of fighters, albeit in very different ways.

Mikoyan MiG 1.42: A Relation of the J-20?

The Soviet Union began developing a direct successor to the Su-27 in the late 1970s with the Mikoyan design bureau, which until the Flanker had been responsible for developing all the best-known Soviet air superiority fighters, seeing its proposal selected over rivals from the Sukhoi and Yakovlev bureaus. Full-scale development was approved by directive in 1986, with the first prototype of the fighter's engine first flying that year.[64] The program was designated *Izdeliye* 1-42, and otherwise better known as the MiG 1.42, and gained investments on an unprecedented scale in areas ranging from its wind tunnel hours, radar cross section reduction testing and assessing the possibility of flexible cannon, among hundreds of other issues studied at length.

Soviet planners placed a much greater emphasis on stealth than their Russian successors could, with the country's industrial base and defence budget far better able to support a high performance fighter with world leading stealth capabilities. Several stealth technologies which did not exist anywhere else in the world were developed for the new fighter,[65] a notable example being the Keldysh research centre's 'stealthogenic' system that used whips of plasma from electromagnetic rays generated by the aircraft to absorb radio waves. This reportedly reduced the fighter's RCS by approximately two orders of magnitude.[66] An airframe using thirty per cent composite materials, and making high use of radar absorbent materials and coatings, further minimised RCS,[67] with Russian sources expressing confidence that the fighter would lead the world in its stealth capabilities.[68] The fighter was the world's first with moveable aft portions of its ventral fins, and had an avionics suite well suited to network-centric operations.[69] The stealth aircraft passed the Soviet Air Force's review in 1991 with flying colours, and once details of the design were eventually publicised the aircraft was widely predicted by analysts to surpass its American rival the F-22 – much as the Su-27 had surpassed the F-15 before it.[70] The aircraft was expected to make its maiden flight before 1994 and enter service in 2001.

The fallout from the USSR's disintegration prevented Mikoyan from completing any prototypes of its new fighter, although it did complete a single technology demonstrator designated 1.44 designed to prove the fighter's aerodynamics and control systems. Despite considerable post-Soviet delays the 1.44 airframe was almost ready for its first flight by 1994, but Mikoyan's inability to pay for its flight control actuators and other equipment delayed this by six years to February 2000 a few months after the Defence Ministry belatedly provided funding. Similar issues were stifling tactical weapons programs across the defence sector at the time. The demonstrator made a second flight in April 2000, with both being brief and at low altitudes, although by this time the 1.44 was already obsolete as a demonstrator. The Sokol aircraft plant had begun tooling to manufacture the MiG 1.42's pre-production airframes in early 1990,[71] with these set to differ substantially from the 1.44 demonstrator with a much stealthier design, most conspicuously for its engine intake, and a different wing platform. None of the four prototypes that had begun construction were ever funded to completion and the program was officially cancelled in 2002, with the Defence Ministry concluding that an operationally useful force was unaffordable.[72] The fighter's highly promising but costly AL-41F engine had used new advanced composites and alloys, including monocrystalline blades fabricated using the new blade cooling concept, providing an unmatched 0.09 weight/thrust ratio compared to 0.11 for the F119 that powered the F-22 and 0.125 for its predecessor the AL-31F.[73] Development was terminated, however, when the fighter program was cancelled.

Had the MiG 1.42 program been just two years further ahead in development by 1991 it likely would have had the momentum needed to survive the Soviet Union's disintegration and enter service in the early 2000s – providing a far superior combat capability to anything Russia would field at least until the mid-late 2020s. The fighter was referred to in the early 2000s by Russian Air Force representatives as 'not even tomorrow's aircraft but truly the day after tomorrow's aircraft' for its tremendous advances.[74] As leading expert on Soviet aviation Yefim Gordon observed: 'In retrospect it is clear that the [MiG 1.42] program philosophy was better than that of the American ATF [Advanced Tactical Fighter] ... it held promise of a breakthrough in aerodynamics, automation of flight control systems, ergonomics

AI etc. And so it did, except that the Soviet aircraft industry did not have enough time for practical implementation of these results before the tempestuous events of 1990-91.'[75] The program's collapse heralded the end of Russia's position as a peer level challenger to the United States in fighter aviation which it had held since the late 1940s.

After the program's termination it was widely speculated by Western and Russian sources that MiG 1.42 technologies were sold to China, with American sources reporting in the late 1990s that China had even offered financing and support to complete the program in order to ensure a successor to the Flanker would be available for it to import.[76] China's J-20 fifth generation fighter had a general configuration in the rear which loosely resembled that of the MiG 1.42, as did plans in early research papers for a similar ventral air intake much like that also seen on the J-10 – although two lateral divertless supersonic intakes were instead favoured and further reduced the fighter's RCS.[77] Both aircraft were heavyweights designed for air superiority and using double canards and twin engines, and the J-20 was developed remarkably quickly by a relative newcomer to the cutting edge of fighter aviation which fuelled speculation of external support. Nevertheless, China had been developing double canard fighters with ventral intakes since the 1960s with the J-9, succeeded by the J-10, and the J-20 much more closely resembled the unrealised J-9VI-II first designed in 1975 than it did the MiG 1.42 with the two Chinese aircraft sharing twin tails, side air intakes and canard delta wings.

Although China's combat aviation industry benefitted immensely from transfers of Soviet technologies and expertise during the 1990s, whether these included MiG 1.42 technologies, and if so to what extent, remains highly uncertain. Considering the extent to which cash-strapped post-Soviet Russia was willing to sell weapons technologies to China and India in particular, with the administration of President Boris Yeltsin instructing arms manufacturers at the time of crisis to 'sell anything to anyone,'[78] transfers of MiG 1.42

technologies cannot be ruled out. Indeed, Russia was willing to make substantial fifth generation technology transfers even for active programs when it agreed to a transfer of Su-57 technologies to Indian industry in the 2010s under a $6.7 billion deal.[79] Even if MiG 1.42 technologies had been transferred, however, the program was still very far from serial production stages and would have still left China with years of development work independently. The very considerable differences between the Soviet jet and the J-20 indicate that any influence it may have had would have been limited.

One key factor reducing the likelihood of major technology transfers was that, unlike for India, the Russian Defence Ministry consistently sought to limit technology transfers to China to prevent its emergence as a competitor on export markets and to ensure it would continue mass procurements of Russian-built armaments. China had imported more Su-27s than all other countries combined, and its purchases were expected to provide key support for an Su-27 successor whether it was the MiG 1.42 planned in the 1990s or the Su-57 planned from the following decade. Supporting development of an indigenous Chinese fifth generation heavyweight fighter would have thus risked seriously harming future exports. As it was China would field its first full strength fifth generation fighter squadron a full seven years before Russia could, ending hopes for Su-57 exports and illustrating precisely why Russia had sought to limit technology transfers.

Chapter Three

Chengdu's J-20 Program from Conceptualisation to Frontline Service

The Post-Soviet Era and China's need for an Indigenous Fighter

In 1990 the Sino-Soviet agreement on the export of Su-27 fighters to modernise the Chinese fleet was seen to potentially mark the beginning of a new era for the PLAAF, with restored access to top end Soviet platforms ensuring its top fighter units would again be able to enjoy parity with, if not superiority over, their American counterparts as they had in the 1950s. Such hopes proved short lived, however, as while Moscow after the USSR's disintegration only proved more willing to supply its most advanced hardware and technologies to its neighbour, it quickly became apparent that the post-Soviet Russian combat aviation sector would no longer be able to compete at a qualitatively peer level with that of the United States. Russian defence spending by 1998 had contracted by a phenomenal 95.6 per cent compared to a decade prior, and sharp contraction of GDP to around half of Soviet era levels and similarly sharp contraction of civilian industry and R&D, meant the country was poorly positioned to sustain the Soviet era momentum that was propelling its combat aviation sector through the 1990s on the back of export financing.[1] Russia's defence sector decline was more acute than spending figures alone would indicate since R&D and acquisitions, as more flexible parts of the defence budget, suffered disproportionately from the extreme cuts. Thus from 1991-1995 the R&D budget as a proportion of the fast-shrinking defence budget almost halved.[2] Russia's fifth generation fighter program the MiG 1.42 was considered effectively dead by the late 1990s, and even relatively basic '4+ generation' fighters would not join its air force until the 2010s.

China overtook Russia in defence spending in 1994-1995, and by 1998 had doubled its defence budget while reaching close to triple by 2009. It exceeded 400 per cent of the Russian budget in 2018.[3] This was achieved despite the far more militarised state of the Russian economy, which spent over twice and very often more than three times as great a percentage of GDP on defence. While China's economy was several times as large as Russia's, the discrepancies in industry and high-tech were far greater still, with Russia largely evolving into a rentier economy heavily reliant on exports of primary goods such as fossil fuels.[4] Chinese industry was thus competitive in a much wider range of strategic technology areas with key applications in combat aviation, from semiconductors to machine tooling, where post-Soviet Russian capabilities were negligible. The complexity of fifth generation aircraft and their requirements for a very wide range of cutting-edge technologies, many of them with dual uses and requiring a robust civilian tech sector and industrial base, meant China even by the late 1990s appeared to be in a far better position to develop them, particularly in the longer term. This was despite Russia having inherited very substantial next generation technologies and formidable programs from the USSR, with China's rapid economic growth and expansion of high-tech R&D the following decade only widening the discrepancy.

While different areas of Russia's defence sector declined to very different extents, with areas with perceived asymmetric value such as ballistic and cruise missiles, submarines and ground-based air defences gaining more investment, fighter aviation saw one of the most pronounced declines due to its cost and complexity. Russian spending on acquiring ground-based air defence systems in the first thirty post-Soviet years was thus at a conservative estimate over three times its spending on fighter acquisitions – an extreme discrepancy which illustrated the extent to which the latter was neglected. As a result, while in 1990 it appeared that the PLAAF could have continued to rely on importing various successors to the Su-27, culminating in a fifth generation fighter in the mid-2000s, just five years later it was clear that continued reliance on Russian aircraft would have guaranteed that China's top fighter units fell qualitatively behind those of the U.S. and its allies as they had been before the Su-27 purchase. The events of the 1990s and effective disappearance of imported alternatives thus made pursuit of an indigenous fifth generation fighter significantly more urgent, in light of the perceived security challenges Beijing believed it faced in the long term which primarily emanated from the United States and its air power.

Origins and the J-XX Program

In 1997 the U.S. Office of Naval Intelligence identified a Chinese next generation fighter program which it dubbed in a booklet on potential threat systems as 'XXJ'.[5] Otherwise known in the West as the J-XX, the program was referred to in China as 'Project 718'. Some of the best insights into the early goals of the program were provided by a paper titled the *Strategic Study of China's Fighter Aircraft Development*, which appeared to have been written sometime between 1996 and 2003, but which was released on the internet only in 2016. Written by former vice president and as chief designer at the Shenyang Aircraft Design Institute, Gu Songfen, who had served in multiple high level positions in the aerospace industry, including as a leading aerospace scholar in the Chinese Academy of Sciences and Chinese Academy of Engineering, it represents the J-20 program's most definitive publicly available early documentation. The paper was a product of military and aviation industry input and described the rationale for developing a heavyweight fifth generation fighter and its requirements and primary roles. It predicted with considerable accuracy how the program would proceed over the next quarter century.

At the time of the paper's writing development of fifth generation fighters in the United States and Soviet Union had been underway for close to two decades, although both countries' programs and those in Russia in particular had stalled considerably in the 1990s due to budget cuts and industrial contraction. The U.S. was pursuing two parallel fifth generation programs which became the heavyweight F-22 and the cheaper single engine F-35, the former designed for air superiority missions and the latter primarily for strike roles. The Chinese aircraft was intended to be able to compete at the same level as the F-22 and comfortably outperform the F-35 in air-to-air combat. The paper made clear that the program would produce a fighter focused on air superiority and on long range engagements, as well as capable of neutralising support aircraft such as airborne early warning and control aircraft, of operating in informatized combat missions and of providing targeting data to friendly assets. The fighter would have an offensive electronic warfare capability, and could act as an auxiliary airborne early warning aircraft, implying a powerful sensor suite – a capability previously seen on the Soviet MiG-31 interceptor which the PLAAF had evaluated shortly beforehand.[6]

The paper emphasised the advantages fifth generation fighters would enjoy over prior generations, including stealth and superiority in communications, firepower and information centric warfare. It also stressed the growing centrality of air power in modern warfare. Development of such a fighter, the paper noted, would both further advance China's already fast modernising military aviation industry more broadly and facilitate significant improvements to the PLAAF's capabilities in defence and offense. It highlighted that a forty-to-fifty-year life cycle, a radar cross section of under 0.3 square meters, and a high endurance allowing the fighter to cover all of Japan with one round of aerial refuelling, were to be key requirements, as was an active electronically scanned array (AESA) radar with a tracking range of 200 kilometres and the ability to track twenty targets. These were all comfortably achieved, although the radar requirements were highly conservative, likely in part because they predated the adoption of AESA radars anywhere in the world.

The paper predicted that China's aviation industry would struggle to develop a fifth generation engine like the F119 or AL-41F for the J-20, indicating that advanced fourth generation engines could power initial batches. It projected full-fledged development would begin around 2006-2007, flight testing around 2013, and service entry around 2020 – with the fifth generation engine entering service in 2021. Although this schedule was seen as highly ambitious, the fighter would in fact begin flying two years earlier and enter service three-to-four years earlier. Although its next generation engine, the WS-15, took longer than expected to develop, it was expected to be far more powerful than originally projected, giving the twin-engine fighter comfortably more thrust than any other in the world.

By the early 2000s it emerged that there had in fact been two rival fifth generation programs from the No. 611 Institute at Chengdu and from the No. 601 Institute at Shenyang.[7] Chengdu worked on a more radical delta-canard design with two V-shaped tails and lateral DSI intakes, while Shenyang proposed an orthodox 'tri-plane' design with canards, horizontal tails and widely canted tail fins.[8] The 601 Institute's proposed fighter was even heavier and more costly than that which became the J-20, while reportedly accommodating a much smaller radar, with its refusal to guarantee development on schedule further ensuring the success of 611's rival proposal.[9] As late as December 2002, however, major Western publications such as *Jane's Defence Weekly*[10] and the *New Scientist*[11] were reporting that Shenyang would lead development of China's next generation fighter which was only years later decisively disproven.

Appearance

In November 2009 PLAAF Deputy Commander General He Weirong said China's next generation fighter would fly 'soon' and become operational between 2017 and 2019.[12] The fighter made a sudden appearance on 21-22 December 2010, when unofficial images showing it conducting runway tests at the Chengdu Aircraft Design Institute's airfield in south-western China were circulated on the Internet. Western observers widely noted at the time that the appearance 'could call into question the U.S. decision to cut funding for its equivalent fighter F-22.'[13] Serious issues with the F-22 meant there was little will for such a reversal, however, and by January 2011 plans to destroy the fighter's tooling equipment were set to be implemented within months. The Chinese fighter's large twin-engine design was a clear indicator that, much like the J-11 and other aircraft from the Flanker series which it was succeeding, it was intended to have a significant range and payload – with a range later confirmed to be double that of the F-22 and F-35.

The release of the first images of the fighter had a considerable impact not only abroad, but also domestically, with expert on Chinese military affairs Richard Fisher, for one, highlighting that 'the response within China has been overwhelmingly positive and has spurred national pride to an enormous degree.'[14] While official Chinese sources did not comment on the release, Director of Naval Intelligence Vice Admiral David Dorsett assured that China was still a long way from fielding an operational fifth generation fighter.[15] Pentagon spokesman Colonel Dave Lapan played down the program as 'not of concern,' stressing that Chinese military aviation was still technologically far behind.[16] U.S. Defence Secretary Robert Gates five days later questioned 'just how stealthy' the fighter really was.[17] Such reassurances were particularly important since, by the year's end, America's sole fifth generation fighter would no longer be in production – with June seeing the last F-22 completed and the mothballing of production equipment announced.[18]

The release of photos of the new Chinese fighter came just days before Defence Secretary Gates visited Beijing to smooth relations, a year after China suspended military ties in protest over American arms sales to Taiwan.* Subsequently on 11 January, just hours before Secretary Gates met with Chinese President Hu Jintao in Beijing and a week before Hu embarked on a state visit to Washington, the J-20 made its first flight in Chengdu and stayed in the air for around fifteen minutes. Official images of a gala reception marking the flight were quickly published with attendees including test pilot Li Gang, director of the 611 Institute Yang Wei, and head of the PLAAF General Xu Qiliang. The aircraft would fly again for eighty minutes on 17 April, then on 5 May for fifty-five minutes when it for the first time fully retracted its landing gear, before demonstrating low altitude manoeuvres on 26 February the following year.

The timing of the maiden flight fuelled widespread speculation regarding its political significance and what message Beijing, or possibly the PLA independently, sought to convey. As the F-22 more than any other weapons system was seen to symbolise U.S. military superiority, so too did the J-20 signify China's own military rise. The *New York Times* thus concluded: 'The symbolism of Tuesday's flight may considerably outweigh its immediate significance.' The *Times* interpreted the timing as miscoordination between the PLA and the civilian leadership which inadvertently sent the wrong message.[19] President Hu and other civilian leaders gave their visitors the impression that they were themselves unaware of the test flight and its timing, with Gates telling reporters that 'the civilian leadership seemed surprised by the test.' He stressed that Hu told him the flight 'had absolutely nothing to do with my visit,' which the Defence Secretary said he believed.[20] 'The Chinese civilians in the room had known nothing about the test ... The PLA would pull such a politically portentous stunt without telling Hu,' Gates later concluded in his memoirs.[21] His statement was supported by experts such as Abraham M. Denmark from the Centre for New

---

* The Republic of China Armed Forces based on Taiwan remain officially in a state of war with the Chinese mainland.

American Security on the basis that senior officials had no day-to-day involvement in aircraft development and were unlikely to have known about the flight test.[22]

While Western analysts widely predicted China's fifth generation fighter would take another ten years to enter production, which proved to be over twice as long as China's aviation industry actually needed, Secretary Gates warned that 'they may be somewhat further ahead in the development of that aircraft than our intelligence had earlier predicted.'[23] Chinese military officials at the time had indicated that the new fighter would enter service around 2018.[24] A paper in the *Strategic Comments* journal observed at the time regarding the significance of the fighter's unveiling: 'The project does, however, underline Beijing's aim – also reflected in its land and naval programmes – to develop armed forces that are commensurate with its status as a rising global power ... the J-20 should be considered within this broader context, rather than as China's riposte to the U.S. Air Force's F-22 Raptor or as an F-35 Joint Strike Fighter "killer."' It concluded: 'It is clear that the West's recent comparative neglect of crewed next-generation combat aircraft has not been mirrored completely by other major powers.'[25]

Development

Two technology demonstrators were built for the J-20 program designated '2001,' which made the first flight, and '2002' which appeared sixteen months later in May 2012. The two were transferred from Chengdu to the China Flight Test Establishment at Xi'an-Yanliang later that year, where they remained active. The '2002' airframe was subsequently renumbered '2004' and used for initial testing of a unique side bay missile launch system for PL-10 visual range air-to-air missiles, with some reports indicating it may have integrated a radar. The '2001' airframe was reported to have been used for testing of radar absorbent materials.[26]

The third airframe, which was the first post-demonstrator aircraft, appeared in October 2012 and as expected differed significantly from the two technology demonstrators. Notable changes included redesigned air intakes, a reshaped canopy, an additional inner frame and an Electro-Optical Targeting System (EOTS) resembling those of the F-35, and the addition of stealth coatings. Other notable changes included a retractable aerial refuelling probe, re-profiled vertical stabilisers, smaller underwing actuators, enlarged tail booms housing additional electronic warfare/electronic countermeasures, and self-defence systems such as chaff and flare dispensers to protect the fighter's rear hemisphere.

The October 2012 prototype numbered '2011' marked the beginning of a new phase in the program leading up to serial production, and over the next two years until the end of 2014 three more prototypes numbered '2012', '2013' and '2015' made their first flights indicating a very rapid rate of progress. The fifth post-demonstrator prototype designated '2016' appeared in taxi tests on 11 September 2015, and first flew on 18 September, with notable changes to its air intakes and reportedly a new engine. The silver-metallic sheen on the engines of prior models was replaced by a charcoal colour, and some observers noted apparent changes to the side weapons bays. The sixth and final model designated '2017' first flew the following month on 24 November 2015, and building on the changes seen on '2016' it also conspicuously boasted a reshaped cockpit canopy for improved visibility. There were thus eight demonstrator and prototype flight airframes built for the J-20 program before serial production began, compared to eighteen for the F-22, sixteen for the F-35 and ten for the Russian Su-57.[27] All J-20 pre-production models made their first flights within a short period of under five years.

All prototypes were eventually delivered to the China Flight Test Establishment in Xi'an, although some first spent time at the Flight Test and Training Centre in Cangzhou, Hebei province, not far from Beijing. '2013' and '2015,' for example, were transferred to Xi'an in April 2015 shortly before the appearances of their successors. New technologies and subsystems were often tested through integration onto the older airframes, a notable example being the re-engineering of '2011' to test new powerplants with improved stealth capabilities. Load tests using large drop tanks and testing the firing of air-launched-missiles were reportedly among the other purposes they served.

In parallel to the J-20 demonstrators and prototypes, from 2013 a heavily modified Tu-204C airliner at the China Flight Test Establishment served as a dedicated radar testbed for the program. This not only allowed systems to be tested individually, but also tested their integration to automate their working together. Such large aircraft had far more space for onsite monitoring and diagnosis, which would not be possible if sensors were flown on a fighter-sized aircraft. The Tu-204C featured the J-20's front section and radome as well as several electronic warfare and communications systems all housed above the fuselage. Testing of other subsystems was also performed by a similarly converted Y-8C transport aircraft.

The role of the one-of-a-kind Tu-204C mirrored the use of a modified Boeing 757-200 prototype in the United States which was converted to serve as a testbed for development of the country's own first fifth generation fighter the F-22 and flown from 1999. New levels of sensor fusion pioneered by fifth generation fighters made such testing necessary, with testbed aircraft touted as reducing the time needed for avionics testing by half. The Boeing 757 was used to test the Raptor's AN/APG-77 AESA radar, its ALR-94 electronic support measures suite, AAR-56 infrared missile approach warning system, secure communications systems, data links, and other subsystems, and had a re-creation of the F-22's cockpit. The F-22's own forward fuselage section was installed in the nose of the aircraft. The testbed aircraft would subsequently be used to support development of upgrades for the Raptor's avionics.[28] Less was known about its Chinese counterpart the Tu-204C or whether it would similarly play a significant role in testing upgrades for the J-20 after the fighter entered service.

Service Entry

Serial production of the J-20 began in 2015, with images of the first serially produced airframe – number 2101 – published in December that year.[29] Like pre-production aircraft, production aircraft were often photographed taxiing and flying with their yellow factory primer before being painted. The first flight of a serial production airframe occurred on 18 January 2016, less than two months after the maiden flight of the final prototype. Deliveries to the PLAAF began in mid-2016 sometime before August,[30] shortly before the first F-35A first became operational in the U.S. Air Force.[31] Leaving Chengdu at a low initial production rate, the first J-20 unit formally entered PLAAF service in March 2017, over six months after deliveries began.[32]

The J-20's entry into service came just six years after its first flight, placing the program entirely in a league of its own for development speed among aircraft of its generation despite it being China's first fifth generation fighter. It represented the first time China's defence sector moved into a new fighter generation without very heavy reliance on foreign technologies. By contrast the F-22 entered service fifteen years after its first demonstrator flight, the F-35 also fifteen years, and the Su-57 eleven years – and twenty years after Russia's first fifth generation technology demonstrator had flown in January 2001. Indeed, even China's first fully indigenous fourth generation fighter, the lightweight J-10, had taken six years to enter service after its first flight in March 1998, which when considering how much more complex fifth generation aircraft were indicated that the country's combat aviation industry had come a long way in little over a decade. As industry continued to advance rapidly upgrades between successive batches affecting both subsystems and stealth capabilities made newer batches significantly more capable than their predecessors, despite software upgrades being made continuously to aircraft across the fleet. As chief designer Yang Wei predicted one month after the first batch of aircraft was delivered to a frontline unit, a priority for the program after the J-20's service entry would be to 'Carry out serial development and continuously improve combat capabilities.'[33]

The first PLAAF unit to receive the J-20 was the 176th Brigade at the Flight Test and Training Base at Dingxin in the Gobi Desert of Gansu Province, which began operating the stealth jets in mid-late 2016. The brigade was assigned to test tactics for new fighters, and almost simultaneously began operating the J-16 and J-10C, which alongside the J-20 together formed the PLA's 'new generation.' The J-16 and J-10C were new iterations of fourth generation designs with avionics and weaponry brought up to similar fifth generation levels to the J-20, allowing them to easily network together, employ many of the same tactics and exchange pilots. The 176th was one of two brigades based at Dingxin alongside the 175th which was assigned to tactical training.

The Dingxin facility had long been a centre for weapons integration testing, and in a relatively isolated location near the Shuangchengzi missile test range it served as China's only large-scale comprehensive test training base for aircraft and air defence systems. It played a comparable role to Nellis Air Force Base in southern Nevada in the United States, and frequently accommodated well over 100 aircraft. The very wide open airspace, expansive training range complexes, and clear weather suitable for flight throughout the year, made Dingxin an ideal facility for breaking in a new fighter, particularly high endurance heavyweights like the J-20. It also made the base a suitable home to both the Golden Helmet and Golden Dart competitions which were the most prestigious in the PLAAF. Although the 176th was not considered a combat unit, the facility it operated from fell under the PLA's Western Theatre Command.

The second unit to integrate the J-20 was the 172nd Air Brigade at the Cangzhou Flight Training Base in Hebei province near the city of Tianjin, which served as both an advanced training and a combat reserve unit. Fighters were received and entered service in February 2018. Thus, while the J-20 was first received by a PLAAF unit in 2016, and entered PLAAF service in early 2017 with that unit, it was announced to have first been delivered to 'combat troops' only in February 2018. J-20s were delivered just months after J-16s had begun to enter service in the same unit, with both high endurance fighters having highly complementary capabilities. The Defence Ministry issued a statement on 9 February that the delivery marked 'an important step towards the full formation of combat capabilities of the new fighter jet,' emphasizing that the J-20's inclusion in combat forces would further enhance the service's comprehensive combat capabilities and 'help the Air Force better shoulder its sacred mission of safeguarding national sovereignty, security and territorial integrity.'[34]

Located near China's East Coast, the Cangzhou facility was one of the closest to the Korean Peninsula, and the deployment came amid high tensions shortly after the White House had seriously considered launching an attack on North Korea.[35] After Chinese state media warned that the PLA would intervene if the U.S. attacked,[36] Beijing, alongside Moscow, drew a red line with Chinese air defence assets deployed to the Korean border and ships sent to exercise at sea to stress that strikes on its treaty ally would not be tolerated.[37] The deployment to Cangzhou followed unverified reports that J-20 fighters had flown near or into South Korean airspace as a show of force to deter possible military action – although these were widely dismissed on the basis that the fighter program was still in its infancy.[38] Beyond Korea, J-20s at Cangzhou were also well within range of targets in Japan and Taiwan while being well positioned to play a role in the defence of the capital Beijing. Almost three years after the first J-20s were delivered, the 172nd would in January 2021 begin to receive more advanced J-20A fighters making it the only Air Brigade to operate both J-20 variants.

The 9th Air Brigade at Wuhu Air Base under the PLA Eastern Theatre Command became the third unit to integrate the J-20 in January 2019, and the first frontline unit to do so. It was the only frontline unit to receive the baseline J-20 variant before the more advanced J-20A replaced it on production lines in the second quarter of 2019. Otherwise known as the Wang Hai Air Group 'Ace Unit', it dated back to the 1950s when it flew MiG-15s and MiG-17s and was responsible for shooting down fifty-nine enemy aircraft – twenty-nine of them America jets over Korea. Its namesake was the Korean War flying ace Wang Hai who was credited with nine kills against American fighters and had led the unit when it was still organised as an air regiment.[39] The deployment was followed by widespread reports linking the J-20 program to the Korean War historical memory of the PLAAF.

The 9th Air Brigade had long had an elite status, and was located less than 300km from Shanghai. It had notably been the first unit to receive Su-27 fighters delivered from 1991, and the fact that it was the first to receive the J-20 outside test and training units highlighted the new fighter's status as a direct successor to the Flanker which would similarly begin bringing the PLAAF into a new generation. The brigade had been similarly prioritised to become the first to operate the new Su-30MKK from 2000, which was at the time the most capable Russian-built fighter class in service worldwide, phasing out the Su-27s to lower priority locations. The Su-30MKK was the last Russian fighter acquired to equip multiple PLAAF squadrons, and although it had just a decade prior been considered an elite fighter, by 2019 its capabilities were very far behind those of top end indigenous aircraft. The fighters were accordingly reallocated to lower priority units when the J-20s began to be received.

The first agreement on Su-30MKK acquisitions had been signed at a time of high tensions in the Taiwan Strait in 1996, with Wuhu considered an optimal location to operate long range fighters for missions into the area. Replacing them with J-20s was expected to similarly improve the PLA's position in the hotspot. Collin Koh, Research Fellow at Singapore's S. Rajaratnam School of International Studies, was among the analysts who speculated regarding the deployment: 'The unit turning operational in Eastern Theatre Command is precisely aimed at Taiwan ... And to challenge U.S. military activities in [the] Taiwan Strait, besides posing a threat to the median line that Taiwan's air force patrols along.'[40] The new stealth fighters' close proximity to Taipei was widely highlighted with considerable concern by Taiwanese media.[41]

In January 2021 the 1st Air Brigade at Anshan Air Base in Liaoning Province became the fourth unit to integrate J-20 fighters and the first frontline unit to receive the new J-20A powered by indigenous WS-10C turbofan engines. It was the first new unit to be equipped with J-20s in two years, as production lines had transitioned from low rate production with stopgap Russian engines, to a much higher production rate of J-20As using indigenous powerplants. The brigade received the fighters near simultaneously to the 172nd Air Brigade at the Cangzhou Flight Training Base which also saw J-20A deliveries commence that month to supplement its existing J-20s using older Russian-sourced engines. With production of the J-20A's new WS-10C engine ending a previous bottleneck, new units began in 2021 to receive the fighters at a much faster rate.

An assessment at the USAF's China Aerospace Studies Institute saw J-20 deliveries to a second PLAAF frontline unit as an indication 'that the PLAAF is satisfied with, and confident in, the capabilities of the J-20, and that more combat units are likely to receive the J-20 in the future.'[42] Dubbed the Military Development Vanguard Air Group 'Ace Unit,' which originated from the first aviation combat force of the PLAAF that served in Korea, the 1st Air Brigade was the first facility under the Northern Theatre Command to receive J-20s. It also represented a priority location where it replaced the majority of the relatively modern J-11B and twin seat J-11BS fighters, although some J-11s remained at Anshan alongside the J-20s. The location was well positioned for the J-20 to carry out air defence duties along China's east coast, as well as operations into Korea and across the East China Sea.

The deployment to Anshan was considered by a number of analysts to be aimed at influencing the security situation in the Taiwan Strait at a time of high tensions, with Beijing-based naval expert Li Jie being among those to conclude to this effect: 'The J-20's new deployment, announced ahead of the Communist Party's 100th anniversary on 1 July, is aimed at telling South Korea and Japan that China is strengthening its air defence along the coastal areas, warning them not to join Washington and intervene in the Taiwan issue.' He elaborated: 'None of the J-20s will be deployed near the coasts, because of their 2,000km-plus combat range, which is more than enough to cover the mainland coastal provinces and Taiwan.'[43] Others highlighted that Anshan, where the fighters were based, was in Liaoning province bordering North Korea, and that the fighters could be ideally positioned to provide air cover to China's treaty ally and to signalling Washington should it again consider an attack as it had in 2017. J-20s under the 1st Air Brigade were likely the first to ever fly up against foreign fifth generation fighters, with a J-20 encounter with American F-35s over the East China Sea confirmed in March 2022 which the Anshan unit was considered the most likely to have been involved in.

The 5th Air Brigade based at Guilin Air Base south-east of the city of Guilin in Guangxi Province in June 2021 became the fifth unit to receive J-20s and the third to receive the J-20A, which replaced older J-10B and J-10AS lightweight fighters.[44] The J-10Bs under the 5th Air Brigade had themselves replaced older J-10A fighters in November 2015, and were subsequently reallocated elsewhere. This was the first frontline unit where J-20s replaced a fighter class other than Flankers, with the J-10 being less than half its size and having far lower operational costs indicating that the PLA was willing to transition more units from lightweight to heavyweight aircraft to accommodate expanding J-20 numbers. It was noted after delivery that two of the PLAAF's three frontline J-20 units were now closely adjacent to the Taiwan Strait, with Chinese military experts highlighting that bases hosting the fighters were accordingly likely to be priority targets for missile strikes from Taiwan in the event of cross-straits hostilities.[45]

The sixth unit to receive the J-20 was the 56th Air Brigade at Zhengzhou Airbase, where J-20A deployments were confirmed in March 2022 to replace J-10B and J-10AS fighters under the Central Theatre Command. Despite its considerable distance from the sea and from major cities, the J-20's high endurance and the new variant's reported supercruise capability meant that the fighters could respond to threats as far as Beijing, Shanghai, Korea and the Taiwan Strait from their airfields. This provided the PLAAF with greater strategic depth, and ensured J-20 operations in key areas around the east coast could commence even if airbases in the region were disabled.

In March 2022 unconfirmed reports emerged that a first frontline unit under the Western Theatre Command had received the J-20, making it the seventh PLAAF unit to do so. Other than for training units, the Western Command traditionally had the lowest priority for receiving modern fighter classes due to the lack of sizeable U.S. or allied military presences near the region. The largest command by area, it faced India, Pakistan and Afghanistan and multiple Soviet successor states in Central Asia. Images released on 19 April subsequently confirmed that the 111th Air Brigade at Korla Air Base in China's westernmost province of Xinjiang had received J-20A fighters, which replaced J-11A and Su-27 fighters that were being phased out of service.[46] The 111th had seen multiple changes to its composition, with very light J-7E fighters replaced by advanced J-11Bs three times their size in 2011, before these were reallocated to other units in 2016 and the brigade instead received the older J-11As and Su-27s which it operated for six years.

Perhaps the most important rationale for deploying J-20s to Xinjiang was that geographically distributing fifth generation units widely ensured there were opportunities for fighter units across all theatre commands to train both against stealth fighters, as well as in how to operate alongside them. Deliveries of J-20s to new units before older units had received enough of the fighters to fully transition to the class – for example the 5th Air Brigade receiving the fighters before the 1st Air Brigade had completed its transition to the J-20 – indicated that getting more units acquainted with the new aircraft was being prioritised. The Western Theatre Command also housed China's expanding land based strategic nuclear arsenal, which was expected to be a primary target for American bombers in the event of a full-scale war and was thus expected to see air defences strengthened as America's B-21 stealth bomber fleet began to grow from around 2030. The B-21 was largely designed with attacks on this arsenal in Xinjiang in mind.[47] Nevertheless, the fact that J-20s under the Western Command were the only ones not within comfortable non-refuelled range to contribute to operations in the most critical potential hotspots, which were all located off the east coast, meant deployments under the command were expected to continue to be limited.

In August 2022 the 8th Air Brigade at Changxing in north-east China became the eighth unit to transition to the J-20. It represented the second brigade under the Northern Theatre Command to deploy the aircraft after the 1st Air Brigade at Anshan had received J-20s in January the previous year. This followed confirmation of the first J-20 engagement with F-35s over the East China Sea five months prior, likely from the 1st Air Brigade, with the decision to prioritise enhancing units under the strategically located Northern Command potentially having been influenced by such incidents and by the large and growing F-35 presence in the area.

In March 2023 the 55th Air Brigade based at Jining Air Base, a central location near the east coast, was reported to have received J-20s to replace its ageing Russian supplied Su-27SK fighters. It was the third brigade under the Northern Theatre Command to integrate the fifth generation fighters and the ninth unit in the Air Force overall do have done so. The central location along the east coast allowed J-20s to perform duties across multiple key theatres from Taiwan to Korea, as well as air defence duties for most of the country's first tier cities which the new unit in south-western Shandong was ideally located for.

In June 2023 the 131st Air Brigade based at Nanning Air Base under the Southern Theatre Command was reported to have become the tenth unit to receive J-20 fighters, replacing J-10Cs which were reallocated to a lower priority location. The J-10C s had been stationed there for seven years, and had begun to be deployed in early 2016 to replace older J-10A fighters. Located near the Chinese mainland's southernmost point, the fighters were well positioned for air defence over southern cities such as Shanghai and Nanjing, as well as the defence of key naval facilities such as Longpo Naval Base – a centre for nuclear submarine operations on Hainan, very near to Nanning. The fighters were also very well positioned to contribute to operations in the Taiwan Strait.

Although J-20 deliveries increased significantly after 2022, information confirming new deployments became increasingly difficult to obtain. Only two air brigades were confirmed to have received J-20s that year, namely the 97th Air Brigade in Dazu Air Base in Chongqing where they replaced J-7 fighters and the 4th Air Brigade at Foshan Air Base where they replaced J-11s and Su-27s. These were only confirmed in the final week of December that year.[48] The 97th Brigade was the first to convert from J-7s to J-20s, which represented one of the most drastic unit conversions not only in China but worldwide, both for maintenance teams who now operated an aircraft almost four times as large, but also technologically with a leap forward of two generations, as well as for how the unit operated with the two classes being at opposite ends of the spectrum in terms of performance. Located under the Western Theatre Command near Chengdu, Dazu Airbase was one of the most remote from potential security threats. The conversion from the J-7 to the J-20 which had several times its endurance, as well as an aerial refuelling capability, allowed this unit to potentially quickly redeploy wherever it was needed, with its location being among the most central in China. By contrast the 4th Brigade at Foshan Airbase under the Southern Theatre Command was near the coast and among the very closest to the key economic centres at Shenzhen and Hong Kong, while also being just within 650km of both Hainan and the Taiwan Strait.

In April 2024 satellite images confirmed that the 41st Air Brigade at Wuyishan had received J-20As to replace J-11 and Su-27 fighters, following unconfirmed reports of J-20 deployments under the unit the previous year. This location placed the fighters just 450 kilometres from Taipei, with the unit representing one of several widely reported but not confirmed have transitioned to the J-20 in 2023. By mid-2023 unconfirmed reports of varying credibility had separately emerged of seven brigades receiving or preparing to receive J-20s, which, alongside the five aforementioned units included the 98th Air Brigade at Chongqing where they would replace J-11 and Su-27 fighters, and the 95th Air Brigade at Lianyungang where they would replace J-11Bs. By the end of the year, however, the 95th Brigade was reported to have received J-16s rather than J-20s, while three other units remained unconfirmed. Unconfirmed reports on the 55th and 131st Brigades appeared to be the most likely to have been true. The surge in the number of brigades being reported to be receiving J-20s reflected the tremendous increases that had been successfully made to productive capacity, with production rate increases indicating that between three and five new brigades had likely received J-20s that year. The possibility remained that one or more of these had gone totally unreported and was not among the three unconfirmed units.

Airframe

The J-20 airframe's surface is smooth with no protruding inlets or pitot tubes, and flush hexagonal fuel-air heat exchangers further reduce its radar cross section.[†] It has a frameless canopy, chiselled nose section, blended fuselage, chimed forebody and electroconductive canopy, flat fuselage bottom, sawtooth edges on compartment doors, as well as radar absorbent coatings and divertless supersonic inlets which all contribute to its stealth capabilities. In November 2018 it was confirmed that the fighter integrated a retractable in-flight refuelling probe embedded under its fuselage, ensuring that stealth could be conserved without sacrificing this capability.[49]

The airframe makes very high use of composite materials at twenty-nine per cent of its overall weight, with titanium and titanium-alloys making up a further twenty per cent and the remaining fifty-one per cent made from aluminium and steel alloys. Composites are vital to reducing the number of fasteners in an aircraft's structure to provide thermophysical and radio-technical characteristics meeting

---

[†] Insight into the development of the J-20's unique airframe was provided by a 2001 paper on the aerodynamic configuration of a next generation fighter by Dr. Song Wencong, the mentor of the aircraft's chief designer Yang Wei. The paper highlighted a focus in the industry on resolving design conflicts between stealth, high manoeuvrability, supercruise, transonic performance, and high angle of attack performance. It proposed employment of lift-body leading edge root extension canard configuration which would be unstable in both the lateral and yaw directions. It further proposed all-moving vertical stabilisers significantly smaller than those which would usually be used on a fighter of its size, as well as S-shaped air intakes, in order to improve and reduce the radar cross section. Also proposed were small aspect ratio wings with medium back sweep angle and relatively large dihedral canards. These features, which closely resembled those on the final J-20, were expected to provide excellent stealth capabilities and supersonic drag characteristics, as well as the lift characteristics, stability and controllability needed to achieve high angles of attack.

fifth generation requirements. When they first began to be widely used on fighters in the 1990s composites could increase an airframe's weight efficiency by around twenty-five per cent, with significant improvements having since raised this figure. Chinese industry made considerable progress developing composite materials for use on combat aircraft from the 1990s, which came to be a distinguishing feature of indigenous derivatives of the Su-27 compared to the Russian original, which made much more limited use of such materials. The J-20's high composite airframe largely built on extensive work done to enhance fourth generation designs using more composite materials. Concurrent production in civil aviation, including manufacturing of a fast-growing range of airliner components, had also played an important role in cultivating expertise in composite material fabrication.

Mature radar cross section testing technologies played an important role in the development of the J-20's stealth profile, and to maintain a reduced RCS the fighter carries armaments internally.[50] A central weapons bay on its underside accommodates four long range PL-15 air-to-air missiles, with two smaller lateral bays behind the side air intakes each further accommodating one smaller PL-10 short range missile. Weapons integration tests at Chengdu for an entirely unique retractable side missile launch rail for the PL-10 began at a very early stage of development no later than the first quarter of 2013. The fighter's pioneering of a new stealthier launch system relative to its American rivals was cited as one of multiple important early indicators that the J-20 could improve on existing designs overseas rather than simply catching up.[51]

Should the aircraft not need to maintain its stealth profile, four external hardpoints on the J-20 can accommodate either fuel tanks or additional missiles. External pylons can also be jettisoned to enter stealth mode mid-flight. It remains uncertain which missile classes the fighter can carry externally, and whether it can carry the very long ranged PL-XX which is too large for its internal bays and was developed primarily to target enemy support aircraft and bombers.

The J-20's airframe benefits from leading edge extensions and body lift, which combined with its canards generate 180 per cent of the lift that the fighter would have had as a pure delta wing design. This allows for a reduced supersonic drag through use of a smaller wing, while ensuring a high turn performance by avoiding compromises to transonic lift-to-drag characteristics. The fighter's chief designer Yang Wei provided insight into the benefits of this unique canard design in an interview in March 2018: 'We are the only ones in the world who have created a fighter with a lifting body, side wings, and canards like the J-20's. The wing layout not only provides the fighter with a good stealth performance, but also with strong supersonic and manoeuvring flight capabilities, allowing it to fly far and carry high weapons payloads.' He added: 'In terms of situational awareness, we have made many breakthroughs and have many unique tricks in many aspects such as information countermeasures, airborne weapons and coordinated operations. This is also the only way for China's aviation industry to achieve from following, running parallel and finally leading.'[52]

The J-20's canard delta wing design with twin outward canted all-moving fins is entirely unique among operational aircraft of its generation, with canards improving flight performance, including both low-speed agility and supersonic manoeuvrability. This is particularly useful for air superiority fighters to provide better control over their angles of attack. They also better optimise the fighter to operate from shorter airfields. Canards on the J-20 appear to be optimised for stealth particularly in the forward sector. Chengdu research papers from as early as 2001 discussed the benefits of a delta-canard design, which had been under consideration since the 1960s for the cancelled but highly ambitious J-9 single engine fighter and were applied to its successor the J-10.

Claims that the canard fuselage join is not ideal for stealth have been common since the J-20 was unveiled,[53] although such assertions are contradicted by the results of studies performed in both China and the United States. A Chengdu Aircraft Design Institute paper, for one, specifically addressed the impact of canards on radar cross section in a publication that emerged in 2019, concluding that there was no significant impact on stealth capabilities.[54] Lockheed Martin notably considered a canard delta wing stealth fighter for its Joint Advanced Strike Technology program before settling on the design that became the F-35, while Northrop Grumman also considered a canard aircraft derived from its YF-23 technology demonstrator which had competed with the YF-22, indicating that the physics of canards were compatible with stealth.[55] The X-36 fighter agility research aircraft developed by McDonnell Douglas and NASA also used a canard design and was considered among the stealthiest manned jet aircraft to have ever flown.

Avionics

J-20 pilots interact with a modern glass cockpit with a 610 x 230mm touchscreen panoramic display controlled by voice command, a smaller liquid crystal display between the pilot's legs, and a prominent wide-angle holographic heads-up display with a distinctive green glow. The fighter is flown with a side-stick and throttle, and a Helmet Mounted Display (HMD) was confirmed in May 2018 to be operational.

Situational awareness is provided by the combination of the Type 1475 (KLJ-5) AESA fire-control radar, the EORD-31 infra-red search and track system (IRST), and an electro-optical distributed aperture system. The cockpit design and HMD allow the pilot to better process data provided by onboard and offboard sensors and benefit from 'information fusion.' The KLJ-5 radar is a major strong point of the J-20's overall combat capabilities, and may well be the most powerful single radar built for air-to-air combat in service worldwide. It reportedly has between 2000 and 2200 transmitting/receiving modules, compared to 1900 on the F-22's AN/APG-77,

1600 on the F-35's AN/APG-81, and just 836 on the French Rafale's RBE-2AA. With a transmission power of 24kW, compared to between 16.4 and 20kW on the AN/APG-77, there is a significant possibility that the radar outperforms those of any other fighter in the world.[56] This reflects both its size and power, as well as the sophistication of the Chinese electronics industry, although detractors have claimed American industry's greater experience in the field at the cutting edge level could partially compensate in other ways.

The first Chinese fighters with active electronically scanned array (AESA) radars entered service around 2015 when the J-16 joined the fleet. Electronically scanned array radars are not only far more reliable and less susceptible to jamming, but also facilitate a much wider range of electronic warfare techniques, are significantly more powerful and efficient and can scan much faster than those with mechanically scanned arrays. Very few mechanically scanned array radars can engage two targets simultaneously, and those that can, such as the F-14's very large AN/AWG-9, must engage targets flying very close together, where by contrast electronically array scanned radars can facilitate engagements of targets flying a few metres over the earth's surface and others flying in near space simultaneously. While mechanically scanned array radars rely on a single continuous radio beam, electronically scanned array radars emit multiple intermittent beams from hundreds of discrete individual electronically steered emitters which can narrowly aim at multiple objects to simultaneously track targets, search for other possible targets, track friendly missiles, and send commands to multiple missiles to intercept multiple targets. AESA radars have the further advantage over passive electronically scanned array (PESA) radars of being able to scan more precisely and send out radio waves at different frequencies in multiple directions simultaneously without moving any antennas, which is particularly valuable for electronic warfare. They also have much smaller radar signatures which makes it more difficult for potential adversaries to use their radar emissions to home in on their locations.

Development of electronically scanned array radars for fighter/ interceptor aircraft was pioneered by the Soviet Union, which developed the N007 Zaslon PESA radar for its MiG-31 that entered service in 1981. It was followed by much improved second generation PESA radars, including the N007M Zaslon-M, which was ready for serial production in 1994, and the N011M Bars which completed development at around the same time and was intended for enhanced Flanker variants. The Soviets were followed nineteen years later by the United States, which integrated AESA radars onto a squadron of eighteen experimental F-15s under the 3rd Fighter Wing at Elmendorf Air Force Base, Alaska in 2000, followed by France in 2001 with a PESA radar on the Rafale and Japan in 2002 with the world's first fighter, the F-2, with an AESA radar as its standard sensor. Electronically scanned array radars had tremendous advantages over those with mechanical scanning, with the last fighter program to adopt them being the joint German, British, Spanish and Italian Eurofighter, which until 2019 was produced with a mechanically scanned array radar long since considered obsolete.

The J-20's AESA radar is complemented by the EOTS-86 optical sensor, an equivalent to the F-35's Electro-Optical Targeting System, which is well optimised to engagements against stealth targets and provides long range visual identification of potential threats. The EOTS-86 is highly complementary to the fighter's infra-red search and track (IRST) system, with the latter detecting and the former identifying targets before they are neutralised at beyond visual range. This can be done passively without the need to emit any radar emissions, which allows the fighter to better conserve its stealth capabilities, although AESA radars already have very low radar signatures compared to traditional mechanically scanned array radars.

Perhaps the most outstanding feature in the J-20's sensor suite are its six diamond-shaped windows, with two on the sides of the nose, two more under the rear fuselage and a further two at the forward aft of the cockpit. These are electro optical sensors covering all directions, and form part of the distributed aperture system that allows pilots to observe their surroundings 360 degrees around the aircraft as well as through the bottom using their helmets. The system facilitates the detection and tracking of enemy missiles including launch point detection and the cueing of countermeasures. It also facilitates detection and tracking of enemy aircraft and cueing for air-to-air munitions and infrared tracking systems, while further providing imagery for cockpit displays and pilot night vision. A further function is to eliminate blind spots which is particularly valuable for visual range combat. The designation of the J-20's aperture system remains unknown, with its only known equivalent being the F-35's AN/AAQ-37. Use of aperture systems is one of multiple examples of a key cutting edge technology which sets the J-20 and the F-35 apart from other fighters even within their generation.

The benefits of the J-20 and F-35's aperture systems were effectively summarised by Russian defence analyst Vladimir Tuchkov as follows: 'It is the pilot's helmet, which makes the aircraft "transparent." That is, visibility is not limited by the cockpit windows. The whole panorama of the surrounding area is displayed in the pilot's visors, in both the visible and the infrared spectrum. Monitoring the pilot's head and eye movements, the computer provides the necessary panoramic viewpoint and provides the pilots with tips, and manages targeting.' He indicated that a lack of such systems was the Su-57's leading disadvantage – one which also affected the older F-22.[57]

Engines

As predicted by Chinese aviation industry experts around twenty-five years before the J-20's first flight, engine technologies proved the most challenging area of development due to the very high power required by heavyweight fifth generation air superiority fighters, as well as the need for reasonable maintenance requirements and near perfect reliability.[58] Although work on a suitable engine began in the 1990s, which was later designated WS-15, in contrast to almost all other aspects of the J-20 program which completed development on or ahead of schedule, the engine took considerably longer than expected to be ready for serial production. As such two and possibly three stopgap engines, all of them based on powerplants designed for fourth generation fighters, were relied on to power the J-20.

The majority of J-20 prototypes and demonstrator airframes used an unknown variant of the Russian AL-31, with some sources reporting that the very first aircraft were powered by the WS-10B, or a close derivative – which also powered the fourth generation J-11 series at the time.[59] This was China's first afterburning turbofan with a comparable thrust/weight ratio and overall performance to those powering Russian and American fourth generation fighters – namely the AL-31F and F-110, which respectively powered the Su-27/30 and F-15. It was later acknowledged, however, that this was highly unlikely and that all prototypes and demonstrator airframes almost certainly used the AL-31.

The WS-10B's entry into service in 2009 was a major milestone in Chinese engine development, as while the country had for decades produced and exported combat jets, these had been powered by derivatives of Soviet turbojet designs from the 1950s that had seen conservative improvements made in China. The most notable example was the WP-13 turbojet powering the widely exported J-7 fighter, which was based on the Soviet R-13. Not only had turbojets been phased out abroad in the 1970s in favour of turbofan engines, which were far more fuel efficient and retained much greater potential for modernisation, but even among turbojet engines Chinese designs like the WP-13 were considered outdated. As their name implied, a turbofan engine achieved a superior performance by using a ducted fan to increase the mass and reduce the speed of the propelling jet.

Although an effort was made to develop a highly ambitious turbofan from the 1960s comparable to the Soviet and American

designs then under development for fourth generation fighters, this
failed, as did the J-9 fighter it was intended to power, which was
cancelled in 1984. Work on the J-9's immediate successor the J-10,
however, spurred development of the WS-10. Development of an
advanced turbofan engine became more viable as Chinese industry
modernised rapidly in the 1990s, and as it gained access to Soviet
technologies and expertise after the superpower's disintegration in
1991. The WS-10 began to be introduced into frontline service on
a significant scale in 2009 on J-11 fighters, with this seen to pose a
low risk due to their twin engine configurations and resulting engine
redundancy. The engine was considered to have achieved high
levels of reliability in the 2010s when it began to equip PLAAF J-10
fighters, which as single engine aircraft lacked engine redundancy,
which indicated a high degree of confidence that the WS-10 was
dependable.

Although both are highly capable as powerplants for fourth
generation aircraft, the AL-31F and WS-10B would both have left
the J-20 far underpowered. The PLAAF consequentially integrated a
much more powerful engine, which is widely thought to be modified
derivative of the Russian AL-31FM2, onto production variants of
the J-20 from 2015. This enhanced AL-31 variant benefitted from
use of an entirely new three-stage fan, a new high-pressure turbine
assembly and combustion chamber, a 75°C increase to turbine
entry temperature, and a new full authority digital engine control
with hydromechanical backup – a major leap in sophistication over
prior AL-31 models. A variant of the AL-31FM2 modified for the
J-20 is thought to have been jointly developed with Chinese inputs
and had an estimated thrust of 142kN – just seven per cent lower
than the F119 powering the F-22. The variant developed for China
may well have integrated a number of technologies from the AL-
31FM3 powerplant which was first tested in 2007, was considered
production ready around the time Chinese orders were made, and
had a significantly superior performance to its predecessor, with

major improvements to its turbine fan and combustion chamber in particular. Offering these technologies for the J-20's customised powerplant would have provided a means to recoup some of the investment sunk into developing the engine, which never received orders from the Russian Defence Ministry itself.[60] According to figures from the Stockholm International Peace Research Institute forty pairs of AL-31FM2 derived turbofans were purchased in 2014, which represented one of the last ever Chinese orders for Russian fighter engines.[61]

Joint development of customised new AL-31 variants to meet PLAAF requirements was far from unprecedented, with the J-10 having been powered by the heavily customised AL-31FN which was specifically designed for it after a contract was signed in March 1992, much as the AL-31FM2 derivative was designed for the J-20. Indeed, some sources indicated that the stopgap Russian powerplant for early J-20s was not a derivative of the AL-31FM2, but rather a new enhanced iteration of the J-10's AL-31FN – the AL-31FN Series 3.[62] The original AL-31FM2 had been developed as a far more powerful AL-31 variant with approximately sixteen per cent more thrust, which was necessary to power the heaviest fighter class in the world, the Russian Su-34 strike fighter. Although far from cutting edge, the engine was efficient enough to provide the J-20 with a respectable flight performance and a wide combat radius reportedly exceeding 2,000km on internal fuel – a range comparable to that of advanced Flanker variants and far exceeding all Western fighter classes. The J-20's flight performance and endurance were both expected to improve very considerably, however, once it moved past stopgap engines to integrate the fully indigenous WS-15 fifth generation powerplant.

As the first J-20s became operational in early March 2017, Chen Xiangbao, vice president of the Aero Engine Corporation of China Beijing Institute of Aeronautical Materials, predicted: 'It will not take a long time for our fifth-generation combat plane to have

China-made engines ... The engine's development is proceeding well. We also have begun to design a next-generation aviation engine with a thrust-to-weight ratio that is much higher than that of current types.' He elaborated regarding remaining issues in the industry: 'For instance, we are able to develop the two most important components in an advanced engine – the single crystal superalloy turbine blades and powder metallurgy superalloy turbine disks – but in mass production, the products' quality is not very satisfactory.' 'The road to success is filled with setbacks and failures. Each of the world's engine powers has walked this road,' he added. His statements were presumed to be referring to the clean sheet WS-15 design which was at the time expected to replace the jointly developed AL-31FM2 derivative (from here referred to simply as AL-31FM2) within five years.[63]

With the WS-15 facing delays an improved variant of the WS-10 of unconfirmed designation, speculated to be designated (and from hereon referred to as) the WS-10C, was developed to provide a viable replacement to the AL-31FM2. The engine was first confirmed to be in flight testing in 2017, with a new prototype designated '2021' built to test its integration and likely other new features for the J-20A variant. Aircraft '2021' was first seen in September 2017. The WS-10C powered all factory-built J-20s from mid-2019. The first J-20s with the new powerplants, designated J-20A and benefitting from a number of conservative other improvements, entered service from January 2021.

The WS-10C's combustion chamber was reportedly an area where it improved on the AL-31FM2 particularly significantly, with the engine also having improved fuel efficiency, acceleration performance and thrust over the Russian turbofan. It also had much better stealth capabilities, most conspicuously represented by its serrated afterburner nozzles – a key distinguishing feature from other engines in PLA service. Engines with such stealth features were first seen tested as early as 2014, when they were integrated onto the first prototype number '2011', which was re-engined to serve as a testbed for such powerplants eighteen months after its first flight. The WS-10C reportedly allowed the J-20 to fly at low supersonic speeds without afterburners – referred to as low supercruise – which facilitated sustained supersonic flight for extended periods.[64] This made the J-20 the only supercruise-capable fighter of its generation in production worldwide.

WS-10C equipped J-20 fighters had by early 2022 operated at extreme altitudes, humidity levels and temperatures, which was cited as evidence that the fighter could carry out missions across the country. Such testing was thought to be the purpose behind the J-20's reported brief deployments to south-western China's mountainous territories. Take-offs at extreme altitudes were particularly challenging and required high engine power due to the thin air, which had previously posed similar problems for the Indian Air Force's European-sourced aircraft near its northern borders. The J-20's deputy chief designer Gong Feng highlighted in January 2022 that integration of the WS-10C significantly increased the fighter's capabilities and was customisable for the aircraft, where the AL-31FM2 had limited its performance. Gong had been tasked with conducting reliability tests for the fighter under extreme conditions, and concluded: 'I can proudly tell everyone, that the J-20 with Chinese engines has it all, both from the inside and outside.'[65]

Visiting fellow at the Griffith Asia Institute in Australia Peter Layton highlighted in April 2022 regarding the significance of the WS-10C's integration, which he claimed was more reliable than any Russian engine: 'It's not just that China does not need Russian help anymore, it is that Chinese-built aircraft are now superior to Russia.' The engine's superior performance and reliability relative to the AL-31FM2 made long range maritime patrols 'a much more plausible option' for the J-20, he added.[66]

Looking beyond stopgap engines to the J-20's final intended powerplant, the Shenyang Aeroengine Research Institute designed the WS-15 engine which was to be produced by the Xi'an Aero-Engine Group. The engine would not only provide an estimated twenty-one to thirty-six per cent more thrust than the AL-31FM2 and WS-10C (estimates varied widely), but would also have a much higher thrust/weight ratio estimated at 10:1 or 11:1, require less maintenance, improve thermal management properties, and have a significantly longer service life. Its cutting-edge single-crystal turbine blades, although proving particularly difficult to mass produce, were expected to almost double the engine's lifespan compared to the WS-10B.

While the WS-15 made its first flight in twin configuration on the J-20 in June 2023, little had been confirmed regarding the engine's performance – although much had been reported but not confirmed. The new powerplant was considered broadly equivalent to the American F119 powering the F-22, but had more ambitious specifications with an expected maximum thrust of 18.4 tons,[67] compared to 17.5 tons for the F119, 16.3 tons for the WS-10C and AL-31FM2, and 18.7 tons for Russia's AL-51F then under development for the Su-57.[68] Its weight/thrust ratio was expected to be between 0.09 and 0.1, compared to 0.125 for the AL-31F and 0.11 for the F119, making it more efficient than any prior powerplant used by a twin engine fighter. Some reports indicated that the WS-15 could have twenty tons of thrust.[69] The Soviet MiG 1.42 fighter's AL-41F previously reportedly achieved a very low weight/thrust ratio of 0.09 and thrust of 19.5-20 tons in testing, although after the USSR's disintegration led to the program's cancellation no engine designed for twin configuration again reached this level.[70]

Pre-development and demonstrator work on an engine to power a fifth generation fighter began in the 1990s, while the WS-15 began as a program in 2006. In 2009 prototypes reportedly achieved a thrust/weight ratio matching the F119. While its development was protracted by the standards of Chinese weapons programs, it was far from exceptional when compared to American and Russian next generation engines. In the United States Pratt & Whitney and General Electric spent over twelve years just to develop prototypes of the F119, and it took another fourteen years of testing to perfect the design for operational service. China's relatively poor technological base when the WS-15's pre-development work started in the 1990s inevitably slowed this significantly further, and with even the country's fourth generation level WS-10B only maturing around 2010, the fact that the WS-15 could begin flight testing in 2016 and start test flights on the J-20 itself no later than January 2022 represented a tremendous rate of development. The much more mature stage which China's aeroengine industry had reached by the mid-2000s when the program began resulted in a much smoother development timeline compared to the WS-10, with the WS-10 program having represented far more of a technological leap due to the much poorer state the industry had been in in the mid-1980s when it began.

Reports emerged in October 2016 that the WS-15 would begin flight testing on the IL-76LL – a heavily modified Soviet transport jet – and had finished ground testing. The news came a few months after the first J-20s had been delivered to the PLAAF. Multiple successful tests were reported over the next five years,[71] which culminated in January 2022 when the first images of a J-20 flying with the new engine emerged.[72] The J-20 used one WS-15 and one older WS-10 engine, with the latter providing redundancy and enough power to land in case there was an issue with the WS-15 prototype. Further reports of an improved test performance emerged two months later.[73] Extensive coverage that year by Chinese state media, and subsequent confirmation that the J-20 was indeed test flying the engine, were seen by a number of analysts as important indications that the WS-15 would enter service in the near future.[74]

In March 2022 Li Zhiqiang, Head of the Manufacturing Technology Institute of the state-owned Aviation Industry Corporation of China and Member of the National Committee of the Chinese People's Political Consultative Conference, expressed confidence in a CCTV report that complex problems of warplane engine development could be resolved. A specialist in the hot forming and superplastic forming of titanium alloys, Li observed that the technology gap with world leaders had been narrowed and that developments would provide fighters with higher thrust/weight ratios, thrust vector control and variable cycles. He stressed the importance of modernising domestic industry and cutting reliance on engine imports, with his statement following the deliveries of J-20As with WS-10C engines to a fifth PLAAF brigade demonstrating self-reliance at the very high end of the industry.[75] Days later experts credited breakthroughs in key material technologies such as those in single crystal blades, the accumulation of technologies and theories over two decades of accelerated development, and the establishment of the Aero Engine Corporation of China, with boosting the jet engine industry.[76] In December 2022 a professor at the school of energy and power engineering at Beihang's University, Liu Daxiang, a leading advisor to military aviation programs, provided strong indications in a prominent keynote speech that the WS-15 was nearing completion, and confirmed a weight/thrust ratio of at least 0.1.[77] Three months later an official from the Aero Engine Corporation of China confirmed that the WS-15 had entered serial production, indicating a low initial rate of production which could allow it to enter service in late 2024.[78] Indicating that it had achieved sufficient reliability levels, the WS-15 was first flown in twin configuration on J-20B prototype '2052' in June 2023.[79]

It was rare, not only in China but worldwide, for fighter units to deploy the same class of aircraft using entirely different engine types – particularly engines from different countries which had almost no commonality and further complicated maintenance and logistics. Re-fitting the two-and-a-half J-20 brigades integrating the AL-31FM2 with the WS-15, likely eventually followed by those using the WS-10C, was thus expected to resolve this issue while also reducing units' operational costs due to the WS-15's reported lower maintenance needs. Benefits the WS-15 was expected to provide the J-20 included a higher endurance due to greater efficiency, lower maintenance requirements and thus higher availability rates, and a lower heat signature particularly from the rear, overhead and underneath. Its greater power would also be key to facilitating integration of new generations of avionics, such as more powerful sensors, and potentially a range of directed energy weapons. A significantly higher thrust/weight ratio for the fighter ensured a higher climb rate, greater manoeuvrability at all speeds, faster acceleration and possibly a higher altitude ceiling. Manoeuvrability, particularly at low speeds, would also be further enhanced by to the engine's thrust vectoring capabilities. As the state-run *Global Times* noted in March 2022 regarding the WS-15's future integration: 'The J-20 will finally become its ultimate form.'[80]

Armaments

Much as had been the case for the F-22 in the United States, new classes of air-to-air missile needed to be developed for the J-20 that could be accommodated in its internal weapons bays. Where in America existing missile designs such as the AIM-120 and its short-ranged counterpart the AIM-9 were modified with clipped fins and improved overall performances, for the J-20 program new missiles were developed. The AIM-9 had been in service since 1956, and the AIM-120 since 1991, but even by the early 2020s neither had an operational successor – with the need to reduce costs particularly after the Cold War's end leading to an emphasis on upgrading older designs. The PLAAF as a result had a clear opening to gain an advantage by operationalising entirely new missiles, with the PL-10 and PL-15 developed for the J-20 generally considered superior to their competitors in the U.S.

The PL-15, a challenger to the American AIM-120D and European Meteor, had a longer range than its competitors, with estimates ranging between 200km and 300km.[81] Designed from the outset for integration onto stealth fighters, with shortened fins to facilitate internal carriage, its use of a dual-pulse rocket motor was key to its range advantage, while a two-way datalink provided guidance updates to both the missile and the launching fighter. The PL-15 notably used an AESA radar for inertial guidance which, as a prominent 2018 IISS report noted, ensured 'improved performance against low-observable targets and greater resistance to countermeasures on target aircraft, such as radio-frequency jammers.'[82] Despite some initial speculation that the American AIM-120D introduced in 2014, with an estimated range of 160[83]–180km,[84] might also use an AESA radar, this never materialised.[85] The PL-15 caused considerable concern among Western analysts[86] and U.S. military officials,[87] and its high performance was widely considered a leading reason for the launch of the AIM-260 missile program 2017.[88] Its capabilities, as noted by analysts at *The Drive* as late as 2022, had left the U.S. 'working to close the gap' by developing clean sheet successors to the AIM-120.[89]

The short-ranged PL-10 which used thrust-vector controls and a gimbaled imaging infrared seeker was capable of high off-boresight engagements and could engage aircraft beyond ninety degrees, thus providing a significant performance advantage over the vast majority of foreign competitors. Its cutting-edge seeker type provided a range of significant benefits including superior resistance to countermeasures and an improved detection range. According to a report by IISS its induction 'has placed China among the handful of nations with a defence-industrial base capable of producing such a weapon,'[90] with analysts at *The Drive* highlighting that it was 'judged to be at least equivalent to Western weapons in its class.'[91] Reports from the British Royal United Services Institute defence think tank highlighted that the PL-10 had a 'superior kinematic performance to the American AIM-9X Sidewinder,' which was the most capable in the USAF's arsenal.[92] The missile was one of very few of its kind in the world capable of engaging at near beyond visual ranges, with some reports indicating that it had a lock-on-after-launch capability and could receive targeting data by datalink during flight to facilitate targeting at greater distances.

The PL-10's high performance supplemented the advantages provided by J-20's unique side launch rails, which deployed the missiles outside of the fighter's side weapons bays with bay doors closed to conserve stealth and facilitate much faster launches during short range engagements. This contrasted with American and Russian fifth generation fighters which lacked such a launch system, and consequentially could not launch missiles without both significantly increasing their radar cross sections and disturbing airflows around them. This compromised flight performance which could be particularly detrimental in close range engagements where such missiles would be used. Avoiding the need to open its weapons bays at the time of engagement, combined with the PL-10's particularly long reach for a missile of its kind, created opportunities for J-20 units to use unique new tactics, including operating radar silent using passive sensors and third-party sensor data to attack at shorter beyond visual ranges.

The PL-15 and PL-10 are thought to have first entered service around 2015, and were first used on the J-16 fighter which was China's first with an AESA radar and next generation helmet mounted sights needed to accommodate them. The J-20, J-10C, and export-orientated JF-17 Block 3 were the next aircraft to integrate the missile, alongside J-11B fighters modernised to the J-11BG standard and modernised variants of the J-11's aircraft carrier-based derivative the J-15.

Long range air-to-air missiles have increasingly since the 1980s in particular emerged as one of the most important determinants of a fighter's potency in air-to-air combat. Gaining an advantage with a new generation of missiles represented the culmination of decades-long PLA efforts, with Chinese fighters having had negligible standoff anti-aircraft capabilities when the Cold War ended until the Soviet R-27ER and R-77 were acquired from Ukraine and Russia respectively in the 1990s. The latter was the country's first with active radar guidance, meaning it had much prized 'fire and forget' capabilities, could be used to implement a significant range of new tactics, and allowed each fighter to engage many more targets simultaneously. It was fielded by the PLAAF close to two decades before the Russian Defence Ministry financed acquisitions for its own air force. Indeed, China had to fund development of an upgrade package for the Su-27 to be able to integrate the new missile due to the almost total lack of financing for modernisation in Russia at the time.[93] The Soviet missiles were followed into service from around 2005 by the superior PL-12 developed with Russian support and with a 100km range. The PL-12, like the R-77, had active radar guidance and provided parity with its most capable Western contemporary the AIM-120C. The entry into service of their successors the AIM-120D and PL-15, within months of one another, transformed Chinese parity in beyond visual range air-to-air missiles into a comfortable lead. Whether this could be retained as the U.S. moved to induct its first clean sheet long range design since 1991, the AIM-260, remained uncertain, since little was known of a Chinese successor to the PL-15 or of its future variants.

There have been strong indications of a PL-15 successor under development, with some speculating that it could be smaller to allow stealth fighters to carry more missiles internally. This would mirror developments in another American program, the Peregrine, designed to produce more compact air-to-air missiles for internal carriage without compromising performance. What is certain, however, is that while the PL-15 was developed based on Chinese aerospace industry technologies in the late 2000s, the new missile will have a far more sophisticated technological base supporting it due to the extent of advances made since then.

Role of the J-20

Since the J-20 made its first flight in 2011 there has been significant speculation from a wide range of sources as to what primary role it was designed to fulfil. The aircraft's size, twin engines, stealth profile, bubble canopy and extensive flight control surfaces were among the aspects of its airframe design that strongly indicated an air superiority role similar to the F-22 Raptor. A number of alternative theories nevertheless also prevailed. While a large airframe, high thrust, operational altitude and speed, long range and sizeable missile payload are all key to the performance of air superiority aircraft, a number of other combat roles also require such specifications.

The J-20 was initially widely considered by Western analysts to have been designed as an interceptor-type aircraft similar to the Russian MiG-31 Foxhound, making it a specialist in long range air-to-air engagements against bombers and force multiplier support assets such as airborne early warning and control (AEW&C) systems and tanker aircraft. This conclusion was partly influenced by erroneous initial Western estimates of the J-20's size, which placed it at a gargantuan 22-23 metres and around thirty per cent heavier than the F-22 – an appropriate size to accommodate oversized air-to-air missiles with extreme ranges similar to the MiG-31's R-37M. The MiG-31 was by far the largest aircraft in the world built for air-to-air combat, allowing it to deploy oversized missiles as well as an exceptionally large sensor suite all far heavier than F-22 sized aircraft could accommodate.[94]

Transfers of the J-20's two demonstrator airframes to the China Flight Test Establishment at Xi'an-Yanliang in 2012 provided an important indication of the fighter's actual size, as it allowed satellite images to show scale comparisons next to Flanker airframes there. At approximately 20.8 metres long the J-20 was in the same weight range as the F-22 – heavy by the standards of fighters, but significantly lighter than a stealth interceptor with oversized missiles would have been. Furthermore, with interceptors designed to engage from extreme ranges and being the least manoeuvrable of all aircraft designed for air-to-air combat, a growing body of information on the J-20's flight performance and other capabilities made it increasingly clear that it was a fighter. The J-20's high manoeuvrability, which was set to improve markedly with the integration of WS-15 engine and incorporation of thrust vectoring technologies, strongly indicated an air superiority role. Details of the kinds of armaments it carried internally provided final confirmation of its role.

Research director at the China Aerospace Studies Institute of the USAF Air University Rod Lee was among those to conclude with near certainty that the J-20 had an interceptor-like role and was designed primarily to neutralise targets such as AEW&C systems. 'The PLA de-emphasises the importance of attrition warfare and instead advocates a "systems destruction" approach. Killing individual adversary fighters (even in large numbers) is not as useful as killing [high value airborne assets] and key ground targets,' Lee stated, which he believed would be reflected in how the J-20 was built and would be used.[95] As late as December 2021 an assessment published by the Air University claimed that 'the much-hyped Chengdu J-20 is a heavy fighter aircraft comparable to the MiG-31, which is essentially an interceptor and not a multirole or an air superiority aircraft.' It was among the very last Western sources to continue to make such claims, which were by then thoroughly discredited, and was published under the title *Why China Cannot Challenge the US Military Primacy* as one of multiple similar errors used to support the argument.[96] Such assessments were further undermined by the fact that the J-20's weapons bays were not built to carry the PLAAF's very long ranged oversized air-to-air missiles such as the PL-XX, which was instead deployed by the non-stealthy J-16. This fighter had a similarly large radar and high endurance to the J-20, but was better suited to carrying such missiles most threatening to support aircraft. When considered alongside the J-16, the J-20 appeared to be an air superiority fighter, while the J-16 was more suitable to being allocated interceptor-like 'AEW&C/tanker killer' missions.

Another early view widely held among Western analysts was that the J-20 was optimized for air-to-ground attacks against heavily defended targets – as a fifth generation equivalent to the USAF's massive F-111 strike platform and similarly to the FB-22 concept for a strike derivative of the F-22. This again stemmed largely from erroneous estimates of the aircraft's size. The editor of *Defence Technology International*, Bill Sweetman, for one, referred to it as a 'stealth F-111,' with other statements to this effect made widely.[97] Imagining the J-20 as 'a fast, long-range, stealthy, precision bomber [which] might be able to penetrate U.S. defences and destroy any airfield infrastructure that survived the missile barrage,' was in part based on the general importance the PLA allocated to strike capabilities.[98] This would require an even longer range than air superiority fighters, with a primary role of destroying enemy infrastructure and supplies as an interdictor, or targeting enemy ground and possibly naval assets as a strike fighter. It was increasingly evident, however, that the J-20's airframe far more closely reflected an intended air superiority role, as did the fact that the fighter was never seen with weapons other than air-to-air missiles.

The J-20 continued to be described in Western popular media and by less seasoned analysts as a dedicated interceptor or dedicated strike fighter into the 2020s. Cognitive dissonance and an unwillingness to admit that the Western world's top fighter the F-22 had a direct, symmetric and peer level competitor from an East Asian rival likely played a role. As analyst Rick Joe observed when writing for *The Diplomat*: 'It is difficult to assess if foreign commentary on the J-20's role reflects a genuine consideration of evidence or arises from some underlying discomfort or disbelief that a PLA stealth fighter may be intended to compete in a generally symmetric way with the F-22 and F-35, the former of which in particular has attained something of a mythic status in defence watching circles.' Joe further highlighted regarding the PL-XX that the fact the J-20 had been 'consciously designed to a size which prevented it from carrying a missile of this size should be further instructive of its role'.[99]

Although the J-20 was developed primarily for air superiority roles, the aircraft are very likely to gain secondary strike and perhaps even maritime strike capabilities. As early as the 1980s the Soviet Union had designed its fifth generation air superiority fighter under the MiG 1.42 program to be able to deploy a wide range of standoff missiles for air-to-ground strikes as a secondary role. Even the F-22 Raptor, developed as a dedicated air superiority fighter, was later modified to be able to perform air-to-ground roles – albeit carrying only relatively light gravity bombs as its weapons bay was not capable of accommodating cruise missiles or heavier ordinance. Whether the J-20 would demonstrate strike capabilities, and what kind they would be, remained an object of speculation into the 2020s.

In March 2018 Director of Science and Technology at the Aviation Industry Corporation of China Deputy Director Yang Wei, the J-20's chief designer, indicated regarding the fighter's future roles: 'Of course, it will be tasked with penetrating air defence networks, but that will not be its only mission. It definitely has multiple functions. How we will use it depends on its production and deployment scale.'[100] He reiterated that as numbers grew the fighter would begin to be seen operating in a more diverse range of roles.[101] Yang was quoted as saying at Airshow China 2018, in November (better known as the Zhuhai Airshow): 'First, the J-20 has outstanding stealth capability; second, it has outstanding long-range strike capability; third, it has outstanding capability in information warfare.'[102] The fighter was described on a flyer at the airshow as 'renowned for its dominant role of medium and long-range air combat and excellent capability in ground and marine precision strike,' adding that 'major operational missions include: seizing and maintaining air superiority, medium and long range fast interception, escort and deep strike.'[103] With what armaments it could do so, however, remained highly uncertain, with none having been seen.

As the J-20 participated in its first confirmed combat exercises in January 2018 PLAAF officer Zhang Hao, who oversaw the fighter's flight testing, was quoted in Chinese state media stating: 'J-20 will be like a needle that can penetrate and break down the enemy's air-defence network.'[104] It was reported in January 2020 that alongside air superiority the PLAAF had been simulating land attack and maritime strike roles for the J-20.[105] A further indicator came at the August 2021 Zapad/Vzaimodeystviye Sino-Russian strategic military exercises when J-20s spearheaded a simulated air raid on enemy frontline command centres and air defence observation outposts. The state-run *Global Times* reported: 'The J-20s kicked open the door and seized air superiority by accurately attacking high-value targets on the ground, and this was the leading role the J-20s had played in the exercises as stealth fighter jets … This allowed ground troops and other non-stealth warplanes to proceed with their missions with much less risks.' It was followed by non-stealthy Russian Su-30SM fighters and Chinese JH-7, J-11, J-16 and H-6 jets – serving as a force multiplier for all of them.[106] This strongly indicated that the J-20 not only had a strike capability, but was seen as an asset which could move in first to suppress enemy ground-based defences paving the way for non-stealth aircraft to operate more safely. It mirrored the role allocated to the F-35 in American war planning,[107] as previously demonstrated by the F-117's operations in the Gulf War which were similarly described as 'kicking down the door.'[108]

J-20s would similarly simulate strikes and electronic attacks on ground targets in subsequent exercises in January 2022. Experts cited by the *Global Times* highlighted regarding its function: 'J-20 could be used to penetrate hostile defences and seize air superiority, and other types of non-stealth aircraft could be used to unload a large amount of munitions on targets' – much like the 'kick open the door' role played at Zapad 2021.[109] Indeed, even before the J-20 was first delivered to frontline troops, the fighter's chief designer

Yang Wei had stated regarding the aircraft's role: "'Kicking in the door" is definitely a key aspect, but just using "Kicking the door" still has certain limitations, and it will also play other roles. This is also related to the batch size. When the batch size is small, it is an application, and when the number of equipment is large, it is another application.'[110] The rapid increase in J-20 deliveries in 2022-2023, confirming the aircraft would form the backbone of the fleet rather than a few niche units as the F-22 had, further indicated that it had to be a versatile multirole aircraft.

The lack of known air-to-ground munitions and particularly more complex weapons such as cruise or anti-radiation missiles for the J-20 is likely a result of the program's primary mission as an air superiority fighter, which makes development and widespread fielding of such weapons a lower priority. The security situation in East Asia and threat of clashes with much larger fleets of enemy fifth generation aircraft means J-20 units are expected to initially be focused primarily on air-to-air combat where their unique capabilities can likely have the greatest impact. This is particularly the case considering the PLA's abundance of other strike assets. Nevertheless, once larger numbers of J-20s are available to focus on air superiority missions there could be more resources available to allocate to training and arming for roles such as air defence suppression or anti-shipping. Once J-20s form a greater proportion of the PLAAF fleet, they will likely be relied on to perform a wider range of roles.

Among the weapons expected are an anti-radiation missile based on the PL-15's airframe, much like the LD-10 anti-radiation missile was developed based on its predecessor the PL-12. An anti-radiation capability, ideal for neutralising air defences and ground radars, could be particularly prized for aforementioned 'kick down the door' operations. A cruise missile with a small form factor similar to the Su-57's Kh-59MK2 and the F-35's Joint Strike Missile also remains a significant possibility. An anti-ship missile for the J-20 could also enter service, particularly if the fighter is ever commissioned by the PLA Navy, although even in the air force its extensive deployments for maritime patrols from 2021 could make this a valued secondary capability.

The J-20 Matures in Service: Timeline

On 1 November 2016 J-20 fighters in PLAAF service were first revealed to the public at the Zhuhai Airshow when a pair conducted a brief fly-past at the opening ceremony. The fighters had been delivered to the Air Force some months before, but were not yet considered active or operational.

In November 2017, eight months after their formal entry into service, the J-20 participated in the year's Red Sword military exercises at the Dingxin base alongside H-6K bombers, KJ-2000 and KJ-500 AEW&C systems, JH-7 strike fighters and J-10 and J-11 fighters. Its participation was only confirmed three months later, when state media described the fighter class as having 'played an important role in the "Red Sword 2017" systemic confrontation drill, laying the foundation for the improvement in the air force's new combat capabilities.'[111]

In January 2018 the PLAAF conducted a series of large-scale live fire exercises testing the capabilities of the J-20 and J-16. Their announcement represented the first public confirmation of J-20s being involved in any kind of exercises. J-20 pilot Chen Liu compared the task of those flying the new stealth fighter over the past several months to 'white hat' hackers and video game testers, with their job being the identification of mechanical and software glitches for fixing or debugged before the next mission or drill to break the aircraft into service. Pilots were also tasked with compiling manuals for other PLA units. Coordinated exercises saw J-20s simultaneously deployed from airbases across the country. It was much publicised that Chen's grandfather was the renowned Air Marshal Liu Yuti, a MiG-15 pilot credited with shooting down eight American fighters during the Korean War, which tied the new air superiority fighter with the historical memory of the PLAAF's finest hours guarding North Korean skies.[112]

On 9 February 2018, the PLAAF announced that the J-20 had reached a combat ready status, with spokesman Shen Jinke highlighting that the fighter would enhance the service's comprehensive combat capabilities and its ability to safeguard China's sovereignty, security and territorial integrity.[113] Regarding the speed with which this had been achieved, just eleven months after the fighter entered service, senior researcher with the PLAAF Command College Wang Mingzhi indicated that this demonstrated how the Air Force 'transformed advanced technology into combat strength faster than the air forces of other powerful nations.' Chinese defence experts widely observed at the time that the fighter was 'now ready years ahead of when the United States was expecting them to be,' which would serve to 'deter the U.S.'[114]

On 9 May 2018, PLAAF spokesman Shen Jinke announced that J-20 units had begun maritime training, stating: 'The J-20 has conducted a combat training mission in sea areas for the first time, and this has further strengthened the comprehensive combat capability of the PLA Air Force ... It will help the Air Force to better execute its sacred duty to safeguard national sovereignty, security and territorial integrity.' He added that pilot training for the J-20 had been proceeding smoothly.[115] Shen subsequently announced on 12 May that since the J-20 was commissioned it had participated in realistic air battle training with other fighters like the J-16 and J-10C, and played an important role in confrontational drills.[116]

The beginning of maritime training was announced just days after the PLA reinforced disputed island outposts in the South China Sea with YJ-12 anti-ship missiles, HQ-9B air defence systems and advanced electronic warfare systems, and highlighted the important role that the J-20 could play in supporting broader Chinese maritime anti-access area denial capabilities.[117] PLA Navy J-11BH fighters, the J-20's direct predecessor, had been deployed to disputed islands since 2015.[118]

In the third week of May 2018, amid high tensions in the Taiwan Strait, a CCTV program on conflict over Taiwan highlighted that the J-20 could be deployed for operations in the strait in the near future. Military scholar with the China National Defence University Wang Mingliang highlighted that hostile forces on Taiwan would struggle to counter stealth aircraft. He added that the government in Taipei feared 'precision strikes on the leadership or key targets' by J-20s which 'could come and go at will above Taiwan.'[119]

Analysts nevertheless questioned whether the J-20 would be deployed near Taiwan, highlighting that the fighter would likely be held back to deny potential adversaries opportunities to study it. The precedent set by the U.S. Air Force F-22 Raptor's operations over Syria were cited as a precedent, where U.S. Air Force Lieutenant General VeraLinn Jamieson confirmed adversaries had gained 'a treasure trove' of information on how the aircraft operated due to extended periods in its proximity.[120]

On 2 June 2018, Chinese state media outlet the *People's Daily* gave insight into the J-20's role when operating alongside the PLAAF's two other new fighter classes the J-16 and the J-10C in joint night-time exercises. 'During the exercise, the J-20 pilots used their aircraft's advantages in terms of situational awareness and stealth to gain air superiority, while the J-16 and J-10C fighters carried out precision strikes on ground targets. The training sought to take full advantage of the different capabilities of the fighter jets,' the paper elaborated, with pilot He Xing reiterating that the exercises capitalised on the three aircraft's complementary attributes.[121] The role assigned to the J-20 served as further confirmation that it was indeed an air superiority fighter.

On 11 November 2018, a J-20 at the Zhuhai Airshow flew with its bay doors open, providing confirmation of its air-to-air missile payload.[122] The aircraft performed significantly longer and more aggressive flight displays than at Zhuhai 2016.

In January 2020 the PLAAF deployed the J-10C, J-16 and J-20 for joint exercises, with the three widely referred to by Chinese sources as the 'Three Sky Musketeers' when operating together. The J-20s were drawn from the 9th Air Brigade. The fighters demonstrated a new formation dubbed the 'battle box,' where formations of two J-20s, two J-16s and one J-10C worked in unison with the J-20s tasked with launching surprise attacks on enemy aircraft while the J-10C provided cover at close ranges. This capitalised on the former's stealth capabilities and the latter's exceptional manoeuvrability. The J-16 was then tasked with baiting the enemy. Another scenario saw J-20s seek and destroy 'strategic nodes of the enemy's defence,' in particular AEW&C systems, while the J-16 struck mobile radar installations and the J-10C gained air superiority over enemy fighters. The exercises demonstrated the growing synergy between the three fighters which were entering service in growing numbers in parallel. Other than the F-35, all three were produced at much higher annual rates than any other fighter classes in the world.

In July 2020 mainland and Hong Kong media outlets widely reported that a new J-20 variant, the J-20B, had entered serial production. The fighter was unveiled on 8 July at a ceremony attended by senior military leaders, including the Vice Chairman of the Central Military Commission General Zhang Youxia, although beyond the addition of thrust vectoring engines none of its new capabilities were revealed. Some of the most widely speculated new features included missile racks for a greater internal payload, more powerful sensors and electronic warfare systems, and further reductions to the fighter's radar cross section.

In August 2020 two J-20s were reportedly sighted at Hotan Airbase around 320km from the disputed Ladakh region on the Indian border, providing the high endurance fighters with coverage of most of Indian airspace.[123] This occurred just two months after border skirmishes between the two countries. Aside from deployments to the 176th Air Brigade at the Dingxin Flight Test & Training Base in the Gobi Desert, which was much further from India and primarily for testing purposes, this was the first known J-20 deployment under the Western Theatre Command.

In September 2020 it was widely reported that a J-20 with a novice pilot, confronting targets approaching from all directions in mock air-to-air combat, scored seventeen kills for zero losses. This was based on a publication from the official *PLA Daily*, which although not naming the fighter used to achieve the simulated kills, confirmed the 9th Air Brigade had been responsible – a unit which deployed no other fighter classes.[124] Such a kill ratio was highly plausible for the J-20, particularly against older PLAAF fighters such as the J-11A which were technologically around thirty years behind. The fact that this was achieved by a pilot with only 100 hours of experience in the aircraft demonstrated the growing degree to which technology could compensate for pilot skills, mirroring reports from the USAF of novice pilots seven or eight flights out of training in F-35As comfortably outperforming seasoned veteran flyers in older fourth generation aircraft.[125] Such tests were important for shaping the future acquisitions priorities of both air forces.

On 4 April 2021 at the Qingming Festival, the traditional day of tomb-sweeping, CCTV gave considerable publicity to J-20 pilots paying respect to the Chinese pilots who fought in the Korean War. It emphasized that the Wang Hai Air Group 'Ace Unit' (9th Air Brigade) of heroic pilot Sun Shenglu had been equipped with J-20s, again drawing strong links between Chinese combat aviation's finest hours and the J-20 program. 'Air Force pilots in the new age will inherit the spirit of "aerial bayonet fighting," train to prepare for combat, be ready at all times for combat, and resolutely safeguard national sovereignty and dignity,' J-20 pilot Sun Teng said at the time.[126] J-20s were seen exercising in 'stealth mode' without Luneberg reflective lenses, which Chinese state media sources highlighted indicated a higher state of combat readiness had been attained.[127]

In January 2022 the *Global Times* reported that the J-20s under the Northern Theatre Command, presumably the 1st Air Brigade 'Ace Unit,' 'started the year with intensive mock combat training sessions' pitting them against the J-11B, J-16 and other PLAAF fighter classes. The J-20s reportedly simulated combat with a handicap, using Luneburg lenses which nullified their stealth capabilities, leading to a close match against adversaries. The fifth generation jets in the end prevailed using performance advantages other than stealth. Both the J-20s and their adversaries were able to evade multiple simulated missile attacks by pulling high G manoeuvres after at one point firing simultaneously on one another. Some two-versus-two mock engagements lasted more than an hour, while other exercises involved live fire attacks against groups of targets.

J-20s conducted some night-time exercises without Luneberg lenses, with brigade commander Senior Colonel Li Ling elaborating: 'During air combat at night, the J-20 takes advantage of its stealth capability, carries out beyond-visual-range combat missions and plays the role of a commander in the air, taking initiatives in combat.' At least one mock engagement saw J-20s engage J-16s two-on-two, with the J-16 considered the PLAAF's second most capable fighter class overall. Experts cited by the *Global Times* highlighted that these exercises would give pre-fifth generation units experience in tackling fifth generation targets, with lessons learned against the J-20 likely being applicable against F-35s and other stealth aircraft.[128]

Against the J-16, the J-20 reportedly 'took advantage of its stealth and attack capabilities and realized the tactical goals of finding the enemy first, firing missiles first, breaking away from combat first and destroying the target first,' according to state media reports. The J-20s were nevertheless spotted and targeted at range by their adversaries on at least one occasion, although they managed to evade. The results of these exercises and feedback from airmen participating had the potential to influence the PLAAF's future investments regarding acquisitions. If the J-20 proved overwhelmingly superior to the J-16, widely considered the most advanced Flanker in the world and one of the most capable non-stealth fighters, it could speed up a decision to phase the class out of production. If the J-16 was still capable of challenging the J-20 with full stealth capabilities, however, it may be more likely to remain in production longer.[129]

The USAF had previously similarly sought to test its fifth generation F-22s against fourth generation fighters in the 2000s, with the stealth jets gaining overwhelming victories in simulated engagements against F-16s and F-15s using mechanically scanned array radars. Captain John Teichart, a Raptor pilot who flew F-15s against the F-22 in simulated combat, reported regarding his adversary's advantage: 'It's like clubbing baby seals, it's so easy,' with pilot Captain Jeremy Durtsch, who also participated similarly referring to the Raptors advantage as 'clubbing baby seals.'[130] Advanced Chinese fourth generation fighters like the Chinese J-16 and J-10C, however, which were equipped with AESA radars several times more powerful than those used in exercises against the Raptor, as well as infrared tracking systems, modern data links, and training in counter stealth tactics, had a much greater chance of challenging fifth generation aircraft like the J-20 and F-22. Some limited stealth capabilities of their own and much more capable PL-15 missiles with inertial AESA radar guidance were other important capabilities the J-16 and J-10C had, but advances in radar technology and data sharing capabilities were seen as likely the most significant in making fifth generation aircraft's advantages less extreme. Although fifth generation fighters maintained a strong edge, these very high end fourth generation aircraft were still challenging to tackle in contrast to the 'baby seals' position more basic fourth generation aircraft had been in when facing stealth fighters.

In March 2022 Commander of the U.S. Pacific Air Forces (PACAF), Air Force General Kenneth Wilsbach confirmed that the J-20 and F-35 had had their first ever encounter, which took place over the East China Sea.[131] This was the first ever encounter between fifth generation fighters from opposing sides, with China being the only country in the world outside the Western sphere of influence to field such fighters at squadron level strength. Speaking to Wilsbach at the time, former (PACAF) Vice Commander Lieutenant General (ret.) David Deptula emphasized that 'clearly fifth generation aircraft are going to become increasingly important in the Pacific.'[132]

In the second week of April 2022 the PLAAF was confirmed to have made its first deployments of the J-20A for routine patrols over the East China Sea and South China Sea, with the *Global Times* highlighting that this had been facilitated by the integration of the new WS-10C engine. This followed the deployment of a U.S. carrier group to the region earlier that week – the first such deployment that decade – and was seen to reflect growing confidence in the J-20's capabilities. The *Times* referred to the deployment as intended to 'better safeguard China's airspace security and maritime interests', with Chengdu spokesman Ren Yukun highlighting that patrols of the two seas were now considered 'training routine' for J-20 units.[133]

Griffith Asia Institute Visiting Fellow Peter Layton told *CNN* at the time regarding the new patrols that China's message to the world was: 'Any foreign military aircraft intruding into China's claimed airspace in the East and South China Sea may now be intercepted by J-20s.' The PLAAF 'now has in regular service a fleet of advanced stealth fighters as good as the Americans, who remain the benchmark,' he stated, highlighting that the J-20's high endurance would allow it to patrol further out to sea than other fighters and patrol Chinese claimed waters for longer periods. He added that the United States and Japan would be 'keenly collecting electronic intelligence data' on patrolling J-20s' stealth characteristics and communications.[134]

In June 2022 J-20s made their first confirmed deployment to identify foreign military aircraft entering China's Air Defence Identification Zone. The incident took place over the East China Sea, and was reported two months later, with state media highlighting the value of the fighter's photoelectric aiming system and a photoelectric distributed aperture system, as well as its main radar, particularly against American stealth fighters based in the region.[135]

On 3 August 2022 Beijing announced unprecedented live fire military exercises surrounding the Taiwan Strait as an immediate response to the visit of U.S. Speaker of the House Nancy Pelosi to Taipei. These saw J-20s play a very central role, and were referred to as being intended both to increase preparation for possible military solutions to the technically ongoing Chinese Civil War across the strait, and to deter possible separatist aspirations by the ruling Democratic Progressive Party in Taipei. Following the exercises J-20s were reported more frequently to be deployed for patrols near Taiwan.

In September 2022 J-20s were assigned to escort Y-20 transport aircraft repatriating the remains of Chinese personnel from South Korea who had been killed during the Korean War, with the deployment of the new stealth fighters described by the state-run *Global Times* as one which 'will not only pay tribute to the ... martyrs but also display the increasing number of J-20s in service.'[136] The J-11B had previously been assigned to escort missions for the highly symbolic repatriations from Korea, with the use of the J-20 providing yet further grounds for Chinese commentators to widely remark on the fighter's importance in the context of the historical memory from the Korean conflict. J-20s subsequently continued to be deployed to perform such escort missions, with the tenth batch of soldiers' remains repatriated in November of that year.[137]

In October 2022 it was reported that J-20s conducting combat patrols over the East China Sea had been deployed to intercept and drive away foreign fighter jets. The location indicated they were most likely American, or possibly Japanese, both major F-35 operators, while references to the targeted aircraft as 'advanced warplanes like the J-20 and others' potentially implying that the incident had seen the two stealth fighter classes again encounter one another.[138]

In January 2023 footage aired by CCTV showed J-20s performing an 'excellent job on regular patrols and controlling the East China Sea Air Defence Identification Zone,' and being scrambled to intercept intruding foreign fighters. Pilots from the Wang Hai Air Group (9th Air Brigade) Yang Juncheng and Wei Xin were shown being scrambled to intercept two unspecified incoming foreign aircraft, with Wei in his J-20 telling the targets in English: 'This is China Air Force. You have entered the Chinese ADIZ. Report your nationality ID and the purpose of flight.' There was subsequently considerable speculation on Chinese social media that the footage showed an interception of American F-35s – which were among the most commonly flown foreign fighters in the area. As the squadron's commander, Yang stated regarding its responsibilities that: 'No matter what happens in the air, even if it means sacrifice, we will never step back from our positions.'[139] Pilot Wei Xin commented on patrols further south around the Taiwan Strait, which highlighted the very wide area of operations which the long range stealth fighters could have and the multiple hotspots they could cover from their base at Wuhu.[140] The growing complexity of military drills J-20s were involved in that month were seen by analysts as a sign of improving operational combat abilities.[141]

On 27 July 2023 the PLAAF commemorated seventy years since the conclusion of the Korean War, with Senior Colonel Zhang Hong from the Wang Hai Air Group observing regarding a displayed MiG-15 fighter: 'I can imagine how the older generation fought against the world's top air force with them. Winning such glorious results must have been hard-fought.' He added that the Wang Hai Air Group emerged from blood and fire in Korea, and that its personnel would continue to carry on this spirit. Through the air group and its namesake, state media at the time again drew the link between the memory of the Korean War and the J-20's status highlighting that the Wang Hai Air Group was the first combat unit to field the aircraft which were direct successors to the MiG-15 in PLA service.[142] The previous day the J-20 had made a prominent appearance at the opening of the Changchun Air Show, where aerobatics were later performed to commemorate Chinese successes in the Korean War.[143]

Numbers in Service

In October 2017 CCTV 4 reported that the J-20 had entered 'stable' mass production, which was interpreted to mean serial production at a fixed regular rate.[144] It was reported that year that up to 100 J-20s would be produced by the end of 2020,[145] with 100 airframes not considered an unrealistic estimate particularly with the hindsight of how quickly they would soon begin to enter service. Ten years after its first flight, and five years after entering production, by the beginning of 2021 four PLAAF units deployed J-20s, which alongside further numbers which had been built but had yet to join the PLAAF made production of 100 or more aircraft by the end of 2020 highly plausible. As with any new fighter initial production rates began relatively low before climbing upwards.

Two main means were used to track the number of J-20s in service, one of which was observing serial numbers from pictures of new airframes to extrapolate total numbers. While there had been relatively frequent pictures taken at the Chengdu Aircraft Corporation before the fighter entered service from 2011-2016, however, these became far fewer afterwards, meaning observers often revised their counts significantly after new airframes were seen at air shows or other events.

The second means was to look at how quickly new units received J-20s, which indicated that the rate of production increased quickly as the time between deliveries to new units grew closer together. This was far from unexpected, with reports of increases in the production scale made in October 2017, October 2021 and later in November 2022.[146] In December 2021 the Chengdu Aircraft Industrial Group announced it had increased the scale of J-20 production in the fourth quarter of the year, with advances in the program including development of the more capable J-20A variant with indigenous engines having influenced the decision.[147] This was referred to as an increase to 'full-scale mass production.'[148] The state run *Global Times* cited military aviation expert Fu Qianshao reporting at the time: 'In a short time, we will be able to see J-20s operated by all eastern, southern, western, northern and central theatre commands, and become the main force to safeguard China's sovereignty and territorial airspace security.'[149]

On 8 October 2021 *Air Force Magazine* highlighted that the PLAAF likely had over 150 J-20 fighters in service and was increasing the scale of production.[150] The magazine was published by the Virginia-based professional military and aerospace education association, Air Force Association, which was closely connected to the USAF. The estimate followed a flight of fifteen J-20s in formation at the 2021 Zhuhai Airshow, with an additional group of J-20s parked on the runway. Even with 100 in service this would represent close to one fifth of the entire fleet, indicating there was indeed a significant number in the Air Force. The *Global Times* quoted J-20 deputy designer Wang Hitao saying industry could 'satisfy any level of demand from the People's Liberation Army Air Force for the J-20,' and that for development, 'particularly for equipment like the J-20, we need to do it faster in all aspects, including designing, production, testing, and crafting.'[151] Chinese experts at the time cited the high frequency of J-20 exercises as an indicator that the fleet was indeed large.[152] In November the J-20's chief designer and executive vice president of AVIC, Yang Wei, alluded to a larger J-20 fleet size than had previously been estimated.[153]

When in October 2017 the J-20 was reported to be set to soon enter 'stable' mass production, which was widely seen to mean production at a fixed and regular rate, projections by experts at Chengdu Aerospace indicated an annual production rate averaging close to thirty airframes per year over the next three years.[154] This meant the J-20's production rate was over twice as high as any other twin-engine fighter and behind only the single engine F-35 and J-10C. The fighter was reported in December 2021 to have entered full-scale mass production,[155] indicating much higher delivery rates would begin to materialise, with new serial numbers observed at the Zhuhai Airshow in November 2022 showing that the fleet had reached approximately 180 airframes at minimum. Annual deliveries for 2022 were accordingly estimated at approximately seventy aircraft. To put this in perspective, the F-22 had been produced at an average of nineteen point four airframes per year, peaking at twenty-four in 2009,[156] while the Su-57 was expected to see approximately fourteen produced annually by 2025. The leading non-Chinese heavyweight aircraft from the previous generation the F-15QA/EX and Su-35, were being produced at rates of around twelve and fourteen per year.

While American estimates in early 2022 that there were 'some 200 J-20s' in service were seriously questioned by many analysts,[157] the new serial numbers observed in November strengthened the consensus that the fleet size was indeed much larger and deliveries had increased substantially. Satellite footage of facilities at Chengdu were cited as an indicator that production lines were expected to grow significantly further still, with some unverified reports indicating that J-10C production could even be moved elsewhere, possibly Guizhou, to allow for a greater focus on producing more J-20s. Increases to production led the PLA to invest more in better and faster training programs for new generations of pilots to keep up. The Shijiazhuang Flight Academy in Hebei Province pioneered many of these changes.[158] As a result of these production increases the PLAAF was in the early 2020s estimated to be receiving more new fighters every year than any other air force – around fourteen to twenty per cent more than the USAF was receiving – which fit in with the trend towards China surpassing the U.S. in spending on arms acquisitions from 2020.[159]

Placing the J-20's production numbers in perspective, its direct predecessor the Soviet Su-27 had similarly for years been produced for domestic use only while still maintaining deliveries close to 100 per year. The F-22 was also expected to be produced at around sixty airframes per year before the large majority of planned units were cancelled.[160] With serial numbers indicating J-20 deliveries had reached around seventy in 2022,[161] estimated annual deliveries rose further in 2023 so that by the middle of the year it was expected that eighty J-20s would be delivered. Both Western and Chinese sources reported that deliveries would rise to over 100 a year and likely reach around 120 per year in 2025.[162]

The J-20 was from late 2021 the only fifth generation fighter in the world that could be described as in 'full-scale mass production' and the first of its generation to reach such a state,[163] with the F-35 being denied Pentagon authorisation for full-scale production and the Su-57 being produced in very modest numbers. F-35 production rates were never expected to approach the program's initially planned levels, with annual deliveries to the U.S. Air Force, projected as late as 2015 to reach 80 per year, in the early-mid 2020s fluctuating between 36 and 48 and not expected to further rise.[164] The F-22, with orders cut by seventy-five per cent, never exceeded forty per cent of the planned full-scale production rate.[165]

Chapter Four

Industrial Bases, High Tech and Support for Fighter Development

American Defence Sector Contraction and China's Industrial Advantage

The scale and sophistication of a country's research and development and its industrial base have throughout history been key determinants of the complexity and quality of the armaments it can produce, with this being particularly evident for higher end more complex asset types such as fighter planes. Moving into the twenty-first century the importance of civilian high-tech industry to defence has continued to grow as more key defence technologies have been derived from advances in the civilian sector, rather than vice-versa as was previously more common. As among the most complex and technology intensive products to develop and manufacture, both the ability to operationalise fifth generation fighters and the efficiency and cost effectiveness with which this can be done thus closely correlates with the state of a country's industry and tech sector. The phenomenon that is the J-20 program, and its standing relative to its rivals in the United States, therefore cannot be fully comprehended without a brief assessment of the predominant trends shaping both the defence sectors and the broader tech sectors and industrial bases in China and America.

China's rise to primacy in the post-Cold War era in both the scale and sophistication of its industry and high tech across multiple fields has directly corresponded to its ability to see its first fifth generation fighter program through development relatively smoothly and in a fraction of the time of its competitors. American programs' considerable difficulties and delays, and the more extreme delays and limitations of Russian programs, has similarly reflected the industrial decline, and in Russia's case also a sharp R&D decline, which both faced over the same period. Referred to by its chief designer Yang Wei as a symbol of 'the development achievements of China's aviation industry in the past forty years,'[1] the J-20's strong international standing has thus been the product of multiple broader converging trends in the tech sectors, defence sectors and wider economies of both China and of its rivals.

Comparing the standing of the Chinese industrial base with its rivals one key indicator and facilitator of its strength has been the much greater prevalence of workers with the skills required for very high-tech manufacturing. As observed in the *New York Times* as early as 2012, China 'provided engineers at a scale the United States could not match,' and could assemble the skilled personnel required close to twenty times as fast, with their 'flexibility, diligence and industrial skills' having 'so outpaced their American counterparts'.[2] Taking America's largest information technology company as an example, Apple CEO Tim Cook observed in 2017 regarding the prevalence in the Chinese workforce of technical skill levels needed to work at state-of-the art production facilities: 'The skill here is just incredible ... In the U.S., you could have a meeting of tooling engineers and I'm not sure we could fill the room. In China, you could fill multiple football fields.'[3] Cook separately observed: 'The quantity of skill in one location ... and the type of skill it is. The products we do require really advanced tooling. And the precision that you have to have in tooling and working with the materials that we do are state-of-the-art. And the tooling skill is very deep here.'[4] He noted that China benefitted from 'very deep' vocational expertise, for which he credited its education system, noting that it was ahead of the curve in emphasizing vocational aspects of education which had given its industry a significant edge.[5] Cook's predecessor Steve Jobs had made multiple statements to similar effect.[6]

Where the piston engine fighter aircraft of the Second World War era could be assembled by workers from a basic car assembly line with relatively little conversion training, the skill level needed in fighter manufacturing rose sharply moving in to the jet age and subsequently with each new generation. This made China's prevalence of manufacturing and engineering talent a tremendous advantage for manufacturing defence products like the J-20. The tremendous difficulties the United States had in scaling up production of the F-35 despite funding from a decade long backlog of orders, and the speed and smoothness with which China could do so for the J-20 at an estimated small fraction of the cost, was one notable example, with shortages of skilled labour consistently cited as the leading bottleneck preventing accelerated deliveries of F-35s or other advanced assets.[7]

Complementing the significant advantages in its skilled workforce, the concentration of supply chains was a further leading advantage China's high tech industrial base had over that of the U.S.[8] As observed by a former high-ranking Apple executive cited by the *New York Times*: 'The entire supply chain is in China now. You need a thousand rubber gaskets? That's the factory next door. You need a million screws? That factory is a block away. You need that screw made a little bit different? It will take three hours.'[9] Supply chain concentration in North-East Asia was a serious obstacle firms such as Apple faced when trying to produce high tech products in America since inputs needed to be brought very far to reach production lines. These trends made American firms increasingly reliant on Chinese inputs, and even in those civilian areas with key strategic implications such as telecommunications there were often no alternatives to key Asian inputs from Western countries.[10]

Looking to the American defence sector specifically, while industrial decline was slower than that in civilian industries due to a degree of government protection, it would, from the 1990s, increasingly struggle to operate efficiently without a robust civilian industrial base supporting it. A review ordered by the White House and led by the Pentagon found in 2018 that the military had come to rely heavily on foreign products, particularly from China. An anonymous U.S. official informed *Reuters* regarding the findings: 'People used to think you could outsource the manufacturing base without any repercussions (on national security). But now we know that's not the case.'[11] The review highlighted that 'all facets of the manufacturing and defence industrial base are currently under threat,' emphasizing that decades of decline left entire 'industries near domestic extinction' – forcing the Pentagon to increasingly look overseas for supplies.[12]

The *Washington Post* summarised regarding the review's findings: 'the vast supply chain serving the U.S. Military has become dependent on low-cost foreign components ... Things such as machine tools, infrared detectors and night-vision systems are largely provided by foreign suppliers, officials say, raising questions about whether the U.S. Military would have access to them in a protracted war.' This was in part a result of a 'broken procurement system'.[13] The report highlighted that consolidations in the early and mid-2010s in particular, amid a sharper post-2008 industry decline as budgets were further cut, had created several monopolies, preventing market forces from driving up performance and lowering costs for domestic products as they would if multiple vendors could be supported to bid for each contract. Like almost every report on the state of the defence sector it underlined a severe shortage in skilled workers such as engineers and software developers.[14]

Notable among the areas of dependence on China were microelectronics, integrated circuits and transistors, which were all very widely used in military hardware ranging from satellites and guided missiles to combat aircraft and communications systems. American defence journalist Brett Tingley was one of many to thus summarise:

'Currently, the U.S. is almost entirely reliant on foreign-made electronics to power most of its technologies, both in the defence and consumer sectors.' He stressed that this had significant implications both for civilian high tech's ability to compete, as well as for the defence sector.[15] Reliance on Chinese manufacturing inputs was wide ranging and went far beyond electronics, with one example that gained greater publicity being the chemical Butanetriol used to produce Hellfire missiles.

Analysts at the *National Interest* emphasized that Chinese industry built a 'huge chunk' of the American arsenal, highlighting the extent of high-tech supply chain concentration in China, and in North-East Asia more broadly, and noting that moves to phase out Chinese inputs 'may be more smoke than fire' due to their very limited feasibility. They concluded: 'Short of nationalizing American defence contractors, the U.S. will depend on private industry to satisfy its military production needs. And private industry ... will insist on minimizing costs and maximizing profits. That's the essence of globalization, and the impetus for the relentless outsourcing of American manufacturing. That's why Chinese goods have so captured so much of the U.S. market ... Made in America makes great sense in terms of national security, but American taxpayers will have to be willing to pay extra for Made in Seattle instead of Made in Shanghai.'

'The Pentagon tries to save money by buying commercial-off-the-shelf technology instead of custom-made gear, but the commercial sector relies on Chinese-made components, especially electronics ... transforming into Made in America will not be cheap or easy,' the assessment added, stressing that the massive shift of global supply chains to East Asia raised the question of 'whether it is even possible anymore to make purely American weapons.'[16] The more complex the defence production and more sophisticated its inputs, the more this was an issue, which posed particularly significant problems for combat aviation.

With American industrial and defence sector decline having seriously impeded the performance and delayed the realisation of new generations of complex weapons systems, including fighters, this and an even sharper decline in post-Soviet Russia were primary enablers of China's rise to produce weapons systems including stealth fighters which were serious contenders for global leadership. The trend towards contraction of the American industrial base and growth in reliance on foreign suppliers for defence emerged soon after the Cold War's end, as while high defence spending levels of the Reagan and G.H.W. Bush years had insulated the defence sector from the early impacts of industrial decline, spending in the 1990s was cut sharply.[17] As German-American tech billionaire Peter Thiel summarised in 2021, speaking to former State Secretary Mike Pompeo, the Cold War's end saw 'a shrinking of military budgets, but there was also an incredible consolidation of the defence industry, and the consolidation actually meant the money was spent less efficiently – especially with respect to R&D. And so we spent less money and [with] less efficiency, and so there was some massive decline in the effectiveness of the system in the 90s.'[18] Deterioration was particularly rapid in the 1992-1996 period, which represented a post-Cold War shock, but continued long afterwards, with erosion of parts of the industrial base vital to military procurement becoming increasingly evident around the turn of the century. Domestic sourcing for production of critical systems such as aircraft parts and engines all fell sharply, while pressure on manufacturers to increase efficiency amid declining budgets very often resulted in outsourcing overseas.

The Pentagon's annual Industrial Capabilities reports confirmed that although defence industries continued to make significant profits, a high and growing number of key components could not be supplied domestically. The closure of niche manufacturers and lack of technical skills were leading causes, and represented part of a broader trend towards industrial decline. Taking 2018 as an example, cases ranged from a key producer of missile components having closed for two years before the Pentagon found out, to 'perpetual financial risk and experience bankruptcy threats' facing key suppliers of aircraft parts. The 2018 report was only the latest in a long line pointing to 'a generation of engineers and scientists that lack experience in conceiving, designing, and constructing new, technologically advanced combat vehicles.'[19] The reports highlighted that large numbers of key inputs were produced by uncompetitive niche manufacturers, and that using government subsidies could only temporarily slow industry deterioration, but was far from a sufficient or long-term solution.[20]

Shrinking diversity of suppliers led to higher costs, lower efficiency and lower redundancy, with Industrial Capabilities reports highlighting significant risks from 'dependence on single and sole source suppliers, capacity shortfalls, a lack of competition, a lack of workforce skills, and unstable demand.'[21] They also cited statistics from the Department of Labour predicting further sharp decline in skilled worker numbers which would further impact industry's ability to meet demand.[22] Under Secretary of Defence for Acquisition, Technology, and Logistics Ashton Carter had warned as early as 2009 that these were 'very rare kinds of skills that are not easily replicated in the commercial world and, if allowed to erode, would be difficult to rebuild,' emphasising regarding the potential consequences of these skill shortages that 'having the best defence industrial and technology base in the world is not a birthright.'[23]

Reports from the National Defence Industrial Association (NDIA) pointed to many of the same trends as the Pentagon's reports and the White House's review, with NDIA president and chief executive Hawk Carlisle, a retired four-star Air Force general, stressing the serious issues posed by 'reliance on single producers within the supply chain, dependence on unstable or unfriendly foreign suppliers for critical components ... Compounding these risks, the report highlights a drain on talent that now flows toward Silicon Valley start-ups instead of defence-focused industries.' He highlighted a 'misplaced presumption of continued pre-eminence of American military superiority' which defence sector trends had left far from certain.[24]

NDIA reports highlighted firms' struggles with deteriorating industrial security and the scarcity and costs of both materials and skilled labour, and showed that supply chain security was by far the defence sector's biggest problem.[25] The sharp contraction in the number of firms able to bid for key contracts was widely highlighted, with NDIA Vice President Wes Hallman noting, regarding the Boeing-Lockheed Martin duopoly in fighter aviation, that in the Cold War era 'it took you more than two hands to count the number of companies that could produce a fighter jet, and now we're down to essentially two. That's a big deal, and that's just one sector.'[26] U.S. Strategic Command General C. Robert Kehler similarly highlighted that 'since the space age began, we have rarely been so reliant on so few industrial suppliers.'[27] Similar trends were observable across the Western world, as well as in Russia where post-Cold War industrial decline was even sharper, forcing the diverse ranges of firms producing competing products to gradually merge into duopolies and monopolies.[28] China showed opposite trends in its defence sector.

As early as August 2009, Heritage Foundation Senior Research Fellow in National Security Policy James Jay Carafano had warned that it was unclear how America could 'sustain a defence industrial base' with the deep cuts that followed the 2008 financial crisis – a trend he was far from alone in highlighting. Such concerns proved well founded over the next decade.[29] Also raised at the time were 'concerns about the viability of the U.S. machine tool industry to supply the ultra-high precision tools needed to replace existing tools and meet future demand.' Concerns grew of a 'tacit acceptance that the United States lacks a sufficiently robust commercial industrial base to supply many vital products needed for maintaining a strong defence industrial base.' As a result a vicious cycle emerged where 'the Pentagon's support for globalizing defence procurement not only reflects the growing inability of our industrial base to meet national security needs, but in itself contributes to the ongoing unravelling of the nation's overall industrial capacity.' The more the Pentagon outsourced abroad the more industry declined, and the more it declined the greater the incentive to outsource became.[30]

Contraction of the defence sector not only limited the range of products that could be built, while reducing efficiency and performance and driving up costs of those which still could, but it also had highly detrimental impacts on innovation. Top tier defence contractors such as aviation giants Boeing and Lockheed Martin were focused much more on systems integration than innovation while 'pushing the burden of innovation lower into the supply chain,' with the smaller firms relied on to innovate also being the most vulnerable to the fallout from industrial decline. The defence sector's capacity for innovation was thus harmed disproportionately. Observing this trend former RAND analyst Michael Webber highlighted: 'If the manufacturing support base no longer adequately serves the innovative companies, then their ability to be competitive is hindered and innovation does not move up the chain to the top-tier integrators. Consequently, the health of the entire innovation food chain, and thus the entire national innovation system and the defence industrial base, relies on the health of the foundation of the entire system: the manufacturing support base.'[31] As increasingly acknowledged by industrial policy experts from the late 2010s, those who manufactured products were very often the best positioned to innovate.[32]

By the early 2020s issues with the American defence sector had grown serious enough that measures as radical as nationalisation began to be considered, with USAF head of acquisitions William Roper in July 2020 highlighting that this would allow the Air Force to avoid the tremendous inefficiencies in ownership, sustainment and modernisation costs caused by the existing system. This could be necessary 'if our industrial base collapses any more,' he said, concluding that 'everything has to change,' and elaborating that what talent existed was being drawn away from the defence sector.[33] Vice President of analysis at the Teal Group aviation consulting firm Richard Aboulafia noted that the prospect of nationalising America's military aviation sector was 'an admission that they have failed miserably',[34] with Army Chief of Staff Mark Milley being among growing numbers to highlight that China's nationalised defence industries were producing armaments far more cost effectively.[35]

The decline in the American defence sector and broader industrial decline, as much as China's own economic and technological rise, were responsible for allowing the J-20 to emerge as a world leading fighter aircraft competing on a fully peer level with the most capable assets in the USAF inventory. These industrial trends had very significant implications for almost all aspects of competition in next generation combat aviation, ranging from how quickly performance issues with new aircraft could be solved, the scale and efficiency of their production, how future iterations of the J-20 would compare with future F-35 variants, and what performance advantages U.S. and Chinese sixth generation fighters would have.

Supplementing the benefits China reaped from a defence sector that proved to be far more efficient, and a far healthier industrial base, from 2020 the country surpassed the United States in expenditures on arms acquisitions to become the world leader.[36] A far greater proportion of China's defence spending was allocated to placing orders from industry, and a greater proportion of these orders went to local industry compared to in the U.S. This followed China's overtaking the U.S. in GDP, according to CIA and IMF figures, in 2014, with its much higher growth rates meaning that by 2020 its economy was one sixth larger , and by 2024 well over one fifth larger.[37] The high discrepancy in efficiency, paired with China's growing advantages in scale, ensured an increasingly favourable military balance for Beijing and positioned it well to field more capable armaments in future, including fighters, and in much larger quantities.

Artificial Intelligence and the J-20 Program

By the late 2010s China was increasingly demonstrating a strong lead in multiple strategically significant high end technology areas with dual civilian and military applications, which had strong implications for the standing of its combat aircraft and the networks they were integrated into. This was increasingly widely acknowledged from the late 2010s by experts and policy think tanks,[38] an example being the Australian Strategic Policy Institute, which in 2023 identified that China was outpacing the U.S. in eighty-four per cent of technology research areas with critical security applications.[39] Chinese entities by 2020 were gaining leads in a growing number of tech areas and filing nearly fifty per cent of all patent applications worldwide – over twice as many as the United States – and continuing to expand this proportion fast.[40] Competition in two of the most critical emerging technology areas with strong implications for the J-20 program and how the fighter will operate, artificial intelligence and quantum technologies, are explored below.

Artificial Intelligence (AI) has been widely seen by analysts as the Fourth Industrial Revolution technology with the greatest strategic and economic implications, and allows machines to 'think' for themselves with minimal human intervention, learn from data and make accurate assessments and predictions. This ranges from basic functions such as playing chess or poker to processing complex data inputs from sensors or even designing weapons. At a more advanced level AI can adapt to new data and train itself to learn and recognise patterns – known as Deep Learning. Speaking regarding defence applications more specifically, former Deputy Secretary of Defence Robert O. Work noted in January that at the Pentagon there was 'certainly no technology that we could identify [which] would have as broad of an impact on national security as artificial intelligence.[41] Predictions of a future of warfare dominated by clashes between rival fleets of unmanned AI piloted aircraft became increasingly widespread in the 2010s, with Russian President Vladimir Putin famously positing that 'when one party's drones are destroyed by drones of another, it will have no other choice but to surrender.'[42]

The performances of the J-20, the F-35, and the networks of other assets supporting them, are expected to be increasingly shaped by advances in AI. Not only is AI expected to be able to perform a wider range of functions when integrated onto aircraft, but also to accelerate advances in industry. A notable example announced in March 2022 was the use of AI to design a new generation of Chinese hypersonic weapons, accelerating development significantly.[43] A year later AI was used to complete almost a year of design work on a new Chinese warship within twenty-four hours – doing so with '100 per cent accuracy' leaving the ship 'ready for engineering applications'.[44] Beyond potentially arming the J-20 and many supporting assets in their networks with new generations of missiles, AI was expected to fundamentally revolutionise design processes across the Chinese aviation industry. From reducing an airframe's radar cross section to increasing engine efficiency, AI had the potential to accelerate and improve the designs of military aircraft working alongside human designers. The range of areas where AI design could be applied and its potency are expected to significantly increase as technological advances in the field continued to be made.

AI is expected to support the J-20's combat effectiveness by processing data from surveillance assets, assisting with pilot training, supporting command and control and helping to check hardware for problems during maintenance, among a very wide range of other functions.[45] It will very likely perform them far more efficiently, with less room for error, and at a much lower cost than human personnel. Speeding up tasks from administration and logistics to surveillance and targeting, it is expected to first replace humans in simpler jobs, before increasingly doing so as a combatant on both cyber and physical battlefields. Expected functions range from conducting electronic and cyber warfare from a J-20, to piloting UAVs accompanying the fighters, and eventually possibly flying the aircraft themselves.

A stepping stone to a fully autonomous fighter is a synergy between human and AI pilots, either serving as co-pilots or flying alongside one another. AI co-pilots were compared by USAF Assistant Secretary for Acquisition, Technology and Logistics Will Roper to R2D2 from the Star Wars franchise,[46] with J-20 chief designer Yang Wei highlighting that they could help pilots process vast quantities of information and make decisions in complex battlefield environments.[47] While weapons systems officers in the second seats of fighters such as the J-16, or the American F-15EX, had long been reported to provide significant combat advantages over single seaters in both strike and air-to-air missions,[48] as simultaneously flying, operating weapons controls and experiencing high G loads could be extremely strenuous on a single pilot,[49] AI co-pilots were expected to obviate the need for them.

Outside the cockpits of the fighters themselves, AI is expected to facilitate the semi-autonomous operations of unmanned 'wingman' aircraft alongside manned fighters. Providing insight into the future of this synergy between manned and unmanned platforms, USAF Secretary Frank Kendall highlighted in June 2022 that America's upcoming sixth generation fighter should be thought of as a combination of a manned aircraft flying with four or five UAVs 'used together as an operational formation' directed by the pilot.[50] Wang Ya'nan, chief editor of the Beijing-based magazine *Aerospace Knowledge*, was among many to speculate that the J-20 could similarly serve as a commander for UAV wingmen formations, and could itself be optionally manned.[51] Leadership in AI development would be key to operationalising this, reducing the amount of direction semi-autonomous aircraft required, and eventually making fully autonomous aircraft viable replacements for a wider range of manned ones.

AI-flown combat aircraft already began to demonstrate tremendous potential in testing by the late 2010s, with SpaceX CEO Elon Musk announcing in February 2020 at the Air Warfare Symposium that as a result of the latest advances 'the fighter jet era has passed.' 'Drone warfare is where the future will be. It's not what I want the future to be – it's just, this is what the future will be,' he stated, stressing that the latest stealth fighters 'would have no chance against' upcoming AI-flown challengers.[52] Although Musk's comments were hotly disputed by Western defence experts,[53] they aligned closely with the consensus in China. On 25 October 2018 at the Xiangshan Forum, for example, senior executive at leading Chinese defence firm Norinco Zeng Yi had similarly predicted regarding AI's potential: 'In future battlegrounds, there will be no people fighting,' with increased use of AI being 'inevitable … We are sure about the direction and that this is the future.'[54]

Experiments by the USAF in 2020 showed that the viability of manned combat aircraft could quickly be greatly diminished by AI, with the service in August pitting a top human F-16 pilot against an AI pilot in five simulated air-to-air battles. The test was a culmination of efforts to explore how AI and machine learning could help to automate various aspects of air-to-air combat, and saw the AI pilot win overwhelming victories in all rounds.[55] By early 2021 AI-piloted F-16s were simulating working in teams and engaging targets at longer ranges, which were major steps towards moving away from simulations to begin flying real world F-16s with AI at the controls. Adding more weapons options and multiple aircraft introduced considerable further complexity to operations.[56] The PLAAF was revealed in 2021 to be conducting similar tests pitting human fighter pilots against AIs, which saw the latter consistently win overwhelming victories. Chinese AIs were similarly reported to be 'learning' from pilots, gaining experience and improving quickly.[57]

AI piloted fighters could learn from simulations significantly better than human pilots could, reducing the costs of regularly flying for training purposes. Since the primary cost of any combat aircraft was its lifetime operational cost, cutting the need for training flights and exercises could reduce each fighter's lifetime expenses by close to two-thirds and thus facilitate the fielding of fleets which were much larger than those seen in the era of human pilots. AIs could 'experience' millions of hours of simulated combat and 'learn' from this experience 24/7, supplementing this by bringing together data in aerial combat much faster than a human could to come up with an optimal means of neutralising targets. While human pilots could not endure G forces of over 9G, an AI piloted aircraft could be as manoeuvrable and fast as a missile and pull turns at 40G or more. Removing the life support systems, canopies and interfaces needed by human pilots was expected to contribute to making AI-piloted fighters considerably lighter, longer ranged and more efficient.

The trends seen in fighter aviation applied to varying extents across the spectrum of military modernisation, from reducing tank crew requirements and eventually developing semi-autonomous and autonomous tanks,[58] to sensors and navigation,[59] autonomous aerial resupply missions,[60] and cyber offensives.[61] One USAF program was pursued to allow attack jets to find targets faster by filtering out bad information using AI,[62] and another saw AI take over the sensors of long-range surveillance aircraft. Secretary Will Roper noted regarding the latter, following a landmark test in December 2020: 'Putting AI safely in command of a U.S. military system for the first time ushers in a new age of human-machine teaming and algorithmic competition. Failing to realize AI's full potential will mean ceding decision advantage to our adversaries.'[63] Similar developments were expected to make J-20 units and their vast networks of supporting assets, from surveillance drones to unmanned bombers and command and control aircraft, far more potent, with the balance of power between Chinese and American air units set to be heavily influenced by which had more effectively applied superior AI.

While the era of unmanned fighters was by the early 2020s increasingly considered inevitable, the J-20 appeared to have more chance of a future than any other pre-sixth generation fighter particularly as the J-20S variant. First flying in 2021, it was the world's only fighter with both stealth capabilities and a second seat to accommodate a drone controller, allowing it to direct the AI-flown UAVs of the future. Should AI development begin to quickly render manned fighters obsolete in the 2030s, as many sources have projected, the J-20S could well be left as the only manned variant in production. Command and control variants of the J-20 reported to be under development, likely derived from the J-20S, could potentially also have important roles in a world where AI had replaced human pilots in combat roles.

AI was also expected to increasingly replace humans in command and control, with Norinco's Zeng Yi reflecting the emerging consensus in Chinese defence circles when he observed: 'Mechanized equipment is just like the hand of the human body. In future intelligent wars, AI systems will be just like the brain of the human body ... AI may completely change the current command structure, which is dominated by humans to one that is dominated by an "AI cluster."'[64] China's Central Military Commission Joint Operations Command Centre argued in August 2016* that recent events had 'demonstrated the enormous potential of artificial intelligence in combat command, program deduction, and decision making.'[65]

---

* This followed the defeat of the human champion in the most complex two player game in the world GO, for decades considered the last game where humans retained primacy, by an AI in March 2016 which led to a renewed focus on the technology in high tech economies, particularly China, the U.S. and South Korea. Superiority to humans in GO was a symbolically important step towards leaving humans redundant in a growing number of fields.

Despite significant investments, and although military applications of AI received a disproportionate amount of attention and funding in America, the Pentagon faced considerable difficulties attempting develop and utilise the technology. A thorough 756-page report by the U.S. National Security Commission on Artificial Intelligence (NSCAI) published in 2021 noted regarding these issues that 'visionary technologists and warfighters largely remain stymied by antiquated technology, cumbersome processes, and incentive structures that are designed for outdated or competing aims.' Referring in its opening letter to the U.S. as 'not prepared to defend or compete in the AI era,' it highlighted multiple obstacles faced integrating AI into the military. Spending, it noted, 'remains concentrated on legacy systems designed for the industrial age and Cold War,' while 'many Departmental processes still rely too much on PowerPoint and manually driven work streams. The data that is needed to fuel machine learning is currently stovepiped, messy, or often discarded. Platforms are disconnected. Acquisition, development, and fielding practices largely follow rigid, sequential processes, inhibiting early and continuous experimentation and testing critical for AI.'[66]

Analysts at *The Drive* in early 2021 similarly observed regarding the military's slow rate of AI adoption: 'While wars have for centuries been largely decided by which side possesses the best hardware, we are entering a brave new future in which software will hold the key to global supremacy ... the laborious slow pace of procurement and innovation among the DoD has left the United States lagging behind in terms of its preparedness to face AI threats.'[67] They otherwise highlighted key missed opportunities for development of important AI-centred programs, and obstacles to modernisation using the new technology posed by the Air Force's pilot-centric 'flyboy culture.'[68] The military's ability to integrate the new technology was repeatedly brought to question, with the *National Interest* observing in the title of a major 2021 article on 'data-illiterate culture' that it: 'Exists across the Department of Defence and among powerful constituencies within the military services. It starts with a paucity of understanding the value of data and the data science that drives the artificial intelligence and machine learning (ML) revolution.' It concluded 'the U.S. Military is failing to adapt to the automated battlefield in scope and speed. The Department struggles to apply AI/ML to military functions outside of the narrow tasks of reconnaissance, surveillance, target acquisition, and prosecution. The reason for this narrow scope and glacial pace of exploitation is data-illiteracy.'[69] This issue was widely alluded to, including by the Defence Secretary, and affected the civilian economy in much the same way as it did the military.[70]

Pentagon bureaucracy was another key obstacle, with former First Air Force Chief Software Officer Nicolas Chaillan stressing in October 2021 that America had already lost the competitions with China in AI, cyber capabilities and machine learning. A former technology entrepreneur, software developer and cyber expert, Chaillan slammed the Pentagon for failing to adapt stating: 'We have no competing fighting chance against China in fifteen to twenty years. Right now, it's already a done deal; it is already over in my opinion.'[71] More moderate statements to similar effect were made by a number of figures in the U.S. military leadership, most notably by Vice Chairman of the Joint Chiefs of Staff John Hyten, who warned that the United States had long been moving far too slowly in developing key new technologies which had diminished its advantages significantly.[72]

While economic, strategic and military importance of AI grew significantly in the 2000s, and more so after 2010 as the technology began to advance faster, the number of published peer review data AI papers grew more than fourfold from 1998 to 2018. This growth was described by experts in January 2020 as representing 'just the leading edge of this massive wave.' It was thus notable that China comfortably led growth in research and in publishing, surpassing

America in journal publications on AI from 2006 and subsequently rapidly widening its lead.[73] China's lead in AI was well established by the time the J-20 began to enter service, with a study published by information analytics firm Elsevier finding that between 1998 and 2017 134,990 AI research papers were published in China compared to just 106,600 in the U.S. – with the very distant third place held by India at under 40,000 publications.[74] The strong Chinese lead was particularly pronounced in deep learning papers.[75] China also overtook the U.S. for AI citations in 2020,[76] with prevailing trends indicating that its lead would grow considerably wider over the coming decade.[77] A prominent article in the *Harvard Business Review* thus concluded in February 2021 that in AI research 'China has surged to rapidly catch up. From a research perspective, China has become a world leader in AI publications and patents. This trend suggests that China is also poised to become a leader in AI-empowered businesses,' with its market being 'conductive to the adoption and improvement of AI.'[78]

Not only did China lead the world by a considerable margin in AI research, but it also retained very significant advantages in its AI workforce, funding, and the degree of government support provided. By the time the J-20 entered service in 2017 the country already accounted for forty-eight per cent of global equity funding for AI startups compared to thirty-eight per cent in the U.S. and thirteen per cent by the rest of the world. The Chinese AI industry continued to expand its lead afterwards, growing by sixty-seven per cent that year alone.[79] Chinese AI startups were already raising $4.9 billion annually in venture capital funding where startups in the U.S. raised $4.4 billion – a difference which was considerably greater when considering the dollar's far higher purchasing power in China. By 2018 China had secured leading positions in AI technology, development and market applications, and comfortably held first place in total AI research papers, highly cited AI papers, AI patents and AI venture capital investment.[80]

As the emergence of a Chinese lead in AI became increasingly evident, a December 2019 *MIT Technology Review* report referred to a 'deep-seated fear within the policy community that the U.S. is sorely losing in the so-called AI arms race,' and highlighted that America was being comfortably outspent in the field.[81] NSCAI's aforementioned 756-page report similarly detailed how China was expected to establish itself as the undisputed leader in AI, and why America was poorly positioned to compete.[82] Experts highlighted a much greater willingness to take risks with AI-related investments, government funding and support, a lively research community, a large consumer base, and a society primed for technological change as key causes of Chinese leads.[83] A prominent paper on the subject from Taiwan's CTBC Business School similarly observed: 'It has become an article of faith amongst those in the commanding heights that whoever unties the "AI Gordian Knot" would dominate the twenty-first century,' with China having emerged as 'the leading contender in this race and seemingly inevitable victor.'[84]

Much as natural disaster responses were often taken as a key measure of military readiness, so too did the onset of the COVID-19 pandemic provide unique insights into the extent of the discrepancy between China and its competitors in how effectively they could practically utilise AI for new purposes and on short notice. The CTBC Business School paper thus reported that 'without outlier events such as COVID-19, the world may not have realised the significant strides China has made in AI,' with the pandemic having 'revealed to the world the remarkable progress China has made in AI and its accompanying ecosystem. More importantly, this outlier event demonstrates the surgical, hybridised manner in which China has utilised these emerging technologies in containing its spread and set itself on the path to unleashing their full potential.' It concluded the 'technological brilliance of China's high-tech campaign to eradicate COVID-19' demonstrated its leadership in the field. Examples ranged from using AI to analyse chest scans to diagnose patients in a fraction of the time it took doctors, to answering calls and delivering food to patients, with no remotely comparable applications seen elsewhere.[85] This was a highly positive sign for China's ability to apply the technology to respond to unpredicted developments in a political or military crisis.

Tactical combat aviation represented one of a very wide range of areas of competition with the United States where a Chinese lead in AI was set to have potentially decisive implications – positioning battle networks in all domains, and particularly in the air, space and cyberspace to gain key advantages. As AI plays a growing role in design processes superior AI is likely to translate into more capable future generations of aerial warfare assets, both manned and unmanned, from airframes themselves to their missiles and sensors. The tremendous discrepancy in size and sophistication separating the AI sectors of China and the U.S. from those of the rest of the world, and the transformative effect the technology is set to have on tactical combat aviation, will likely further the already significant and growing discrepancy between the two leaders and all other players in the field.

Quantum Technologies and the Battle Networks of the Future

Representing a second emerging strategic technology area alongside AI, quantum technologies are expected to have a transformative effect on the data sharing capabilities and eventually the situational awareness and computing power of assets in Chinese combat networks, making them highly relevant to determining how the J-20 and other major weapons systems can be utilised. The *MIT Technology Review* was accordingly among sources which described China and America as seeing: 'The emerging quantum era as a once-in-a-lifetime opportunity to gain the edge over its rival in military tech,' stressing that its potential impact on military communications were 'game changing.'[86] As China showed growing signs of leadership in the field, quantum technologies had the potential to provide a strong edge to future iterations of the J-20 and to other assets it would be integrated with, ranging from AEW&C platforms like the KJ-500, to communications satellites or combat and surveillance UAVs.

The strategic importance of quantum technologies was repeatedly emphasized by Chinese officials at the highest levels, and made a top priority for development alongside AI in the country's Fourteenth Five Year Plan, with investment in the national quantum program growing far faster than programs abroad.[87] As observed in a 2018 paper by the Centre for a New American Security (CNAS): 'At the highest levels, China's leaders recognize the strategic potential of quantum science and technology to enhance economic and military dimensions of national power,' one result of which was that scientists were 'receiving nearly unlimited resources.'[88] China showed growing signs of a strong lead in the field from the late 2010s, key to which was its success in promoting close working relationships between government research institutes, universities and firms. The U.S. by contrast took much longer to create a national plan for coordinating public and private efforts and longer still to begin to show signs of implementation. According to the *Scientific American:* 'The delay in adopting such an approach has led to a lot of siloed projects and could slow the development of useful military applications' – an issue which was also raised by quantum experts in the military.[89]

The area of quantum technologies which first materialised in an actual militarily applicable capability was quantum communications, with communications between Chinese government officials having been secured by a new quantum network by 2009 making the country the first in the world to achieve this. By early 2015, according to leading scientist in the field Pan Jianwei, China was already 'completely capable of making full use of quantum communications in a local war.' Pan projected 'using relay satellites to realize quantum communications and control that covers the entire army.'[90]

The world's first satellite dedicated to quantum information science – the Micius satellite – was launched in China in 2016, and quickly produced several breakthroughs. As early as 2017 it demonstrated quantum entanglement over unprecedented distances, which placed China very far ahead of competitors in developing quantum communications.[91] The Pentagon by then had yet to even decide to invest significantly in building a quantum communications infrastructure. Citing Micius as an example, a 2018 CNAS paper warned: 'Chinese researchers have achieved a track record of consistent advances in basic research and in the development of quantum technologies, including quantum cryptography, communications, and computing, as well as reports of progress in quantum radar, sensing, imaging, metrology, and navigation. Their breakthroughs demonstrate the successes of a long-term research agenda that has dedicated extensive funding to this domain while actively cultivating top talent.'[92]

Quantum satellites' potential to transform battle networks was exhibited in 2020 when Micius was used to demonstrate the world's first ever quantum-secured space communications, and did so across very wide areas.[93] It was the latest of many Chinese breakthroughs in high tech to be widely compared in the West to the Soviet launch of the world's first satellite – a 'Sputnik moment' for America showing how far ahead the competition was in a key technology area with potentially decisive military implications.[94] The *Scientific American* observed of the Chinese achievement: 'Arguably represents the nation's lead in an emerging contest among great powers at the frontiers of physics,' leaving America 'scrambling to catch up.' It concluded: 'The achievement brings the world – or China, at least – one step closer to realizing truly unhackable global communications.'[95] The versatility of China's unique satellite quantum communication capabilities were further demonstrated in May 2021 when Micius was used to secure large parts of the country's power grid against cyber attacks or blackouts. Conducted in south-eastern China, it was seen by some as a show of force amid high tensions in the adjacent Taiwan Strait.[96]

Micius' successes were followed in January 2021 by the establishment in China of the world's first large integrated quantum communication network, which was a milestone no competitor was anywhere close to reaching. The network integrated over 700 optical fibres on the ground and ground-to-satellite links to achieve quantum key distribution over 4,600 kilometre distances. Next steps included developing smaller and cheaper satellites, as well as satellites in much higher orbits, to expand the network's reach and capabilities.[97] With the potential to evolve into a 'quantum internet,'[98] and to create new technologies such as 'super-telescopes,'[99] it also laid the foundation for a network of quantum satellites that could revolutionise the security of PLA communications, command and control, and transmission of targeting data for precision strikes. Such a network was expected to be active by 2030,[100] and would provide a very significant advantage to Chinese combat assets, including J-20 units, in the event of a major war, ensuring a much more robust network centric warfare capability than aircraft such as F-35s in other countries' fleets had.

With seamless transfer of information within networks being a key feature, and according to some assessments the most defining feature, of sixth generation aerial warfare, China's strong lead in quantum communications placed its forces, including its top fighter, in a strong position to gain dominance in the new era. China's increasingly clear superiority in quantum communications fuelled comparisons in both China and the West to being the first to field nuclear weapons,[101] with senior PLA leaders emphasizing the significant impact a combat network based on quantum technologies would have on the balance of power.[102] More than other areas of quantum technologies, quantum data sharing networks were expected to become central to how the PLA waged war in the air during the J-20's time as its premier fighter, with access to such networks potentially providing the class with one of its most decisive advantages over foreign rivals.

A second major area of quantum technologies with significant military applications, including for the J-20 program, was quantum computing. With the potential to provide computing power quintillions (millions of trillions) of times greater than traditional computers and supercomputers, it had particularly significant implications when considered alongside parallel advances in artificial intelligence. By the early 2020s a Chinese lead in quantum computing appeared to be emerging, and in December a team of Chinese scientists claimed to have made the first definitive demonstration of quantum mechanics to perform computations that would be mathematically impossible on any classical computer – a demonstration of 'quantum advantage.' They demonstrated the ability to perform computations in just 200 seconds which would take 2.5 billion years for the world's fastest supercomputers, with scientists internationally widely referring to it as a major milestone.[103] In July 2021 a team from the Hefei University of Science and Technology of China set a new record for processing speed on a quantum computer,[104] with this lead subsequently widened in October with a new prototype which could solve in one millisecond problems that would take the world's fastest non–quantum supercomputers thirty trillion years. It was one million times faster that its closest Western competitor which had been developed by Google.[105]

A Chinese lead in quantum computing had very significant strategic implications, with the *Scientific American* referring to it as 'a multibillion dollar enterprise recognized for its potential impact on national security, the global economy and the foundations of physics and computer science.'[106] Alongside applications of greater computing power for the design process of new aircraft and air launched weapons, it could also allow assets in PLA battle networks to process data far faster and facilitate more effective use of AI in roles ranging from command and control of battlefield assets to autonomously operating specific weapons systems. It further had potentially game changing offensive applications, with quantum computers expected to be able to overcome almost any form of encryption and thus providing a means of penetrating and destroying enemy information networks.

Development of quantum computers was a prominent part of China's national security strategy, with President Xi Jinping referring to it as 'an advance-handed piece on the board' – in reference to an advantage in the game GO which could be pivotal to gaining victory.[107] A 2019 paper by the School of Advanced Military Studies U.S. Army Command and General Staff College noted regarding the sheer destructive potential cyber attacks using quantum computers could have: 'The discussion about a large-scale quantum computer attack on a nation has grown to the same level as the nuclear deterrence discussion during the Cold War of 1945-1990. Because of the expected devastating effect of a large-scale quantum computer attack, there is a strong incentive amongst the countries that possess universal quantum computers to avoid conflict.'[108] Much like bombers, cyber assets could be key facilitators of air superiority by paralysing or disabling enemy networks, military facilities and logistics to prevent them from contributing to an adversary's complex air operations.

A third area of quantum technologies, albeit one far less likely to be operationalised in the foreseeable future, but with potentially very significant eventual applications for fighter aviation, was quantum sensors, with claims of breakthroughs beginning to emerge in the late 2010s particularly in China. These used pairs of twin entangled photons sharing a single quantum state, with one of each pair beamed out to a distance and one kept in the sensor itself. The process of quantum illumination would allow the far one to 'tell' the sensor a great deal about it through the changes seen in its twin. After significant progress was made by a team at Tsinghua University's aerospace engineering school in 2021, which was one of several teams working on such projects, experts increasingly expressed confidence that the technology had significant military applications.[109]

Quantum radars were expected to provide a much more effective capability for detecting, tracking and locking onto stealth aircraft,[110] and if operationalised could potentially initially be deployed from ground and ship-based sensors sharing data with combat aviation assets, before being miniaturised to deploy from AEW&C systems and eventually from combat aircraft themselves. The possibility of quantum radars being integrated onto PLA satellites, which by 2022 were benefitting from increasingly sophisticated AI to better track targets on earth,[111] was also raised and could further provide a tremendous situational awareness advantage to Chinese tactical aviation and other assets.[112] Quantum sensors were also expected to provide major advantages tracking missiles in flight, potentially allowing fighters integrating them to both better contribute to missile defence efforts and to have greater warning of and thus better evade anti-aircraft missiles.[113] Current trajectories indicate that China will be the first to operationalise these technologies for its armed forces, although it is highly possible that practical military uses will not be achieved before the 2040s.

Analysts at the Jamestown Foundation observed as early as 2016 that quantum communications could provide an 'asymmetric information advantage in a conflict scenario,' while quantum computing 'may prove to have strategic significance on par with nuclear weapons.' Quantum technologies more generally could 'radically alter the rules of the game on the future battlefield' and 'decisively change the future strategic balance.'[114] Quantum communications were expected in the near term to have very significant benefits for Chinese battle networks and all assets within them, with quantum computing potentially gaining significant military applications closer to the 2030s while quantum sensors may only become practically usable years later. The J-20 is almost certain to be the world's first stealth fighter to see its data sharing capabilities benefit from quantum communication technologies, and there is a significant possibility that it will also be the first to operate as part of a network that benefits from the use of quantum computers. The future of quantum sensor technologies remains less certain, but the technology could have particularly significant applications as fast-growing portions of the Chinese and American fleets are comprised of aircraft with advanced stealth capabilities. Assessments of technological trends in the Quantum and AI fields serve to illustrate the much broader trend towards Chinese dominance of strategic technologies, and how this has a wide range of potential implications for the standing of its combat aviation sector and top fighter units.

Chapter Five

The Future of the J-20 Program

Production Run

The number of J-20 stealth fighters the PLA intends to commission remains subject for considerable speculation, with several factors contributing to the uncertainty. The first is that it remains unknown whether the PLAAF will procure another lighter fifth generation fighter for a complementary high-low combination – much like it had acquired the lightweight J-10 to complement its heavyweight Flankers. Cost effectiveness calculations for the J-20 and any potential lighter counterpart, particularly pertaining to their operational costs which form the large majority of any fighter's lifetime costs, will likely be central to determining this.*

Heavyweights have represented a growing proportion of China's fighter fleet from 1992, much as they have in neighbouring Russia, albeit for very different reasons, and the PLAAF has in the past transitioned its brigades from deploying lightweight fighters to replacements twice or three times their size despite the tremendous resulting increase in operational costs. Notable examples have included J-20s replacing J-10s in the 1st and 5th Air Brigades, which

---

* Looking to foreign examples, the F-22's very high operational costs led the U.S. Air Force to continue to comprise the bulk of its fleet of lighter F-16s and later F-35s. By contrast the relatively low difference in operational costs between Russian Flankers and lighter MiG-29s, when compared to the discrepancy in performance, led the Russian Air Force to favour a slightly smaller fleet of more heavyweight Flankers as the more cost-effective option.

were under half their size and had under half their engine power, and in a more extreme case replacing J-7s little over a quarter their size and with under a quarter their engine power – namely under the 41st Air Brigade. It remains uncertain how far this will go into the 2020s, but the fact that J-20s have replaced not only Flankers, but also J-10s, including in their very first two frontline units, and in 2023 even a J-7 brigade, indicates that the fighter program could fuel further expansion of the heavyweight fleet as a proportion of all PLA fighter units. This would continue the trend that began with the large Su-27 and Su-30 acquisitions of the 1990s and has continued since. The distances separating Chinese air units from their leading potential adversaries, the expected importance of being able to loiter for extended periods over the Pacific in a potential future war, and the benefits of being able to contribute to operations from a much wider range of dispersed air bases, are all important factors in the favour of an increasing focus on high endurance heavyweight fighters.

Even if the proportion of heavyweight fighters is not significantly increased from the levels of the early 2020s, the J-20 and its derivatives could still see close to 1,000 aircraft produced. The PLA already fields a larger fleet of heavyweight fighter jets than NATO and Russia combined with over 700 fighters from the Flanker family in service in 2023 (approximately 600 in the Air Force and 150 in the Navy). Replacing the bulk of these, and possibly a portion of the country's more than 250 JH-7 strike fighters as well, provides room for a very large production run for the J-20 without reducing the portion of lightweight fighters in the fleet.

The second major cause of uncertainty is that it remains unknown what roles the J-20 will fulfil, with future derivatives potentially having different designations (J-21, JH-20, KJ-20 etc.) as they perform different roles – for example a dedicated strike variant or an AEW&C variant which have all been rumoured. The J-20 would inevitably see far more airframes built if it could perform a wider range of roles beyond air superiority – much like the Flanker saw very large production runs in both China and Russia as more well-balanced multirole variants, as well as specialised air defence suppression, strike, aircraft carrier, long-range interceptor and AEW&C variants, were all developed.[1]

The third source of uncertainty is the unknown extent to which manned fighters will play a role in a future PLA tactical fleet, with the J-20's production run potentially being heavily influenced by how quickly viable autonomous alternatives are developed. If J-20s begin to serve primarily as command-and-control assets for autonomous aircraft, and autonomous UAVs come to be strongly preferred for actual combat as they are expected to when AI and other associated technologies advance sufficiently, then this will likely limit production considerably. As noted by multiple U.S. Air Force sources, a balance of around five unmanned combat aircraft for every manned one, and possibly eventually as many as twenty to one, is currently envisioned, meaning deep cuts in production of manned fighters such as J-20s and F-35s in both fleets are highly possible.[2] Expectations regarding how soon advances in the capabilities of unmanned aircraft could cause deep cuts in orders to manned ones differ significantly, with U.S. Air Force Secretary Frank Kendall having indicated in March 2022 that F-35 production could continue until around 2037.[3] This meant even short ranged single seat fifth generation airframes were expected to be considered viable for decades to come when properly modernised.† Relative to the West, however, Chinese defence circles

---

† Even if produced until 2037, this did not mean F-35s would be acquired by the USAF even beyond 2027, or that production would continue on any meaningful scale into the 2030s. Taking the F-35's predecessor the F-16 as an example, the fighter was expected to be produced until around 2030 for export on a small scale – but the U.S. Military stopped receiving them a full quarter of a century earlier in 2005. The possibility remains significant that unmanned aircraft could end F-35 acquisitions by the USAF, or at least scale it down substantially, and at a much earlier date than expected, with the same applying to the J-20, particularly for single seat combat variants.

have long predicted autonomous unmanned systems will take on a much greater role in combat and much sooner, which combined with a lack of exports means the J-20 may not be expected to remain in production for nearly as long.

Beyond unmanned aircraft, the J-20's viability into the 2030s as sixth generation fighters join the PLAAF and the USAF is a further important factor. Whether it proves straightforward to modernise with sixth generation technologies and able to cost effectively contribute to operations in the next generation era will be key to determining how long production lasts.[†] A key overseas example was the American third generation F-4D/E fighter, which was seen to have limited modernisation potential and be far less cost effective than fourth generation fighters such as the F-16 leading to it quickly being be phased out of production. Its successor, the F-15, however, was still seen to be operationally cost effective in the fifth generation era when modernised to a '4+ generation' standard, and thus remained in production for well over twice as long.

A further unpredictable factor is whether the J-20 could eventually be offered for export, particularly as the extent of foreign demand depends largely on geopolitical factors which are difficult to predict, as well as on the performances of foreign economies that are seen to be potential clients. The F-35, for example, is expected to see its production run lengthened significantly by production exclusively for export, much like its direct predecessors the F-16 and F-5 did.

[†] Sixth generation fighters were referred to by prominent figures in the U.S. aerospace sector as necessary to be able to 'go one-v-five, one-v-ten, etc.' against fifth generation fleets, meaning they were intended to have overwhelming performance advantages over fighters like the J-20 where F-22s and F-35s could only 'go head-to-head from a one-v-one perspective.' Whether with upgrades including integration of sixth generation technologies the J-20 could avoid such a disadvantage was potentially decisive in how long it could remain in production. ('A next-gen digital backbone will give U.S. platforms a one-versus-many advantage against near-peers,' *Breaking Defense*, 12 October 2022.)

Although currently built for domestic use only, the J-20 may be offered abroad after a more capable sixth generation fighter enters service around 2030.

As early as May 2018 the U.S. House of Representatives Permanent Select Committee on Intelligence was informed by senior experts that production of up to 500 J-20s was expected.[4] The speed at which production lines grew in subsequent years, however, led to some projections for a production run well over 700. This would place the J-20's production run in the same range as initial projections for the F-22, which was to see production peak at over sixty airframes per year and have 750 aircraft produced before budget cuts and performance issues reduced this by over seventy-five per cent. The rapid and significant expansion of J-20 production facilities provided an important early indicator of a very large intended production run. Another was the high requirement for fifth generation fighters as a result of pressure on China's defences from the tremendous numbers of F-35s that were set to be deployed by its potential adversaries, with over 2000 F-35s expected to enter service even if cuts were made, which made a small J-20 production run appear unlikely.

By 2023 J-20 deliveries to the PLAAF were estimated at approximately eighty per year, with both Western and Chinese sources reporting that deliveries would rise to over 100 a year in 2024, reaching around 120 in 2025.[5] This was a major landmark in Chinese aviation history, as the last fighter produced on any remotely comparable scale had been the J-6 – an early second generation design which first flew in 1952 and was under a quarter the size of the J-20. Even at estimated 2023 production levels the J-20 was already being delivered at comparable rates to American and Soviet fourth generation heavyweights in the 1980s – a scale unseen for any aircraft of its size after the Cold War and matched only by the much smaller multi-national F-35. With the J-6 having formed close to three quarters of Chinese fighter units in the 1980s the J-20's massive production scale indicated that it could be intended to similarly equip close to half, if not a majority of Chinese fighter units, which no class since the J-6 had come close to doing.

With the PLA Air Force being the only client, reports of production rates to be achieved in 2024-2025 meant it would be receiving the fighters at around 250 per cent the rate at which the U.S. Air Force received F-35s – forty-eight per year – and closely rival the full sum of F-35 production for all nineteen global clients of around 140 per year.[6] This was particularly notable since the F-35 was a much lighter single engine fighter a little over two thirds the size. F-22 annual production had briefly peaked at only twenty-four aircraft,[7] while Russia had not acquired any fighter at more than twenty-four airframes annually and had not made sustained acquisitions of any fighter at over seventeen per year – despite acquiring fourth generation aircraft that were much cheaper. The increase in J-20 production numbers in mid-2023 notably closely coincided with deep cuts to production numbers for F-35s that year due to a range of difficulties.[8] By mid-2024, further purposed cuts were set to bring F-35 numbers acquired by the USAF to just 36 in 2025 - less than a quarter of the PLAAF's J-20 acquisitions for that year - and 11 each for the Navy and Marines.[9] With the J-20 fleet expected to exceed 500 fighters in 2025, the new delivery rates made a production run of close to 1000 appear plausible, placing it a league of its own with the F-35 not only in terms of the kinds of technologies it integrated, but also in the scales on which it was produced and fielded among post-Cold War aircraft.

J-20 Variants

By the end of 2023 five serial production variants of the J-20 had been reported and four had already begun flying, making it the only fighter of its generation to have multiple variants completed for air force use. The four already unveiled variants are listed in order of appearance.

J-20 (baseline)

Initial production variant using a derivative of the Russian AL-31FM2 engine. Approximately forty are thought to have been built. Produced at a low rate for over three years from late 2015 to early 2019.

J-20A

Produced from mid-2019 and inducted into service from January 2021. Beyond the integration of the WS-10C engine, the full extent of changes to the design remain uncertain. According to the J-20s deputy chief designer, Gong Feng, the J-20A had a redesigned airframe, structure, pipelines, electric circuits and subsystems.[10] One conspicuous difference were the lines on the fighter's side missile bays.

J-20S

A twin seat variant based on the J-20A which first flew on 5 November 2021, with no significant structural changes visible beyond the addition of a second seat. It is likely that once the program moves beyond the prototype stage, the series-produced two-seat model will be based on the more modern J-20B rather than the older J-20A. The first leaked footage of the aircraft carrying out taxing tests emerged on 26 October, confirming it as the world's first fifth generation fighter with a twin seat configuration. The *Global Times* referred to it as J-20S,[11] although a number of experts have referred to it as the J-20AS. These designations indicate that it is believed to be intended as a fully capable combat aircraft in its own right, much like the J-10AS and J-11BS, in contrast to dedicated trainer models which receive 'JJ' designations such as the J-6's trainer variant the JJ-6.

At the Zhuhai Airshow in 2021, a day before the J-20S was first seen, chief designer Yang Wei revealed that a twin seater 'would not be a trainer aircraft, because it would be developed for the enhancement of the aircraft.' PLAAF pilots had in the past strongly emphasized the advantages twin seat configurations provided in combat, most notably the J-16 which had no single seat variant. Chinese analysts similarly alluded to the benefits a second seat provided for a range of combat situations, as well as the wide-ranging roles a twin seat J-20 could perform such as command and control.[12] China's aviation industry notably had a long history of developing twin seat variants of fighters where their equivalents abroad were fielded only as single seaters. Notable examples included its twin seat adaptations of the Soviet MiG-17 and MiG-19, the JJ-5 and JJ-6, which were produced after building the original single seaters under license in the 1950s as the J-5 and J-6.

Twin seaters could potentially form a very large proportion of J-20 units, perhaps mirroring how PLAAF Flanker acquisitions in the late 2010s transitioned from predominantly single seaters to exclusively acquiring twin seaters. Official artwork preceding the J-20S' unveiling showed twin seaters operating in formation with no single seaters among them, possibly indicating an intention for them to form entire units for frontline combat operations like the J-16, rather than a small portion of predominantly single seat units as seen with the J-11BS.[13] The twin seater is expected to potentially form the basis of multiple new variants such as strike and electronic attack aircraft, much like the Su-27's twin seater formed the basis for developing an interceptor and AEW&C derivative in the USSR and Russia.[14] Indeed, the *Ordnance Industry Science Technology* military magazine reported in August 2022, shortly after the twin seater's unveiling, that it would form an ideal basis for allowing the J-20 to fulfil a very broad range of roles including AEW&C, electronic warfare, reconnaissance and command and control of unmanned aircraft. 'In recent years, experts' views on the position of fifth generation aircraft in information warfare have changed, as the aircraft can perform more duties than in the past,' it observed.[15]

J-20B

Unconfirmed reports of an enhanced J-20 variant under development as the 'J-20B' had emerged from a range of mainland and Hong Kong sources from the late 2010s, with the addition of thrust vectoring engines for enhanced manoeuvrability being common to the majority of them. Hong Kong media outlets reported that the aircraft's design had been shown to Vice Chairman of the Central Military Commission, General Zhang Youxia, who was responsible for weapons development, on 8 July 2020.[16] Subsequently in December 2022 the first images emerged of a J-20 prototype numbered 2051 with a significantly evolved airframe design, which included a much flatter cockpit canopy with a distinctive low-profile appearance blending into the fighter's raised spine and a nose radome with slight geometric revisions. The changes appeared intended to improve its aerodynamic performance and further reduce its radar cross section, with the enlarged spine also expected to accommodate more fuel or possibly new avionics.

It was initially unclear whether prototype no. 2051 was a pre-production airframe of a specialised new J-20 variant, or whether it represented the next stage in development meaning it could potentially be the long awaited 'J-20B.' Where '2051' was powered by WS-10C engines, a second prototype numbered 2052 was powered by the next generation WS-15. This was in line with the Chinese aviation industry and broader defence sector's longstanding preference for applying upgrades incrementally – first testing the new airframe design with an already widely used engine before using it as a testbed for a clean sheet next generation powerplant. Confirmation that the WS-15 was being integrated made it almost certain that the new aircraft was the next iteration of the J-20 design and a successor to the J-20A that had entered service in 2021, with further significant improvements to its subsystems and materials considered highly likely. Prototype no. 2052 was the first J-20 airframe known to have flown with WS-15 engines in twin configuration, which it did on 29 June 2023. After this the J-20B designation was more widely used in both China and the West to refer to the new design, although this was still not officially confirmed.[§]

Future Variants

In March 2018, speaking to *China Daily*, Yang Wei highlighted plans to: 'Develop the J-20 into a large family and keep strengthening its information-processing and intelligent capacities'.[17] This was one of several statements to this effect by prominent figures connected to the program, and prompted speculation as to what a 'large family' could look like and whether this was an indication that multiple variants with special roles were under development. Wei further indicated that advances in China's military aviation sector meant it no longer needed to bridge gaps with competitors, and provided greater freedom to innovate and invest in new capabilities.[18] The J-20's status as the only heavyweight fighter of its generation in production on a meaningful scale, and the only one ever expected to receive such levels of funding, made a range of developments unprecedented overseas appear highly possible.

Airborne Early Warning and Command and Control Variants

Somewhat ironically, since the J-20 was initially widely considered in the West to be intended primarily as an 'AEW&C killer' to target enemy airborne early warning and control assets, one of the most

---

[§]   A number of analysts believed that the J-20B designation was in fact that designation of the twin seater, and that the new variant with WS-15 engines was designated J-20A, while single seaters produced from 2015-2019 and 2019-2023 with either the AL-31 or the WS-10C all had the baseline 'J-20' designation.

likely derivatives of the J-20 is a small AEW&C system. The role of such aircraft is to serve as command posts for other units with special communications equipment and data links, and possibly with oversized sensors as well. This can extend to guiding missiles launched by combat jets with weaker sensors towards their targets more accurately. In Operation Desert Storm, for example, E-3 AEW&C systems assisted in thirty-eight of the USAF's recorded forty-one air-to-air kills.[19]

Radical proposals for modifying heavyweight fighters for AEW&C roles have emerged in the past, a notable example being the Su-27K AEW&C which was reportedly considered in the late Soviet era to mount a 360° search radar with antenna above the fuselage of a Flanker in a revolving 'saucer' radome.[20] More conservative and successful programs to use heavyweight fighter/interceptor airframes for AEW&C roles, capitalising on their high endurances and large sensors, have been made. The Soviet MiG-31 interceptor, and in Iranian Air Force service the F-14 fighter, the two world leaders in situational awareness during the Cold War, both served as airborne early warning aircraft, while the MiG-31 was also designed for command-and-control.[21] The Su-30, as a derivative of the Su-27UB twin seater, was also initially conceptualised to serve as both an interceptor and AEW&C system much like the MiG-31, with sensors improved, avionics installed and endurance increased accordingly.[22] The Israeli Air Force also modified its F-15D twin seat fighters for command-and-control purposes to accompany F-15I strike fighters.[23]

In August 2020 reports emerged that the Chengdu Aircraft Design Institute was developing an AEW&C variant of the J-20. Subsequently in a January 2022 interview the chief editor of Beijing-based magazine *Aerospace Knowledge*, Wang Ya'nan, highlighted that a J-20 with a larger radar and new fire controls could serve as a small AEW&C system.[24] It remains uncertain how heavily modified a twin seat J-20 airframe would be for this role, as while its radar is already one of the largest of any fighter in the world, airframe modifications to accommodate an even larger radar remain possible. An AEW&C based on the J-20 airframe would have significant advantages over existing larger aircraft such as the KJ-500, despite having a smaller radar and less crew, including, most critically, stealth capabilities which would provide survivability against 'AEW&C killer' assets – such as the Boeing LRAAM announced in 2021. The American missile received air force funding in 2022, and is expected to equip USAF F-15 units, with China as the only major adversary operator of AEW&Cs expected to be the primary target of future deployments.[25] Maintenance commonality with the J-20, and likely a significantly lower cost both to operate and to produce than larger AEW&Cs, would be other important benefits of a J-20 AEW&C variant. The aircraft could serve as force multipliers for combat assets like J-20 fighter squadrons while being more widely deployable than larger assets like KJ-500s.

Strike Variant

The widespread uses the PLA could have for a fifth generation high endurance strike aircraft were highlighted multiple times by analysts ever since the first images of the J-20 emerged in January 2011, with the airframe widely misidentified in the West as a strike fighter allowing a growing narrative to build around that interpretation. A 2015 RAND Corporation report, for example, highlighted that the J-20's 'combination of forward stealth and long range could hold U.S. Navy surface assets at risk, and that a long-range maritime strike capability may be a cause for greater concern than a short-range air-superiority fighter like the F-22.'[26] A U.S. Naval War College report similarly highlighted the value of an 'effective surface-attack platform for out to several hundred nautical miles at sea' – originally in the belief that the J-20 was not primarily designed for air superiority.[27]

On 15 January 2019 the U.S. Defence Intelligence Agency's annual report on the PLA concluded that China 'is developing new medium- and long-range stealth bombers' for the PLAAF.[28] While J-20 in the fleet were all expected to gain a strike capability using a range of standoff weapons much like the F-35 – but unlike the F-22 – the possibility of developing a specialised strike derivative was significant. This had a notable precedent in the F-22 program, with Lockheed Martin studying the concept from 2002 of a redesign to double the aircraft's range and significantly increase its internal payload – a design later designated the FB-22. The aircraft had reduced acceleration, speed, and manoeuvrability, but could carry 375 per cent the ordnance of the original Raptor. While the fuselage was largely unchanged, other than the addition of a second seat, the aircraft carried eighty per cent more fuel and its wings had three times the surface area of the F-22's.[29]

Using the F-22 as the basis for the design was projected to create a very high eighty per cent parts commonality, and ensured development costs were approximately seventy-five per cent lower than for a clean sheet strike fighter.[30] USAF leaders stressed the FB-22's speed, survivability, range and payload would make it uniquely useful for attacking targets that were both well defended and time critical.[31] Air Force Secretary James Roche suggested that up to 150 FB-22s could be procured,[32] although persistent issues with the standard F-22 were used to argue against the program and it never moved beyond conceptual stages.[33] A more successful program, albeit from the previous generation, was the Russian Su-34 – a heavy modification of the Su-27 into a dedicated strike fighter with a much increased endurance, a weight increase of over fifty per cent, and with some limited applications of stealth technologies.[34] A J-20 strike variant, possibly designated JH-20, could follow much the same path as the FB-22. A major difference is that while the FB-22 was not designed to carry anti-surface, anti-radiation or anti-ship missiles, deploying only gravity bombs from shallow weapons bays, a J-20 strike variant would almost certainly carry a range of beyond visual range missiles as a primary armament.

A J-20 derived strike fighter could do much to increase commonality between Chinese tactical combat air units, while providing considerable economies of scale to the J-20 program. It would better position the J-20 to replace not only Flankers and J-10s, but also the fleet of 260 JH-7 strike fighters of which approximately half each serve in the Navy and Air Force. Replacing a portion of the country's approximately 200 H-6 medium range bombers may also emerge as a possibility. A strike fighter would complement the PLA's other significant investments in anti-surface and anti-shipping capabilities, particularly against targets in the first and second island chains, which has included developing assets such as stealth drones and hypersonic glide vehicles. The aircraft could hold U.S. military facilities on Guam, and with aerial refuelling possibly even Wake Island or Hawaii, at greater risk, complementing the massive expansion of surface and ship launched ballistic and cruise missile capabilities aimed at these targets. Eliminating facilities and naval assets key to allowing Western countries to project power into East Asia would likely be the primary role for which such a fighter would be designed, supplementing the non-stealthy but increasingly well-armed H-6 bombers. The possibility of a strike fighter being derived from the J-20 is purely speculative and there have been no significant indicators that this is actively being considered. Nevertheless, the precedents set by modifications to the Flanker and those considered for the F-22, as well as the PLA's need for a successor to the JH-7, means this possibility is likely at the very least to be explored.

Electronic Warfare Aircraft and Drone Controller

In April 2021, amid persistent rumours that a twin seat J-20 variant would imminently be unveiled, defence experts writing for the Xi'an-based military magazine *Ordnance Industry Science Technology* highlighted regarding the advantages and roles a twin seater could have: 'The emergence of a twin-seat version of the J-20 is because the J-20's mission has diversified and China needs a more capable fighter jet ... It's a piece of cake for the J-20 to perform [electronic interference] duties because of its strong power supply capacity, fire-control radar and integrated avionics system.' For electronic attacks: 'We can imagine that the front pilot will be in charge of flying the aircraft, while the pilot sitting behind is in charge of controlling the electronic interference platform, making the J-20 a nightmare for enemy electronic equipment.' The second seat could accommodate a controller for drones, as the experts noted: 'The drones could be bait to attract enemy aircraft or draw in stealth aircraft ... they can also gather intelligence, carry out attacks against air defence systems and gain air superiority.'[35]

Wang Ya'nan, chief editor of Beijing-based magazine *Aerospace Knowledge*, highlighted in an interview in January 2022 that an extra pilot on a twin-seat fighter could be utilized in more complicated combat situations including controlling drones. These could accompany J-20 units in flight and expand a unit's firepower, situational awareness and electronic warfare capabilities considerably.[36] In October 2022 state media outlet CCTV unveiled computer graphics showing J-20s commanding formations of flying stealth drones, possibly based on the GJ-11 airframe, which was expected to be a defining feature of sixth generation fighters and which the J-20, as the only fifth generation fighter with a twin seat variant, was well optimised to doing.[37]

Future Technologies

Much like the F-35, the Flanker and other fighters developed under larger programs, the J-20 is expected to continue to see substantial improvements to its performance made over its years in production and beyond as China's defence sector and its tech sector more generally strengthen their leadership in developing key emerging technologies. Since shortly after the aircraft first entered service J-20s across the fleet have received continuous software upgrades as successive batches have been produced with increasingly advanced capabilities, while stealth capabilities and a range of subsystems have made significant incremental improvements between batches resulting in major performance advantages for newer models. Chinese officials have highlighted since the first J-20s became operational that control systems, stealth coatings, airframe materials, sensors and engines were key areas where work was being done to improve the aircraft.[38]

Beyond these incremental improvements, advances in a number of new technology areas have the potential to more radically change how the J-20 can contribute to military operations. Although opacity surrounding military R&D efforts has left many of Chinese aviation's potential new capabilities to be fielded to speculation, available information provides some important indications. A widely expected early improvement to the J-20 is the increasing of its internal air-to-air missile payload, with this possibility highlighted in multiple Pentagon reports and being prioritised for America's own stealth fighter programs.[39] Since the J-20's central weapons bay was first seen, observers highlighted that it was 'remarkably uncluttered' and could potentially house more missiles.[40] One possibility for achieving this would be to integrate new missile racks, as seen on the F-35A/C with the addition of 'Sidekick' racks.[41] A trapeze launcher system similar to that of the F-22 could also be key to achieving this – although the possibility remains that such a solution may have already been implemented since the contents of J-20 weapons bays were rarely revealed. Alongside increases in the quantity of missiles carried, superior new variants of the PL-10 and PL-15, and a next generation of more capable missiles, were all anticipated. According to Pentagon reports this included a ramjet-powered long-range missile, providing a larger 'no-escape zone' and thus an improved long range kill probability, particularly against manoeuvrable targets.[42] The PL-10's successor was sometimes informally designated 'PL-16,' although there were no indications as to what capabilities it could field.¶

Beyond improvements to missile capabilities, state broadcaster CCTV reported in 2020 that an airborne laser attack pod was under development. Chinese defence firms had publicly displayed directional-emission high-energy laser anti-aircraft weapons like the LW-30 at exhibitions.[43] Lasers left no time lag after firing for targeted aircraft to evade or activate countermeasures, and potentially allowed fighters to engage more targets per sortie than they could with a limited missile arsenal and at a much lower cost per shot fired. The fact that they required a large amount of energy to be effective, however, was expected to significantly delay their integration onto fighter sized aircraft. In January 2022 a publication by the state-run *Global Times* highlighted that the J-20 could not only see drone controller and unmanned variants developed, but could also in future be equipped with laser weapons.[44] The rival SHiELD Airborne Laser Weapon being developed for the USAF's F-22s and F-35s was notably terminated in 2024 after eight years of development, months after the cancellation of the Airborne High Energy Laser for its AC-130 gunships, with program difficulties in America significantly increasing the possibility that Chinese fighters would have a lead in laser weaponry.[45]

In April 2023 National People's Congress deputy and J-20 pilot Gao Zhongqiang highlighted that the fighter's communications could be a key focus for future enhancements in order to facilitate more seamless network centric operations. 'A pilot should jump out of his own perspective in aerial combat … and put himself in a system of joint operation, contributing more to winning as a whole,'

¶   A new PL-10 variant with what appeared to be a radar rather than an infrared seeker was unveiled at the Zhuhai Airshow in November 2022, although it remains uncertain whether this was intended for the J-20 or for other assets which lacked large radar guided missiles such as helicopters and drones.

J-20 technology demonstrator on first flight. (Leaked and unattributed on Chinese Internet/Guancha)

J-20 first production batch aircraft in yellow primer, image released on National Day, September 2016, preceding the class' service entry. (机外停车Rabbit on Weibo)

J-20 at Zhuhai 2018 with weapons bays open showing PL-15 and PL-10 missiles. (Colin Cooke / Openverse)

J-20 taxiing in yellow primer. (万全＆T汪汪T on Weibo)

Prototype 2052 first flight with two WS-15 engines. (飞扬军事铁背心 from Weibo)

Above: J-20 during low altitude flight. (Yu Hongchun / China Military Online)

Below: J-20 Twin Seater Prototype. (鼎盛风清 on Weibo)

J-20s taxiing. (万全＆T汪汪T on Weibo)

F-35A in J-20 mimicking colours at activation ceremony of 65th Aggressor Squadron with Lieutenant Colonel Brandon Nauta. (Airman 1st Class Josey Blades/ U.S. Air Force)

J-20 Chief Designer Yang Wei. (Public Domain)

J-10C with PL-15 and K/JDC01A Laser Designator Pod. (China Military Online / Wang Guoyun)

Rare clear top view of J-20 cockpit. (夜航大叔 on Weibo)

J-16D Electronic Warfare Aircraft. (耿直的鲁斯兰 on Weibo)

J-20 First Technology Demonstrator Airframe No. 2001. (top81.cn)

KJ-500 AEW&C Aircraft. (China Military Online/Qin Qianjiang and Zeng Qi)

J-20 at the 2018 Zhuhai Airshow. (China Military Online/Wang Weidong)

J-20A turns left the 2018 Zhuhai Airshow with PL-10s ready to fire and open main missile bay. (China Military Online/Wang Weidong)

Su-27UBK Flanker in Chinese Service. (China Military Online/ Liu Hang)

First publicly released image showing PL-XX missile in active service with J-16 fighters (December 2023). (鼎盛风清 on Weibo)

Left: 1st Aviation Brigade Commander Senior Colonel Li Ling(left) shares experience with fellow airman after completing a flight training exercise on 8 January 2022. (China Military Online/Yang Pan)

Below: 1st Aviation Brigade Commander Senior Colonel Li Ling operates his J-20 fighter jet during the air confrontation training on 10 January 2022. (China Military Online/Yang Pan)

1st Aviation Brigade J-20As taxi in close formation during a flight training exercise on 7 January 2022. (China Military Online/Yang Pan)

J-20 with PL-10 in firing position and open main weapons. (白龙_龙腾四海 on Weibo)

J-20 demonstrates aerobatics. (B747SPNKG on Weibo)

Y-20 transport lands behind two J-20A fighters. (鹰眼军视 on Weibo)

he stated, stressing that while operating the J-20 and other modern fighter classes he had already become accustomed to receiving a cloud map of vast data. He called for greater integration between the different services of the PLA through a constantly improving communications network – with the publication of his statement in state media indicating it had a degree of endorsement.[46] The network Gao called for resembled projections in the U.S. of what a sixth generation battle network with fully seamless information sharing between platforms across the services would look like, fitting in with the Joint All-Domain Command and Control (JADC2) concept. This development was expected to set China and America further apart from third parties in their aerial warfare capabilities in particular.[47] As summarised by the *Global Times:* 'Vast data will likely be pre-processed, selected and highlighted by artificial intelligence before being presented to human operators, so the latter can make the best decisions for victory.'[48]

In April 2021 the PLAAF pilot who had flown the J-20 on its maiden flight, Li Gang, raised the possibility of the fighter integrating two-dimensional thrust vectoring engines for improved manoeuvrability.[49] There had long been speculation that the fighter had already integrated such engines, at least for testing purposes, with chief designer Yang Wei notably stating in 2018 when asked: 'You asked about when, but how do you know it hasn't?' Li highlighted that the fighter could in future integrate thrust vectoring with nozzles that moved both vertically and horizontally – known as three-dimensional thrust vectoring – which was a technology pioneered by Russia in the 1990s and speculated to have been transferred to China with the 2015 sale of Su-35 fighters. This had already been demonstrated on the J-10 from 2018. The only Western fighter with thrust vectoring engines, the F-22, had nozzles which only moved vertically – known as two-dimensional thrust vectoring.[50]

Footage released in late August 2022 showed a J-20 demonstrating very high levels of low-speed manoeuvrability at the Changchun

PLAAF Open Day in North-east China, with its extreme sharp climbs and turns contrasting with the basic flybys and conservative turns that the aircraft previously demonstrated.[51] Footage released a month later showed the fighter performing unprecedentedly complex and strenuous low speed manoeuvres, including turns during vertical climb and gliding while nose up, which fuelled considerable further speculation that the fighter had integrated thrust vectoring engines.[52] Further footage of extreme manoeuvres was released in November, with more subsequently continuing to appear.[53]

The enhanced J-20B variant with WS-15 engines was expected to integrate thrust vectoring engines across its production run, although this feature was notably absent when the first prototype flew with the engines in July 2023. The value of thrust vectoring for the J-20, and whether its benefits were worth the additional costs and added weight to each airframe, was a contentious issue among analysts. Russian sources claimed it allowed fighters to 'disappear from the locators of enemy fighters' by remaining still momentarily and thus discarding radar capture, which could provide the greatest benefit.[54] Thrust vectoring was also potentially particularly important for the J-20 due to the fact that a fast growing portion of the fleets of China's potential adversaries were made up of stealth aircraft, with a much more limited ability to target one another at longer ranges meaning that engagements were much more likely to occur over short distances where extreme low speed manoeuvrability could provide an important advantage.

Alongside expected continuous improvements to stealth coatings, research efforts being pursued in China had the potential to provide revolutionary enhancements to stealth capabilities in other ways. In July 2019, for example, team at the Chinese Academy of Sciences at Chengdu's Institute of Optics and Electronics reached a breakthrough in the use of electromagnetic wave models to enhance stealth technology, creating the potential for developing aircraft which were lighter, cheaper to build and far more difficult to detect. Led by Professor Luo Xiangang, the team created the world's first mathematical model to precisely describe the behaviour of electromagnetic waves, including radar waves, when they strike a piece of metal engraved with microscopic patterns. This model, paired with recent breakthroughs in material fabrication, allowed them to develop a membrane known as a 'meta surface' which could absorb radar waves in the widest spectrum yet to be reported. While fighter-sized stealth aircraft are vulnerable to detection by long wave radars, and have become less survivable as sensor and data sharing technologies improve, application of meta surface technologies could make future Chinese stealth aircraft including J-20 fighters considerably harder to detect.[55]

An unnamed researcher in stealth technology from Fudan University in Shanghai, who was not involved in the program, highlighted that new meta surface technologies could allow future aircraft to evade detection by every known type of radar. 'This detection range is incredible. I have never heard of anyone even coming close to this performance. At present, absorbing technology with an effective range of between 4 and 18 gigahertz is considered very, very good,' he stated. The new technology reportedly allowed for evasion of all radars at frequencies of between 0.3 and 40 gigahertz.[56] With the J-20's surface made of metamaterials - fine surfaces engineered on a nanoscale - research and developments appeared poised to provide newer materials which could improve its stealth considerably further.

A further promising field of research which could enhance stealth capabilities was the use of plasma for radar absorption, with reports from August 2022 highlighting that a plasma device had been developed to improve the stealth capabilities of future Chinese bombers. It raised the possibility that a derivative of the same technology could provide a similar stealth enhancement to fighter-sized aircraft.[57] This would hardly be unprecedented, with the Soviet MiG 1.42 having had a 'stealthogenic' system well under development using whips of plasma to reduce radar cross sections to a small fraction of their size.[58] Early forms of plasma stealth were used on the CIA's A-12 bomber-sized reconnaissance aircraft during the Cold War,[59] with this technology also reported to have been applied to Russia's Tsirkon cruise missiles,[60] which was more straightforward to achieve in both cases due to their very high respective Mach 3.35 and Mach 9 speeds.

A range of new technologies which could not only make the J-20 more potent in its existing roles, but also expand the scope of roles it could perform, were further reported to be under development. In April 2018 it was reported that the F-35 was being modernised to perform a missile defence role, with the fighter predicted at the time by director of the Missile Defence Agency General Samuel Greaves to be ready for such operations by 2025. He described it as 'if not a game changer, then a significant contributor to future ballistic missile defence.'[61] As early as 2014 an F-35 had successfully tracked a missile launch and transmitted tracking data using its data link, and following other tests an F-35 succeeded in August in 2019 in transmitting live tracking data on a strategic missile launch to the U.S. Army's Integrated Air and Missiles Defence Battle Command System.[62] The F-35's role as an 'elevated sensor' linked into missile defence networks was refined further in subsequent testing.[63] Ballistic missile defence was a much higher priority challenge for the U.S. Military than the PLA, as it faced several adversaries with less modern militaries that relied heavily on ballistic missiles to asymmetrically counter American power such as North Korea, Russia and Iran.

Like the F-35, being deployed widely and integrating powerful sensors allows the J-20 to potentially significantly increase the situational awareness of missile defences and provide cueing data to interceptors. The repeatedly raised possibility of an anti-ballistic missile being developed for the F-35, allowing it to neutralise ballistic missiles in their slower early stages, could potentially apply to the J-20. Use of compact solid state airborne laser weapons for this purpose has been raised as another possibility to enhance fighters' ability to contribute to missile defence.[64] While the J-20 has a larger sensor suite and much longer range, however, the F-35 has the advantage of being deployed globally, including near many of the key launch sites of potential ballistic missile attacks against U.S. and allied targets – from the Persian Gulf to Eastern Europe, the Arctic and the Korean Peninsula. Furthermore, F-35s fielded by all overseas clients are networked, allowing the U.S. Military to benefit from a truly global array of elevated sensors well positioned to provide key targeting data. The J-20 by contrast has not been deployed to bases beyond China's borders, which is the primary factor that will likely prevent it from playing as large a role in missile defence as the F-35. Ballistic missiles are only expected to be vulnerable to fighter-sized aircrafts' sensors and weapons in the early launch stages before leaving atmosphere, at which points J-20 units are less likely to be nearby. Nevertheless, the possibility of the J-20 also playing a major role in ballistic missile defence cannot be ruled out, particularly as the U.S. withdrawal from the Intermediate Range Nuclear Forces Treaty in 2019 is expected to pave the way for major surface-to-surface missile deployments across the Western Pacific aimed at primarily China. The majority of expected sites for these missiles will be within the J-20's operational range from bases within China.

While the possible development of a new radar for the J-20 has long been speculated, there was a significant possibility that a new infra-red search and tracking system (IRST) could begin to play a much larger role in the fighter's sensor suite after early breakthroughs in 2022 promised to revolutionise such systems' potential. IRSTs allow aircraft to operate without any radar signature, and although they are considered optimal for countering stealth targets, since they focus on heat signatures rather than radar cross sections, they have generally had ranges of under 120km, which restricts them to operating as secondary sensors. This is due to the limited number of photons which can reach a detector's lens over extreme distances. According to the peer-reviewed *Infrared And Laser Engineering* journal, however, an IRST developed by an unconfirmed division of China's defence sector provided clear images at a 285km range – with the outline of the target aircraft, including its rotor, the tail and number of engines all clearly visible.[65] This has the potential to provide Chinese fighters with a major advantage in their ability to track and target stealth aircraft, and could also have revolutionary applications for the seekers of infrared guided anti-aircraft missiles.

Based on current strengths in Chinese high tech, it remains likely that the J-20 will not only be the first fighter to benefit from quantum satellite communications, but that it will also enjoy significant advantages in artificial intelligence, with the latter being particularly significant as it begins to be fielded alongside supporting 'wingman' unmanned aircraft and integrates more capable AI 'co-pilots' (see Chapter 4). While it is less certain when or even if the aforementioned technologies will have practical military applications, China's lead in developing quantum communications, quantum computers, and possibly, although much less likely, even quantum sensors, places it in a strong position to be the first to apply them. This could significantly enhance the capabilities of the fighters themselves and any combat network they are integrated into.

The Next Generation

Much as work on the J-20's development had begun long before China's first indigenous fourth generation fighter had entered service, so too was work well underway by the late 2010s on a sixth generation air superiority fighter intended as a successor. Aviation Industry Corp of China Deputy Director of Science and Technology Yang Wei hinted in March 2018, twelve months after the J-20's service entry, that alongside a focus on improving the fighter 'at the same time, we will think about our next-generation combat plane to meet the nation's future requirements.'[66] Having served as the J-20's chief designer, Yang was reportedly playing a similar leading role in sixth generation fighter development reflecting a degree of continuity between the two programs. Where the J-20 established China as the only near peer competitor to the United States in fighter aviation, with the J-20 and F-35 very much in a league of their own in their integration of key technologies, it thus also set the stage for close competition between the two to develop next generation successors to these fighters.

In March 2021, Commander of the U.S. Air Combat Command General Mark D. Kelly warned that the Chinese PLAAF could be the world's first service to field a sixth generation fighter. 'I for one am confident ... that the [American Next Generation Air Dominance (NGAD) sixth generation fighter program] technology will get fielded,' and that adversaries going against it would 'suffer a very tough day, and a tough week and a tough war. What I don't know ... is if our nation will have the courage and the focus to field this capability before someone like the Chinese fields it and uses it against us.' 'We just need to make sure we keep our narrative up and articulate the biggest benefit we've had as a nation to have leading-edge technology ensuring we have air superiority,' he stressed.[67] This point was reiterated in September the following year, when he indicated a truly neck to neck race and implied that the rival Chinese and American aircraft could enter service within months of one another.[68]

Concerns regarding how quickly China could develop a sixth generation fighter were almost certainly very heavily influenced by the precedent the J-20 had set for an extremely fast development time, which other than in engine development consistent surpassed all Western projections, as well as its fast rate of incremental upgrades. Despite being China's first manned stealth jet, where the F-35 was America's fourth, the J-20 still completed development far faster. Having made its first demonstrator flight eleven years later than the F-35, it could still begin deliveries to the PLAAF just months after the F-35's first deliveries to the USAF. The J-20 moved from the first demonstrator flight to frontline service in just six years – the same amount of time the J-10 had taken – where the F-35 and the F-22 had taken fifteen to sixteen years. For the race to develop a more capable sixth generation fighter, China's technological and industrial standings relative to the United States were significantly more advantageous than they had been in the fifth generation era. Thus there were considerable grounds for concern that China could comfortably win the sixth generation race, particularly in terms of the speed at which it could bring aircraft into service.

In late October 2021 a new diamond-like delta shaped airframe with a thin nose section and a wingspan comparable to that of the J-20 was spotted at the Chengdu Aircraft Corporation's test airfield. Lacking either tails or horizontal stabilizers, and with a continuous hump along its dorsal centreline, the aircraft loosely resembled concepts for a sixth generation air superiority fighter. Much as a stealth airframe was a key prerequisite for the fifth generation, tailless designs were widely considered a likely potential prerequisite for fighters to meet the standards of the sixth generation. Such airframes would rely on more advanced flight control surfaces and benefit from greater efficiency for sustained high speed cruise and superior stealth capabilities. Prior tailless aircraft such as the USAF B-2 Spirit bomber and PLAAF GJ-11 drone had been designed for air-to-ground or reconnaissance operations, and designing a tailless aircraft with a fighter's flight performance, particularly at higher speeds when thrust vectoring could not be depended on, was considered a leading challenge of sixth generation fighter development. While the quality of imagery made it impossible to determine if the aircraft at the Chengdu airfield was manned or unmanned, it could well have been a technology demonstrator for a next generation fighter program or an accompanying 'wingman' drone. It also remained uncertain if the aircraft had flown or whether its discovery by satellite had been intended. The airfield had been the home of many of China's most innovative aircraft designs during development.

In January 2023 the Aviation Industry Corporation of China released computer generated images of tailless fighter jets flying in formation, which loosely resembled American sixth generation concept designs. Their fuselages bore a strong similarity to the J-20, and fuelled speculation that they could in fact be modified J-20 derivatives designed to radically improve stealth capabilities and operate at a sixth generation level. This would mirror the short-lived American program to develop a tailless F-22 derivative – the X-44 Manta – and could provide a less costly counterpart with a shorter development time to complement a clean sheet sixth generation fighter design.[69]

There was a notable possibility that a clean sheet sixth generation fighter would lack manoeuvrability, and would strongly prioritise endurance, weapons payload, and the ability to command fleets of UAVs. This vision was advanced by a paper by Yang Wei himself, who stressed that stealth, electronic warfare, artificial intelligence, sensors and network centric capabilities should be priority features.[70] This mirrored projections in the United States, where it was highlighted that a next generation fighter could more closely resemble a stealth bomber in its flight performance attributes, including the use of multiple engines to power directed energy weapons and seating of multiple crew to direct accompanying 'wingman' UAVs, and could be far larger than fighters of prior generations.[71]

While the PLAAF received its first fifth generation fighters twenty-five years after its first from the fourth generation (Soviet Su-27SKs delivered in 1991), the space between the fifth and sixth generations is expected to be much shorter. While the Su-27SK was sourced from abroad over a decade before China could source fourth generation aircraft indigenously, the service had no potential foreign sources** for fifth generation fighters, largely due to the USSR's disintegration which meant acquisitions were delayed until China's own defence sector caught up – first to a fourth generation level and then to the fifth. For the gap between the fifth and sixth generations there would be no comparable lag since both generations were developed fully indigenously. China's industrial base was far more up to date by the mid-2010s than it had been when the J-20 began its development, with its far greater scale of research and development, higher rate of advance in key industries, and strong position to dominate potentially revolutionary new technologies as they began to mature and gain real world applications, all being further factors which put it in a strong position to develop a sixth generation fighter quickly.

One key technology which was expected to significantly influence the speed at which sixth generation fighters could be developed was advanced digital assembly and testing, which was considerably cheaper, faster and more straightforward than real world testing. It also had the potential to make aircraft significantly easier to upgrade. The technology was notably used in the development of the Boeing T-7 trainer, allowing it to move from a concept to its first flight in three years.[72] USAF head of acquisitions Will Roper referred to the application of digital assembly and testing technologies to the program as follows: 'Can something fly thousands of hours before it takes off, be laid out and assembled hundreds of times before any metal is even cut? Can something be designed, built, and tested, not

---

** Had the MiG 1.42 program, for example, produced an operational fighter on schedule around 2000, and had Moscow then begun deliveries to China seven years afterwards as it had for the Su-27, the PLAAF would have received a fifth generation fighter before 2010. Had the Soviet program not collapsed, the USAF would likely also have begun to field fifth generation fighters sooner, since the ATF program would not have been subjected to as many cuts and would have been pursued with greater urgency.

by thousands of people, but by fewer than 200, using leading-edge design tools across a digital landscape, connected virtually across the globe? It can. It was.'[73] As *Air Force Magazine* summarised: 'New 3D modelling software meant the company could create a digital twin, test performance in virtual wind tunnels, and make adjustments rapidly, without having to bend metal.'[74]

Beyond their use developing a trainer, new virtual assembly and testing technologies were hailed by Roper in September 2020 for their potential ability to reverse decline in America's combat aviation industry. He at the time revealed the existence of a technology demonstrator for America's sixth generation fighter program, and highlighted that the new technologies would allow small teams to produce multiple competing designs quickly and affordably, contrasting with the trend[††] of the past five decades where growing costs and complexity prolonged development and sharply reduced the number of programs.[75] While China's combat aviation sector was able to pursue a greater number of advanced fighter programs simultaneously than the United States could, and consistently saw through their development in a fraction of the time, it remained uncertain whether the maturing of digital assembly and testing technologies in both countries would further the Chinese advantage, or instead help the U.S. partly bridge the gap.

[††] For example, while the world moved from the beginning of the first generation of fighter aircraft in the late 1940s to the beginning of the fourth generation in the early 1970s – a period of twenty-five years between the introduction of the F-86 in 1949 and F-14 in 1974 which were the first American jets of those generations – fourth generation fighters remain widely in production in the 2020s. The complexity of the fifth generation has made efforts to develop such fighters both slow and scarce, and resulted in only two fighters in production fielded at squadron level strength (F-35 and J-20) by December 2020 – exactly fifteen years after the first fifth generation fighter entered service and fifty years after the first fourth generation fighter the F-14 made its maiden flight.

By May 2023 problems had continued to mount with the T-7 program which had pioneered use of digital engineering technologies, leading Air Force Secretary Frank Kendall to assert that these technologies had been 'over-hyped' and at best could cut costs and schedules by only around twenty per cent.[76] This had serious implications for American efforts to bridge the major gaps in efficiency and development time it faced when competing with China. With major delays and struggles adopting new technologies being the norm for clean sheet post-Cold War American weapons programs, however, the failure to use digital assembly and testing to revolutionise fighter development in the U.S. did not necessarily mean it lacked such potential if used abroad.[77] With digital assembly and testing having been presented as central to accelerating development of an American sixth generation fighter, the fact that the technology failed to revolutionise the speed at which America could pursue fighter programs meant its next generation fighter would likely enter service significantly later than previously projected.

China's investment in digital assembly and testing has played a key role in accelerating the development of the J-20 and other key fighter programs, with this potentially having been an important factor in the aircraft's particularly short development time. Chief designer Yang Wei notably stated in 2018 that China had established a digital aircraft research and development system, including paperless design and production which improved the quality of aircraft and shortened their development cycles, with the J-20, Y-20, J-15, KJ-600 being among the programs affected. He also added at the time that great progress had also been made in the development of military-civilian integration, emphasising as an example that the carbon fibre and metamaterials used in the J-20 were developed by private firms.[78] When J-20 deputy designer Wang Haitao highlighted in 2021 that advances in industrial technology had significantly reduced the R&D periods for aviation equipment, this was speculated to have also referred to digital assembly and testing. Wang was among several to stress the importance of speed in development, stating: 'Particularly for equipment like the J-20, we need to do it faster in all aspects, including designing, production, testing and crafting.'[79]

A further key technology which would potentially prove decisive in the race to develop a more capable sixth generation fighter was additive manufacturing – better known as 3D printing. This was an area where Chinese industry had demonstrated strong advantages, and was used to produce parts for the J-15, J-16, J-20, and FC-31 fighters among others. It significantly reduced the time between conceptualising and producing weapons and equipment, thereby speeding up their update cycles and reducing the time between new generations. This similarly had the potential to reduce the time needed to develop new aircraft and reverse the trend towards longer development times as newer generations grew more complex.[80] Li Daguang, a professor at the National Defence University's Department of Military Logistics and Military Science and Technology Equipment, was among sources claiming 3D printing technology allowed a new fighter jet to be developed in just three years. He highlighted the advantage that parts of any shape could be directly generated from computer graphics data without machining or moulds.[81] Although the three-year period referred to aircraft for which the required technologies already largely existed, rather than for the pioneering of a new generation which required over a decade of further R&D work, additive manufacturing nevertheless had the potential to significantly speed up next generation programs particularly in their later stages.

Additive manufacturing could also significantly reduce the cost of producing weapons and equipment, and while traditional production methods including cutting, grinding, corroding and melting wasted over ninety per cent of raw materials, it had almost no waste. This was particularly important considering the costs of materials used in combat aircraft. This cost saving also applied to production of spare parts, which in turn could mean lower operational costs. Titanium laser additive manufacturing for example not only produced components that were lighter and superior, while streamlining production through the elimination of extra metal in soldered seams, but also reduced waste of the metal considerably. Chinese industry in 2013 began setting records for the largest ever titanium components built using laser additive manufacturing.[82]

While the J-20 had begun development at a time when China's military aviation sector, and to a lesser extent its broader tech sector, were far behind the cutting edge, its sixth generation successor began development in a country already established undisputedly as one of the two world leaders both in GDP and in scale of high tech manufacturing and R&D. Thus while the J-20 may well have been influenced by the MiG 1.42, and its performance requirements influenced by the expected capabilities of the F-22 and F-35, its successor could well be the first fighter of its generation and if anything could be the one to influence foreign programs. Yang Wei observed to this effect that while China's military aviation sector had been working to bridge the gap with the U.S. through the J-20 program, its successor would be developed under different circumstances with China as a pioneer. 'In the past we had to follow others' paths when it came to designing military aircraft because our research and development capabilities were primitive in this regard, but now we have become capable of designing and making what we want to have,' he stated.[83]

Both the J-20 and the F-35 are expected to integrate a range of sixth generation technologies as their countries' respective industries move closer to fielding sixth generation fighters. This would follow the precedent set by fourth generation fighters beginning to integrate fifth generation avionics, sensors, weaponry, and at times even flight performance attributes such as supercruise, as industry approached production of their successors. Much as these enhanced fourth generation fighters were dubbed the '4+ generation' from the early 2000s, so too could future iterations of the J-20 and F-35 eventually be considered '5+ generation' fighters as they continue to expand their advantages over baseline fifth generation fighters like the F-22. Indeed, in Russia this appears to be a primary goal of testing of sixth generation technologies such as hypersonic and directed energy weapons on the Su-57, with the intention of enhancing the fighter to a '5+ generation' level since an actual Russian sixth generation fighter is not expected to materialise for the foreseeable future, if at all.[84] Aside from enhancing the fighter itself, integrating sixth generation technologies onto the J-20 could also be done for testing purposes to assist the development of its successor – mirroring the way the F-22's airframe, which is not expected to receive sixth generation upgrades before its early retirement, was confirmed in 2022 to be serving as a testbed for technologies being developed for the NGAD.[85]

The expected very high cost of sixth generation fighters, and resulting small numbers in which they are fielded,[86] means fifth or '5+ generation' designs could play a major role in the sixth generation era. With NGAD projected by the Pentagon to cost 'hundreds of millions' of dollars per fighter, which is thought to have referred to its flyaway cost, excluding additional expenditures for maintenance infrastructure, spare parts, accompanying 'wingman' drones, or lifetime operational expenditures, the fleet size is expected to be extremely small. If operational costs are comparable to those of the F-22 then a fleet of close to 200 may be possible depending on the extent to which the Pentagon is willing to make cuts to other programs like the F-35. Willingness to invest in numbers could depend heavily on the Pentagon's threat perceptions, including how viable a threat Russia's Su-57 is seen to be, how effectively the F-35 can deal with high end fourth generation threats such as J-16s, how many J-20s the PLAAF is projected to field, and how effectively a smaller number of NGAD fighters are expected to be able to tackle a larger J-20 fleet.

Chinese industry consistently demonstrated an ability to develop peer level weapons systems at a fraction of the cost, in a fraction of the time, and often with less reliability issues, due primarily to its much larger and healthier industrial and R&D bases and purchasing power advantages, which placed it in a strong position to develop a less problematic sixth generation fighter far more cheaply and quickly than the U.S. Taking the J-20 as a precedent to compare pre service entry development costs, these were estimated at just seven point nine per cent of the F-35 – $4.4 billion compared to $55.5 billion – which was one of many indicators of a vast discrepancy in efficiency which made a large J-20 fleet viable where a large F-22 fleet was not.[87] This was aside from the several hundred defects affecting the F-35 which repeatedly denied it Pentagon certification for full-scale production, and added tens of billions of dollars' worth of additional development costs before the aircraft could meaningfully contribute to combat operations.[88]

Beyond development costs, acquisition costs showed similarly considerable discrepancies between the two defence sectors. As Deputy Assistant Secretary of the Air Force for Acquisition, Major General Cameron Holt became the latest to note in 2022: 'In purchasing power parity, they spend about one dollar to our twenty dollars to get to the same capability,' stressing that these discrepancies and America's 'very centrally and micromanaged system of appropriations' would seriously limit the military's ability to compete.[89] This echoed warnings from the head of U.S. Strategic Command General John Hyten that while China in particular was developing new weapons programs incredibly quickly and cost effectively, the U.S. was falling far behind. 'Slow, expensive, that's the way it is … I'm criticizing the entire process … the entire process is broken … We have to go faster, and we're not, and it is frustrating the heck out of me. Look at the threat, if we're not going faster than the threat then it's wrong,' he stated, contrasting the defence sector's performance to what it had been during the Cold War.[90]

Prevailing trends thus strongly indicated that development of a Chinese sixth generation fighter would not only move much faster than its American rival, and at a fraction of the expense, but also that a far larger fleet of such fighters could be afforded while the USAF would be limited to much smaller numbers. The fighters' armaments and supporting assets such as 'wingman' UAVs would also very likely be far more affordable and less troublesome to develop than their American counterparts due to the significant advantages which Chinese industry enjoyed.

Outside China and the U.S., prospects for the development of sixth generation fighters which could pose a peer level challenge were few and far between. European producers' lack of experience with fifth generation fighters, multiple significant shortcomings even in their fourth generation programs, and severe demonstrated industrial, administrative and R&D deficiencies, all pointed to underwhelming sixth generation efforts. Taking patent applications as an indicator of levels of innovation in high tech, when the J-20 was put into service in 2017 mainland China and the United States accounted for forty and nineteen per cent of global patent applications respectively, European states collectively stood at just five per cent, behind Japan and South Korea at ten and six per cent. Five years later China's share had grown to forty-seven per cent, while America's share had dropped to seventeen per cent, with Europe's position remaining relatively unchanged. This was one of several indicators of the diminishing of European states' standing in high tech, including in many fields critical to combat aviation such as material sciences and electronics, which seriously limited its ability to compete on a peer level in the field.[91]

After a joint Franco-German-Spanish sixth generation program was announced in 2018 serious issues quickly began to be reported, and in July 2022 the CEO of its leading contractor Dassault Aviation, Eric Trappier, announced that as a result the fighter would not be ready until the 2050s.[92] This would place it around a quarter century behind Chinese and American programs. The British-Swedish-Italian Tempest program also announced in 2018, although appearing better organised, looked unlikely to be considered genuinely sixth generation due to a number of factors – among them its airframe design with tail fins. It appeared more likely to be an advanced fifth or '5+ generation' aircraft possibly with sixth generation level avionics. Whether this relatively small program could produce a fighter comparable in sophistication even to future F-35 variants was in question, but one operating on a similar level to America's NGAD or its Chinese rival appeared highly unlikely without very major technology transfers and support from the U.S.

For Russia severe delays in the Su-57 program, an apparent emphasis on integrating sixth generation technologies onto the aircraft, and a consistent unwillingness in Moscow to invest in developing clean sheet new combat aircraft, even when enjoying large budget surpluses from oil revenues, meant it too would be far behind the two industry leaders. Russia's much more limited industrial base and scale of R&D in key emerging technology fields was a further major deficiency much as it was for European efforts, with China and the United States being in an entirely different league in how they pursued research and development of key emerging technologies.

The J-20 program's tremendous progress in the decade following its first flight set the stage for China and the U.S. to be peer level competitors in a league of their own not only in the fifth generation, but also in the sixth where their lead over all other competitors was set to be even greater. This was increasingly acknowledged in the United States, with future Chinese fighters widely referred to as the NGAD's only anticipated peer level competitors much as the J-20 had been for the F-35.

The J-20 Beyond China

Due to the status fighter aviation gained in the twentieth century as perhaps the most widely recognisable symbol of national military power, the J-20's success was not only an immense source of national pride in China, but was also hailed across much of the non-Western world. For those disaffected by the West's bombardments of Iraq, Yugoslavia, Libya and several others, and threats to bomb many more, the J-20 was a source of hope that even after Russia's fifth generation programs had failed to materialise meaningfully, the post-Cold War trend towards Western air dominance could be reversed by Chinese achievements. This would have implications beyond China itself, not only as the capabilities of Chinese '4+ generation' fighters offered for export benefitted from increasingly potent fifth generation technologies, but also as the possibility emerged that China could become a leading exporter of fifth generation fighters. Where all prior Chinese heavyweight fighters were derivatives of the Soviet Flanker design, which prevented them from being marketed abroad to compete with Russia's own Flankers, the J-20 as China's first fully indigenous heavyweight was the first Chinese fighter of its size which Beijing could potentially offer abroad.

From the early stages of the J-20 program it was clear that the fighter was not on offer for export. As noted in the *China Daily* in March 2018: 'AVIC is testing the FC-31, another fifth-generation combat plane, and wants to use it to tap the international market for advanced fighter jets. The Air Force has made clear that it will not allow exports of the J-20.'[93] This made the J-20 the only fighter design in production worldwide not offered for sale abroad. The fact that China could reserve such a costly aircraft solely for domestic use reflected the fact that among all major defence sectors its own, as one of the world's two largest, was by far the least reliant on exports. The ability to afford reserving top end systems for domestic use was thus an important sign of strength and economic health. While the Soviet Union, for example, could previously afford not to export its top end fighter/interceptor classes, economic decline in the late 1980s forced a policy change culminating in the 1990 Su-27 sale to China – with far more decline the following decade fuelling an extreme increase in the defence sector's reliance on exports and a willingness to sell its most sensitive technologies.[94]

A possibility remains that the J-20 could be offered for export in the 2030s after progress has been made on a sixth generation successor, by which time the design will have further matured and the PLAAF will likely have a less urgent need for further units. This could mirror how the United States began to actively market the F-15 to a wider range of clients in the 1990s after F-22 production had begun, or how the Soviet Union began offering its top air-to-air performing combat jet the MiG-25 abroad when its successor the MiG-31 was ready for production. Exports had a number of potential benefits including strengthening and increasing interoperability with key security partners, allowing production lines to remain open for longer, providing further economies of scale to industry, sourcing funds for further R&D, and demonstrating China's ability to provide top end hardware internationally.

Increasingly widespread proliferation of advanced unmanned combat aircraft, and the expected evolution of fighter operations to rely more heavily on UAVs as supporting 'wingmen,' raised the possibility that the most popular J-20 variants overseas could be twin seaters able to provide command and control for autonomous or semi-autonomous UAVs. This would allow even a very small fleet of J-20s to make a significant difference to a country's combat capabilities, with each accompanied by large numbers of UAVs operating in strike or air-to-air roles while the manned stealth jets were tasked primarily with directing them. With Chinese UAVs fast gaining market share internationally, the J-20 could be seen as a highly complementary force multiplier for more advanced combat classes. The rumoured AEW&C variant of the J-20 could also potentially be highly popular abroad, even for countries which were not looking for a heavyweight stealth aircraft for combat roles.

A wide range of geopolitical factors could shape the possibility of J-20 exports, with sales potentially yielding a range of strategic benefits beyond export revenues. As China increasingly formed closer economic, political and security ties with a number of traditional

Western security partners, J-20 sales could cement the diminishing of Western spheres of influence in key regions. The Persian Gulf in particular, where states were denied access to the F-35, but where both Saudi Arabia and the United Arab Emirates (UAE) increasingly bolstered economic, strategic and security ties with China, could by the 2030s see the emergence of potential buyers. The UAE's 2022 order for Chinese L-15 fighter/trainers, and its use of Huawei telecommunications infrastructure despite warnings from Washington that this would rule it out as an F-35 client, may well have been initial steps in this direction. Saudi Arabia, too, opened a joint venture with China for drone production in March 2022, had long operated Chinese ballistic missiles, and from the late 2010s accelerated improvements in strategic ties with Beijing which had emerged as by far its greatest trading partner. The Royal Saudi Air Force's fighter fleet was one of very few in the world comprised primarily of heavyweights, namely F-15s, and with these having no apparent Western successor the J-20 or FC-31 could be natural choices in the 2030s.

While the small number of countries able to afford and absorb heavyweight fifth generation fighters limited the number of potential clients, the Algerian Air Force as the most capable and by far the best funded in Africa was a leading candidate. Alongside many lighter aircraft, Algeria in the early 2020s operated a large fleet of heavyweight combat jets including over seventy Su-30s, thirty-six Su-24Ms and fifteen MiG-25s – the latter two both significantly larger than the J-20 and with comparable or higher estimated operational costs. Algeria had longstanding strategic and security ties with China, and Chinese armaments had formed a fast growing portion of its inventory throughout the 2010s. Following the initiation of a NATO military campaign against neighbouring Libya in 2011, which fuelled perceptions of a threat of similar Western attacks,[95] the Algerian People's National Army had strongly emphasized asymmetric anti-access capabilities which included acquisitions of Chinese hardware such as DWL-002 air search radars, CX-1 anti-ship cruise missiles and ELINC CHL-906 electronic warfare systems. Although Algeria's armed forces showed signs of a strong interest in Russia's Su-57 from 2020, the J-20 could well prove a much more attractive option either instead of or alongside its Russian competitor.

One of the few references by officials to possible J-20 exports came in the first week of March 2022, when Pakistani Interior Minister Sheikh Rasheed Ahmed stated: 'We have the J-10C ... God willing, a time will come ... I am not sure when, the J-20C will also come to Pakistan, which will be the most modern aircraft in the world.'[96] While such comments would normally be easily dismissible, Minister Ahmed had just four months prior made a similar isolated and unexpected claim that Pakistan would acquire J-10Cs and field them by mid-March – which quickly proved to be correct.[97] With the Pakistan Air Force remaining the leading client for Chinese fighters, such an acquisition may at least have been under consideration.

The J-20's high operational costs, and Pakistan's reliance exclusively on lightweight fighters, most of them one third or less its size, meant accommodating it would likely require deep cuts to fighter numbers. Nevertheless, as one Indian analyst observed, writing for *Rossiyskaya Gazeta*: 'Even a single stealth squadron – of approximately fourteen jets – could give the PAF a psychological edge while also terminating [India's decades long]... record as possessing the most advanced jets in the region.'[98] A J-20 acquisition would not be entirely unprecedented, and would reflect part of a growing trend towards developing countries making unexpected purchases of high end heavyweight fighters where they had previously fielded none. Examples since the 1990s have included Vietnam, Egypt, Ethiopia, Eritrea, Uganda, Venezuela, Indonesia and Malaysia's unexpected orders for Flankers, where all had previously fielded only much lighter fighters around half their size or less. If offered, the J-20 would be the first heavyweight made available to Pakistan as both the U.S. and Russia, for political reasons, declined to provide their own.

While a J-20 sale was possible, however, it remained more likely that Pakistan would look to a much lighter fifth generation fighter long rumoured to be under development in China as a successor to the export-oriented JF-17.[‡‡]

The possibility of a Pakistani J-20 acquisition was reduced considerably when on 2 January 2024 the head of the Pakistan Air Force, Air Chief Marshal Zaheer Sidhu, confirmed that the FC-31 was 'set to become part of the fleet in the near future' with the 'foundation for acquiring' the aircraft already laid.[99] The aircraft was still twice the size of the country's prior heaviest fighters the J-10 and F-16 and would pose many of the same difficulties to integrate as the J-20 would have. Although significantly cheaper than the J-20, the aircraft was still expected to be affordable only in small numbers, but would bring comparable strategic advantages. It was highly unlikely that Pakistan would acquire both the FC-31 and the J-20, with the former having the major advantage that it was immediately available for export while exports of the latter were still prohibited. Interior Minister Ahmed's statement two years prior regarding J-20 acquisitions, however, raised the possibility that the Pakistan Defence Ministry may have sought to acquire the aircraft before settling on the FC-31 when denied permission to purchase its heavier counterpart.

Beyond exports, the J-20 is expected to benefit Chinese security partners through provision of unique opportunities for training against advanced stealth aircraft. As senior China analyst at the USAF National Air and Space Intelligence Centre Wayne Ulman

---

[‡‡] Should Chinese security partners capable of affording and absorbing J-20s be seen to require them imminently for their security needs, this could also significantly influence the possibility of sales. For example, the first U.S. exports of its top fourth generation fighters in the 1970s, the F-14 and F-15 to Iran and Israel respectively, were approved largely in response to perceived imminent Soviet and Arab challenges to their air superiority.

thus observed: 'As the PLAAF gains access to reduced-signature systems, it will allow the development of tactics, training, and procedures for use against low-observable threat systems.'[100] Such support would hardly be unprecedented, with the PLAAF previously having deployed J-10C and J-11B fighters to Pakistan to support training and simulate the capabilities of the Indian Air Force Rafale and Su-30 fighters respectively. The J-20 could in future be used to similarly simulate the capabilities of fifth generation fighters, particularly F-35s, in exercises with countries potentially facing them.

The J-20's participation in August 2021 Zapad/Vzaimodeystviye exercises provided the Russian Military with its first experience of operating alongside fifth generation fighters,[101] and five months later analysts speculated that closer military integration could lead Russia to seek similar training experiences. Development of counter-stealth tactics would be highly valued as NATO's F-35 fleets continued to grow rapidly, and as Russia was not expected to field a comparably stealthy fighter for the foreseeable future.[102]

Chapter Six

Supporting Programs: The J-20 as Part of a Network

The Network Centric Age

The 2000s and 2010s saw all aspects of aerial warfare become increasingly network centric, with this trend set to continue into the later years of the fifth generation fighter era and more so moving into the sixth. The high rate at which network centric warfare capabilities have improved since the turn of the century is perhaps best demonstrated by a comparison of the F-35 and J-20's avionics with those of the F-22 that were developed in the 1990s. The newer fighters are capable of sharing data and fusing sensor inputs with all manner of assets from satellites to accompanying combat aircraft, while the F-22 struggles to share data even with other fighters, requiring a specialised 'translator' aircraft to fly alongside it and relay its messages. Even this 'translation' capability was time consuming to develop and only began to materialise in the early 2020s.[1]

As observed in 2016 by former PACAF Vice Commander Lieutenant General (ret.) David Deptula regarding the role of fifth generation fighters and how they differed from their predecessors, they 'are not fighters ... they are flying sensor-shooters that have the ability to act as information nodes in a combat cloud – a universe if you will – made up of platforms, not just airborne but also operating at sea and on land, that can be networked together.'[2] The increasingly network centric way all aerial warfare assets operate means the capabilities of top end fighter units has increasingly been determined not only by the characteristics of the aircraft themselves, but also by those of friendly assets in their surrounding networks. The potency of the J-20 in the PLAAF can thus only be fully comprehended with an understanding of some of the range of complementary assets which will operate alongside it. As summarised by Air Force Secretary Frank Kendall in 2022: 'It's not just about fighter [versus] fighter. It's a much more complicated equation than that.'[3]

In August 2016, shortly after the first J-20s were delivered to the PLAAF, when asked how the new fighter would compare to the F-35, U.S. Air Force Chief of Staff General David L. Goldfein stressed that this was far less relevant in the age of network centric warfare when fighters were designed to link with a range of supporting assets under broad national defence networks. A former F-117 pilot, his answer provided one of the best summaries of how network centric operations had transformed aerial warfare. Raising the example of late Cold War era fighters such as the F-117, which joined the USAF in 1983, Goldfein stated: 'It was single domain, it was a closed system and it was a sequential way of applying air power because I [F-117 pilot] was always going to be out in front of anybody else on the ground or at sea. The F-35, now since you're asking about F-35, J-20 is a completely different mindset. It starts talking in the network before the pilot even climbs the ladder. It starts comparing information, it starts placing symbology on the visor of the pilot.

'That symbology is replicated not only in the displays but across the network of everywhere it's joined. So when we apply fifth generation technology, it's no longer about a platform, it's about a family of systems and it's about a network and that's what gives us an asymmetric advantage so that's why, when I hear about an F-35 versus J-20, it's almost an irrelevant comparison because you really got to think about a network versus a network. This is combat in the information age.'[4]

During the PLAAF's last major war in 1950-53, when fighters fought at visual ranges and carried no radars or missiles, they relied primarily on ground-based radars and control centres for support without other aircraft accompanying them. By the 2010s, however, this was very far from the case, and unlike its direct predecessor in the PLAAF's elite units the MiG-15, the J-20 for all its strengths could not come close to guaranteeing Chinese security in the air domain without very significant support from a very wide range of other assets. Support includes not only other classes of combat aircraft, but also more essential assets such as satellites and AEW&C systems to provide targeting data and route communications, airborne tankers for in-flight refuelling, and electronic warfare aircraft to complement fighters' firepower with non-kinetic attacks.

Keeping up with the radical shifts in how aerial warfare was conducted, which only accelerated after the Cold War's end, the J-20 program accordingly saw a range of complementary assets and key technologies developed in parallel. These will be central to determining its success in a wide range of missions. Between the fighter's unveiling in 2010 and its entry into service in 2017 the standing of the Chinese defence sector and the performances of its armaments improved tremendously, which was reflected in a revolutionising of the capabilities of top PLA frontline units particularly in the Navy and Air Force. As observed by Hong Kong analysts at the ten year anniversary of the J-20's first flight, this landmark event not only 'shocked the world and changed the regional balance of power,' but also 'heralded a wave of advanced home-grown hardware, from aircraft carriers to hypersonic missiles.'[5]

Communications satellites, the world's most capable missile destroyer,[6] a much larger and more advanced AEW&C fleet, Y-20 heavy lift aircraft, and a new generation of missiles and sensors for fighter jets, were among the examples of programs which marked the PLA and Chinese defence sector's ascension from unremarkable medium level players to close contenders for global leadership. As late as 2010 many of these capabilities were either entirely unanticipated, or were expected to be realised considerably slower, on a smaller scale and with less cutting-edge features. Thus, where China's armed forces in 2010 would have been poorly suited to properly introducing and operating a fighter as capable as the J-20, its transformation over the decade had no parallels among other major militaries and ensured that the world's first non-American fifth generation fighter could be utilised effectively as part of broader networks of similarly advanced assets. The fighter's ability to network is expected to only grow as technological advances in artificial intelligence, data links and quantum communications, among other technologies, are applied to improve its avionics and those of supporting assets. The value of some of the most important assets which will support J-20 operations as part of common networks, and how their capabilities have matured, is explored below.

Manned Supporting Aircraft

Although twenty-first century fighters are capable of operating far more autonomously from radar and control units than their Korean War era predecessors, airborne early warning and control aircraft nevertheless continue to be considered a key force multiplier with their importance having risen considerably as aerial warfare has become more network centric. It was thus highly notable that when the commander of the U.S. Pacific Air Forces, General Kenneth Wilsbach, confirmed in March 2022 the J-20's first encounter with other fifth generation fighters, he particularly singled out the strong impression made by the Chinese fighter's associated command and control and specifically the supporting role played by China's top AEW&C system the KJ-500. 'We're relatively impressed with the command and control associated with the J-20,' Wilsbach stated, observing that 'aircraft in the region ... were pretty well commanded and controlled by the Chinese assets.'[7] 'The KJ-500,' he added, 'plays a significant role in some of their capability for long range fires. Some of their very long-range air-to-air missiles are aided by that KJ-500. Being able to interrupt that kill chain is something that interests me greatly.'[8] Approximately twenty-five to twenty-eight KJ-500s were thought to be in service at the time, a number operationalised over a very short production period with under four years of high-rate production, which made it by far the most widely fielded AEW&C outside the U.S. Armed Forces. Experts cited by the *Global Times* seven months later highlighted that pairing the KJ-500 with the J-20 would help to ensure an advantage even over other fifth generation fighters when operating near Chinese territory.[9]

After observing the key advantages USAF E-3s provided the service's fighter units in operation Desert Storm,[10] and having no AEW&Cs itself, the PLAAF in the 1990s prioritised development of a similar capability which first materialised in the KJ-2000 platform commissioned from 2004.[11] Fifteen years later China's AEW&C fleet had grown to over forty aircraft. The KJ-500 introduced new levels of sophistication and brought Chinese AEW&C capabilities up to the cutting edge, which made its service entry in 2015 an important landmark. With very few rivals in sophistication, the aircraft was declared fully operational from 2018 and production was reportedly accelerated that year,[12] before an enhanced variant the KJ-500A was unveiled in 2022. Its production scale was well over double that of preceding AEW&Cs. The KJ-500's induction is thought to have influenced the USAF's decision on how early to retire its very large but increasingly obsolete E-3 Sentry fleet and replace them with the modern E-7 Wedgetail – a technological equivalent to the new Chinese aircraft. The decision was finalised in 2023, after officials including General Wilsbach repeatedly stressed both the extreme limitations of the E-3 and the contrasting high sophistication of the latest Chinese AEW&Cs.[13]

Complementing AEW&C systems, new generations of satellites were expected to perform many of the same functions to support fighter units, and to do so over much wider areas and with significantly higher degrees of survivability. This was demonstrated by the USAF's reliance on satellite capabilities to compensate for the sudden contraction of the E-3 fleet as a stopgap until more E-7s were available.[14] China's strong position in many areas of satellite communications technologies, as perhaps best demonstrated by the Micius satellite, had the potential to provide PLAAF units including J-20s with key advantages in this regard.

Alongside AEW&C platforms the airborne tanker fleet gained a less urgent but still significant investment which had the potential to extend the J-20's already very long range and thus facilitate operations across much of the Western Pacific. This is expected to be a particularly key capability should a rumoured strike fighter configuration, or variants, armed primarily for anti-surface roles enter service. Until then, however, the priority allocated to fielding aerial tankers is expected to remain far lower than in the U.S. Air Force for multiple reasons. China's armed forces place a much lower emphasis on power projection, with the J-20 not expected to be deployed far beyond Chinese borders for offensive operations as its American counterparts were primarily designed to do. Furthermore, the PLA's ratio of heavyweight long-range fighters to lightweights is far higher than that of any Western air force – over double that of the USAF – meaning the average Chinese fighter has a much higher endurance than the average U.S. or NATO fighter. Even among heavyweights, China's J-20 and Flankers benefit from very comfortable range advantages over their Western rivals the F-15 and more so the F-22, with the J-20's range using internal fuel being over double that of the Raptor. Thus, while tankers are considered indispensable for Western air operations, Chinese fighters not only rarely use them, but even use of external drop tanks, essential in Western fighter operations in the Pacific, is relatively seldom seen on Chinese jets.

The backbone of China's tanker fleet is comprised of derivatives of the H-6 bomber repurposed for refuelling, with thirteen of these in service at the beginning of the 2020s alongside three Soviet-built Il-78s acquired second-hand through Ukraine. This represented a very modest fleet even by the standards of smaller countries, with the heavily power projection oriented U.S. Armed Forces fielding over 450 tanker aircraft.[15] The future of the PLA tanker fleet likely lies in modifications of the world's largest military transport in production worldwide, the Y-20, which entered service in 2016 and saw a tanker variant, the YY-20, fielded from late 2021.[16] The first images of the J-20 refuelling from the YY-20 emerged on 28 March the following year. The Y-20 and J-20, alongside the Z-20 utility helicopter and the H-20 bomber were increasingly from the early 2020s referred to as the '20 series' of aircraft which each represented high profile landmarks in development in their respective areas of military aviation. The first three of these were first displayed on the ground together at the Zhuhai Airshow in November 2022.

From the late 2020s or early 2030s a new generation of manned long range aircraft are expected to become available to operate alongside the J-20, with many of these set to be similarly well optimised for operations in highly contested airspace. The PLAAF will likely commission its first intercontinental range bomber in the second half of the 2020s – the H-20 – which has been developed in parallel to its American rival the B-21 Raider. The two aircraft could potentially enter service within months of one another due to repeatedly delays in the B-21 program, and were both designed with flying wing stealth designs. Where the B-21 will be able to serve in command and control and electronic warfare roles, it is expected that the H-20 airframe, much like that of its predecessor the H-6, could be used to develop tankers, electronic warfare aircraft and even command and control aircraft which could in turn support J-20s and other combat assets. This would capitalise on its expected very long range, large and powerful sensor suite, tremendous carrying capacity, and advanced stealth capabilities.

While the H-20 airframe has the potential to be developed into multiple specialist aircraft that can support J-20 operations, the bomber variant itself is among a range of new assets with the potential to indirectly support the J-20's air superiority mission. Air power theorists as far back as Giulio Douhet in the early twentieth century consistently emphasized that long range bombers were vital to gaining control of the skies due to their ability to decisively obliterate enemy air units on the ground when they were most vulnerable – what he referred to as gaining air superiority through 'breaking the eggs in the nest.'[17] British strategist J.C. Slessor meanwhile projected that air superiority would be best 'obtained by the combined action of bomber and fighter aircraft' – at a time before the cruise and ballistic missile had been invented – to supplement the role of the former.[18] This had particular relevance for China's position since its primary potential adversary would be fighting very far from home in the Pacific with its supply lines stretched and its assets concentrated at a limited number of facilities. The challenge the J-20 faced in the air in an East Asian war thus depended very greatly on how successfully assets such as H-20 bombers and DF-17 and DF-26 ballistic missiles were in neutralising enemy fleets, air bases and supporting facilities across the Pacific – from Taichung to Guam – particularly in a conflict's opening stages. The H-20's promise of advanced stealth capabilities, a tremendous weapons payload and endurance, and access to cutting edge guided weapons, made it particularly key.

Electronic warfare (EW) aircraft represent a further type of manned support platform expected to play important roles in J-20 operations. Alongside the considerable EW potential provided by advanced AESA radars, many twenty-first century fighters integrate their own electronic warfare suites either built in or as specialised external pods for electronic attacks. Specialist aircraft can nevertheless provide more potent EW support to serve as force multipliers for fighter units. Entering service in 2021, the J-16D electronic warfare aircraft inherited original J-16 fighter's flight performance, high endurance and limited stealth capabilities, but had antennas and conformal electronic warfare arrays built into its fuselage and integrated jamming pods that could analyse radar frequencies and locate radar transmitting devices. While capable of targeting enemy aircraft, it was optimised for air defence suppression and alongside electronic attacks could also integrate YJ-91 and LD-10 missiles built to home in on enemy radar emissions.

The only equivalent aircraft to the J-16D fielded abroad was the EA-18G Growler, which was based on the F-18E/F Super Hornet fighter and served in both the U.S. Navy and the Royal Australian Air Force. Other than Australia's small fleet of eleven EA-18Gs, China's was thus the world's only air force to field such aircraft. Experts widely predicted long before the J-16D was commissioned that its operations could provide J-20 units with important advantages.[19] As the aircraft entered service late in 2021 the *Global Times* emphasized in a headline that its purpose was largely 'to team up with the J-20,' stressing that fielding the two complementary aircraft together 'would bring tremendous combat efficiency.'[20] Eventual development of a future electronic attack jet based on the J-20S airframe was also considered a high possibility.

Alongside fighters, larger airframes have also been modified for electronic warfare roles, a notable example being an electronic warfare configuration of the PLAAF's H-6G bomber which appeared from early 2018. These operate differently to electronic attack jets such as the J-16D, having lower survivability at closer ranges, being unable to keep up with transonic fighter units, lacking anti-radiation munitions, and maintaining a more defensive focus.[21] Their primary purpose is to protect friendly assets across wide areas from enemy electronic warfare attacks using their countermeasures suites, and disrupting enemy communications, data links and connections with satellite assets.[22]

Unmanned Supporting Aircraft

Unmanned aerial vehicles emerged in the early 2000s as a priority area for development, and were seen as key to achieving the PLA's informatization goals.[23] By the mid–2010s China increasingly showed signs of leadership in the capabilities of its military UAVs, placing it in a league of its own with the United States and comfortably ahead of other competitors. The PLA by the end of the decade fielded what was by many estimates the widest array of high–performance medium and heavyweight drone designs of any military worldwide, many of which were unique aircraft without foreign equivalents. Notable examples included the WZ-8 surveillance platform unveiled in 2019, which was the world's first operational hypersonic aircraft, as well as the large Divine Eagle which deployed a wide range of large sensors from high altitudes and used data links to increase the situational awareness of PLA military networks.

New generations of elevated sensor and reconnaissance drones such as the high altitude WZ-7, which first appeared in 2021, are expected to complement the PLA's growing satellite and AEW&C capabilities and the increasing potency of fighters' radars and data links to maximise situational awareness. Such capabilities are key to providing PLA battle networks with targeting data, increasing awareness of potential threats and allowing units to more effectively coordinate their actions. Operating as part of such a network could provide J-20 units with decisive advantages if engaging fighters that lack comparable support.

An emerging trend in the use of unmanned aircraft which is expected to become central in the '5+' and sixth generations of combat aviation is the pairing of manned fighters with unmanned 'wingmen,' with future iterations of the J-20, F-35 and Su-57 all expected to be integrated with such support as force multipliers. Between four and six UAVs accompanying each fighter will be able to use their sensors to maximise situational awareness, their armaments to allow each pilot to direct several times more firepower than a fighter alone could carry, and their likely superior stealth capabilities and relative expendability to deploy closer to enemy defences. Wingman UAVs are also expected to carry key supporting equipment such as electronic warfare suites and directed energy weapons, and some are expected to be developed specifically as decoys to draw fire and thus protect their higher value teammates. The result will be fleets which are overall significantly larger but have much smaller numbers of manned fighters, as approximately eighty per cent of new generations of units are comprised of unmanned 'wingman' aircraft.

UAVs operating as 'wingmen' are expected to begin entering service in the mid-late 2020s, with China's large and sophisticated drone industry well positioned to provide the J-20 and its successors with important advantages over rivals. These are expected to initially be semi-autonomous, but gradually gain near full autonomy as artificial intelligence further advances. With the twin seat J-20S expected to be the first fighter of its generation to seat a drone control officer, and unmanned aircraft benefitting from China's significant leads in AI development (see Chapter 4), the J-20 program is particularly well positioned to lead the world in pioneering the revolution in operationalising manned–unmanned pairing.

One particularly notable fighter-sized unmanned aircraft was developed under the Dark Sword program and unveiled in June 2018. It was expected to operate alongside J-20 units from the late 2020s and support them in air-to-air combat at all ranges. The canard twin-tailed aircraft used a divertless supersonic inlet and appeared designed to emphasize high manoeuvrability and effective employment of anti-aircraft missiles for high end air superiority missions. The possibility of the Dark Sword eventually evolving into an unmanned fully autonomous next generation fighter in its own right was widely raised from the late 2010s.

Designed with a more conventional fighter-like airframe, the later unveiled FH-97A stealth UAV appeared to have been developed specifically as a 'wingman' primarily for air-to-air roles. It was shown in computer-generated presentations operating networked with J-20s and flying in formation both to penetrate air defences and to engage enemy fifth generation units. With a design focused on stealth and manoeuvrability, the aircraft were expected to be able to operate as wingmen or autonomously, and would carry missiles for both air-to-air and strike roles.

A range of other unmanned aircraft were candidates to serve as 'wingmen' for the J-20, albeit many with flight performances less optimised to air superiority missions. The most prominent was the stealthy GJ-11 flying-wing UAV which could potentially see future variants carry sensors and armaments for beyond visual range air-to-air combat. While the aircraft's low speed potentially limited its suitability to accompany supercruising J-20 units, subsonic speeds remained the norm in the early 2020s for 'wingman' drones ranging from Russia's S-70 to the U.S.-Australian MQ-28. Beyond the GJ-11, the more mysterious CS-5000T unveiled in November 2022 also used a flying wing stealth design and had an entirely unknown purpose, but could potentially also be paired with J-20s. Another notable subsonic design was the WZ-10 Cloud Shadow, which appeared intended to provide electronic warfare support with a secondary armament of missiles.

As the J-20's communications suite and data links are expected to continue to be modernised its ability to synergise and share data with unmanned aircraft will only grow. These include not only 'wingmen' nearby but also supporting assets much further away such as Divine Eagle elevated sensor drones and WZ-7 and WZ-8 reconnaissance platforms. Advances in artificial intelligence will be key to improving coordination and allowing supporting aircraft to operate more autonomously. Integration with UAVs is expected to be one of the key developments that increasingly sets the J-20 and F-35 apart from baseline fifth generation fighters to bring them to a '5+ generation' level.

'J-20 DNA' in the Fourth Generation

Although the air forces of many medium sized countries very often invest in acquiring just a single class of fighter at a time, for example

France with the Rafale, Turkey with the F-16, or Sweden with the Gripen, such fleets while simpler to maintain and train on have also come with greater limitations and have in most cases been comprised exclusively of lightweight fighter classes. In contrast, for countries seeking to benefit from the complementary performance advantages of different classes, including those seeking to field high performance heavyweight fighters which would be unaffordable to operate in large numbers, acquiring multiple fighter classes in parallel has been common. Notable examples were the USAF F-15 and the Navy's F-14 acquired in limited numbers as part of high-low pairings with lighter more numerous F-16 and F-18 fighters. Only the U.S. and USSR initially produced complementary aircraft for such pairings, the latter with the Su-27 and MiG-29, before being joined by China in the 2000s with the J-11 and J-10. A French attempt to field a similar pair failed in the 1980s as its heavyweight Mirage 4000, developed as a complement to the lightweight Mirage 2000, proved unaffordable.

While the USAF for most of the 2010s had no fighter other than the F-35A on order, this was a result of both issues with the F-22, and the fact that a sixth generation heavyweight fighter to serve as a complement to the F-35 was still relatively early in its development. The U.S. Navy, meanwhile, abandoned a high-low combination after the Cold War to field a fleet with much lower operational costs comprised exclusively of medium weight F-18E/F fighters. In the Russian Air Force, too, almost all new fighters received in the first thirty years after the Soviet disintegration were Flankers, with the lack of any meaningful fighter acquisitions until the 2010s and contraction of the defence budget and fleet size leading to abandonment of the high-low combination and focus on a smaller fleet of heavyweights exclusively. The U.S. and Russia thus both saw their fleets grow far less diverse after the Cold War's end, ending their parallel high-low acquisitions and seeing the diversity of combat aircraft types on order shrink considerably.

A contrasting trend was seen in China where the diversity of the fleet and of production lines grew significantly in the decades following the Cold War's end, and the J-20 was accordingly developed, produced and commissioned by the PLAAF alongside two complementary fighter classes - the Shenyang J-16 and Chengdu J-10C. The former was an advanced Flanker derivative and a leading contender for the title of the world's most capable pre-fifth generation fighter, while the latter was significantly lighter and represented a much evolved iteration of China's first indigenous fourth generation fighter. The two '4+ generation' fighter programs were key to ensuring that the J-20, which even with a high production rate still equipped only a small portion of PLA air brigades, would operate in a fleet where dozens of squadrons had similarly advanced weaponry, sensors and network centric warfare capabilities.

The J-16 and J-10C's most cutting-edge features were based on technologies developed for the J-20, with avionics comparable in sophistication and access to the same armaments. This demonstrated some of the extent to which the J-20, as China's first fifth generation program, had contributed to advancing the tactical aviation industry. From the J-20's distinctive green heads-up display, to controls, cockpit displays, helmet mounted sights and weaponry, there were multiple significant commonalities. Composite material technologies, data links and sensors were among a multitude of other areas where tremendous advances had been made to realise the goals of the J-20 program, with these then used to enhance the baseline J-10 and Flanker designs with revolutionary new capabilities.* As

---

* This mirrored the way technologies developed for the F-22 and F-35 significantly benefitted the older F-15, F-16 and F-18 programs in the U.S., and technologies for the cancelled Soviet MiG 1.42, S-32 and later the Su-57 were similarly used to enhance Russian Flankers and even its bombers – with the Tu-22M3M bomber, for example, using communication suites almost identical to the Su-57's own.

a result only China and the United States were able to introduce '4+ generation' fighters with fifth generation level avionics, like the J-16 or F-16E/F, in parallel to their first fifth generation fighters. Russia and European states by contrast relied on using advances in avionics and material sciences to improve their fourth generation designs decades before they could develop a genuinely post fourth generation fighter.

Both the J-10C and J-16 were produced on far greater scales than any Russian or American fighter other than the F-35, and facilitated modernisation of frontline units far faster than reliance on the J-20 alone would have allowed. PLAAF pilots flying the J-20 consistently flew the J-16 and J-10C as well, with their similar avionics and common weaponry making transitioning between them more straightforward than adapting to older aircraft such as the J-11B or J-10A. Pentagon reports in 2020 highlighted that the J-20 could prove particularly challenging to tackle when operating alongside the J-16 and J-10C and with KJ-500 support,[24] with the three fighter classes frequently deployed together for exercises and demonstrating highly complementary capabilities.

It was previously expected that a further advanced Flanker derivative, the J-11D, would also begin to enter service after production of the older J-11B single seater ended in 2018. The J-11D was a single seater more specialised in air superiority than the J-16 and was expected to be considerably more costly. Although images of prototypes continued to be published into the late 2010s, it was widely speculated that the decision had been made not to produce the fighter to focus on the J-20 as a more capable top end air superiority fighter. The J-20's advantages in particular pertaining to its stealth capabilities likely made it a more cost effective aircraft in terms of the capabilities it brought to the PLAAF compared to its lifetime cost. The J-11D's design was instead used as a basis to develop a more advanced iteration of the J-15 carrier-based fighter for the Navy, the J-15B, where the original baseline J-15 had been based closely on the J-11B. The sheer number of Flankers the air force already fielded indicated the possibility that this had been the program's intention from the outset. As a less costly alternative means of improving the Flanker fleet, the Air Force and the Navy's still relatively new J-11Bs began, from the late 2010s, to integrate fifth generation level avionics and armaments, with the upgrade package designated J-11BG thought to be closely based on the avionics and weaponry of the J-11D. Updating the J-11Bs' sensors and data links was key to facilitating more seamless operations as part of common networks alongside J-20s, J-16s and J-10Cs, and did much to narrow the gap in performance.

A further fighter class which benefitted from 'J-20 DNA,' as it was sometimes informally referred to, was the JF-17 Block 3 which was from the 'very light' weight range much smaller than even the J-10C. Built for export and first flying in December 2019, it was approximately analogous to the Swedish Gripen E/F – where the larger J-10 was broadly an analogue to the F-16. With a design prioritising very low maintenance needs and operational costs, albeit at the cost of an unremarkable flight performance, the fighter's use of avionics and armaments based on J-20 technologies, including the KLJ-7A AESA radar, still made it potentially formidable. According to the *Global Times* older JF-17 models, of which approximately 150 had been produced, could also be upgraded with the Block 3's next generation avionics and armaments.[25] Alongside exports, the JF-17 Block 3 had the potential to enter service in the PLAAF as a wartime production model to provide larger quantities of modern fighters more quickly and with lower maintenance needs, training requirements and logistical footprints in emergency situations.

The J-10C and J-16 Supporting the J-20

Referred to by Chinese sources as the 'Three Sky Musketeers,' the J-16, J-10C by the early 2020s formed the core of the PLAAF fighter fleet's combat capacity alongside the J-20, and having been developed in parallel the synergy between the three classes was a significant factor determining the combat potential of the broader networks they operated in.

The J-10C radically improved on the relatively mediocre capabilities of the original J-10A of the 2000s to provide a close contender for the title of the world's most potent pre-fifth generation single engine fighter, and repeatedly proved to be highly capable particularly in air-to-air combat. In June 2020 unverified reports emerged that the fighter had won overwhelmingly in simulated combat against PLAAF Su-35s recently acquired from Russia, which remained the Russian Air Force's top operational fighter class. This was a significant achievement considering that the J-10C was approximately half its size and was far from the PLAAF's top fighter. Reduced radar visibility reportedly played an important role in helping the J-10C 'achieve success in the confrontation with the Su-35,' and by allowing the Chinese fighter to detect and fire first 'gave an advantage in the simulation of a missile attack.' The J-10C benefitted from a much lower radar signature and significantly more advanced electronics, sensors and weaponry.[26]

Missile technologies in particular are likely to have provided a tremendous advantage, and at visual ranges PL-10 was overall far more capable than the Su-35's R-73/74 missile and could engage targets at far more extreme angles. The longer ranged PL-15, benefitting from AESA radar and satellite enabled inertial guidance and having between double and triple the range of the Su-35's relatively modest R-77-1 missile, provided an even greater edge. In December 2021 the J-10C repeatedly gained victories against both the Su-35 and the J-16, marking the third consecutive year that the single engine jet had won in simulated combat since entering service in 2018.[27]

Entering service in 2014 or 2015 the J-16 was by far the world's most advanced Flanker derivative, and despite not being marketed for export it was produced at twice or more the rate of any foreign heavyweight aircraft including the Russian Flanker models. It was fourth in the world in terms of annual production rates, but second in the world among heavyweights outproduced only by the J-20. The aircraft began to enter service at an accelerated rate from 2018 as the preceding J-11B, manufactured at the same facilities, saw its production run conclude that year – the last of China's older fighters still using mechanically scanned array radars to end production.[28]

Providing some insight into the J-16's capabilities, Research Fellow and expert on Chinese security at the Royal United Services Institute Justin Bronk referred to the fighter as 'genuinely better in almost every important regard than their Russian Flanker counterparts ... not only do you have something that's lighter and stronger than a Russian Flanker, that has access to far more capable multirole munitions both in the air-to-ground domain ... [but also] much more effective air-to-air weaponry to go with that AESA radar.'[29] For longer ranged missions the J-16's high payload, range and altitude allowed it to keep up with the J-20, while its much larger radar than the J-10 allowed it to contribute more to collective situational awareness. Despite considerable applications of stealth technologies, particularly radar absorbent coatings, the J-16's still higher radar cross section than the J-10 and J-20 saw it used in exercises to bait enemy units into engaging while the stealthier aircraft lay in wait.

Deployment of PL-XX air-to-air missiles, which are too heavy for the J-10C and too large for the J-20's missile bays, allow the J-16 to play an important supporting role for J-20 units eliminating support aircraft such as AEW&C platforms and aerial tankers. Western fighters' extreme reliance on aerial refuelling to operate in East Asia due to the vast distances separating major land masses, as well as their generally lower endurances, meant the J-16 could be particularly effective in inhibiting adversaries' fighter operations. The value of Chinese 'tanker killer' capabilities was notably highlighted by a 2008 RAND Corporation study, which found that to sustain operations for 130 combat coded F-22s from Guam over Taiwan the USAF would need to launch three to four tanker sorties every hour to deliver 2.6 million gallons of fuel. Even assuming no F-22 combat losses and a perfect combat performance, the projected loss of tankers would leave the American jets unable to return to their bases and result in extreme losses among the Raptors. Guam was at the time seen as the nearest location where bases had a chance of surviving PLA strikes.[30] By limiting tanker operations over very wide areas, PL-XX armed J-16s could thus provide an effective complement to J-20 units over the East and South China Seas.

Friendly Fifth Generation Fighters

In parallel to the J-20's development at Chengdu, the rival No. 601 Institute at Shenyang developed a medium weight fifth generation fighter under the FC-31 program which made its first flight less than two years later in October 2012. The more conservative design was expected to have a significantly shorter range, radar size and weapons payload, but also lower operational costs and a smaller logistics footprint. Although some sources speculated that the program could produce a lighter counterpart to the J-20 as part of a high-low pairing, with analysts at CSIS believing that the two were 'designed to complement each other in a similar manner to the planned deployment of the F-22 and F-35 by the United States,' by the early 2020s this appeared unlikely.[31] The PLAAF's lack of prior interest in medium weight fighters, and the lack of a clear place for such an aircraft in the fleet, had raised questions from the outset regarding the veracity of such assertions. The Air Force's few signs of interest in the program contrasted sharply with the high priority status it accorded the J-20.

As the world's first medium weight fifth generation fighter, the fact that the FC-31's first flight and that of the J-20 closely coincided was cited by a number of analysts as a sign that Chengdu and Shenyang had developed a competitive relationship rather than a geographic division of labour. This was based, however, on the highly questionable assumption that Shenyang's aircraft ever had a chance of gaining PLA support in place of the J-20.[32] The requirements for a next generation fighter had since the 1990s strongly indicated the need for a top end heavyweight air superiority platform capable of outperforming the F-22, which the FC-31 airframe did not appear well suited to fulfilling.

By the early 2020s it was expected that the FC-31 would serve primarily as a carrier-based fighter to complement modernised J-15s, with reports in early 2023 indicating that the aircraft had entered serial production with service entry expected around 2025 – in time to deploy from the Navy's first supercarrier the Shandong. The aircraft's especially robust landing gear observed from the very first prototype, including double wheels in the nose gear, had suggested a role in carrier aviation from the outset, and a carrier-based iteration of the aircraft with folding wings and a catapult launch bar was first unveiled and seen in flight in October 2021.[33] The possibility also remained that the fighter could compete with the J-20 to modernise the Navy's land based fighter units, eventually replacing aircraft such as the Su-30MK2 and J-11BGH, with the FC-31 having the advantage of commonality with carrier based naval aviation although limited by a likely much shorter range.

The FC-31 design evolved considerably from the first prototype to the initiation of production, with many of the advances seen on newer iterations of J-20 such as a flattened cockpit canopy to improve aerodynamic performance and further lower the radar cross section also applied to its lighter counterpart. When the fighter entered production China became the first country to manufacture two fifth generation fighter classes simultaneously – a position it had the potential to hold in perpetuity. The chances of this growing to three before 2030 were significant, with a lightweight single engine fighter widely expected to be unveiled as a low cost successor to the JF-17 on export markets – and possibly even to form part of a high-low combination with the J-20 in the PLAAF as a successor to the J-10. This was speculated to begin to appear once the J-20's WS-15 engine fully entered service, with the single engine jet expected to use the same powerplant.

A fighter based on the FC-31 design was also confirmed in February 2022 to have been developed for export,[34] allowing China to enter the fifth generation market without offering the J-20 abroad. Such a program would capitalise on the prestige the J-20 had brought the industry – but fall within the budgets of a broader range of clients. The FC-31's deployment both abroad and in Chinese carrier aviation units had the potential to significantly benefit interoperability between the PLAAF and both the Navy and overseas security partners, much like the USAF's F-35 fleet benefitted from the widespread deployment of F-35s both in allied fleets and in the Navy and Marine Corps.

An important disadvantage China faces when moving into the fifth generation of combat aviation is that J-20 units have very limited opportunities to operate alongside aircraft from their generation outside the PLAAF, leaving China's air force effectively alone in developing tactics for operations at this advanced level. USAF F-35 units by contrast not only benefit from tactics developed for a decade before their induction using F-22s, but also from training and information sharing with the Navy, the Marines and with a large and fast growing number of foreign F-35 operators across four continents. This could potentially change in the late 2020s as Russia's Su-57 fleet gains greater strength and as the two countries' armed forces continue to increase levels of interoperability, including with increasingly large and frequent joint exercises and patrols in the Pacific. With leading NATO members long having set the standard for high level integration between their aerial warfare assets, growing Sino–Russian interoperability appears intended to similarly allow assets to be integrated into common 'combat clouds' – with the J-20 having likely first been used in a network with Russian assets at the August 2021 Zapad/Vzaimodeystviye exercises. Nevertheless, the Su-57's very slow entry into service and very different design philosophy from other fighters of its generation will likely limit the applicability of lessons the PLAAF gains in joint operations.

Opportunities to proliferate fifth generation fighters to match the vast network of allied F-35 operators built by the United States remain very limited, with China's having just one bilateral treaty ally, North Korea, which remains under a United Nations arms embargo. Other security partners such as Laos, Cambodia and Kazakhstan notably either have negligible defence budgets and capabilities or are geographically not well located to realistically participate in joint operations in potential conflict zones. The result is a greater burden on the PLAAF's own J-20 fleet to counter adversaries on a fifth generation level, with over half a dozen countries' F-35s expected to join a U.S.-led war effort in the Pacific should this occur. While possible exports of Su-57s, FC-31s, or future single engine stealth fighters to relatively neutral third parties such as Vietnam, Thailand or Pakistan could provide some further opportunities for exercises, they would lack benefits of common strategic goals in training and defence planning that F-35 operators have usually shared. The PLA Navy is thus set to be the leading provider of shared experience, and if needed combat support, at a fifth generation level to the PLAAF's J-20 fleet.

Chapter Seven

Challenges and Responses to the J-20

The J-20 as a Challenge to American Power

The J-20's first known encounter with another fifth generation fighter, which was also the first ever encounter between stealth fighters from opposing sides, was confirmed on 14 March 2022 to have occurred over the East China Sea. Commander of the U.S. Pacific Air Forces (PACAF) Air Force General Kenneth Wilsbach stated at the time regarding PLAAF J-20 operations: 'What we're noticing is they are flying it pretty well. We recently had – I wouldn't call it an engagement – where we got relatively close to the J-20s along with our F-35s in the East China Sea, and we're relatively impressed with the command and control that was associated with the J-20s.'[1] This represented a rare insight into prevailing thought in the USAF on the Chinese next generation fighter, which had persistently surprised Western analysts over the past eleven years with both the speed of its development and the sophistication of its demonstrated capabilities. The PACAF chief's assessment followed a Defence Department report to Congress referring to the J-20 as having 'high manoeuvrability, stealth characteristics, and an internal weapons bay, as well as advanced avionics and sensors providing enhanced situational awareness, advanced radar tracking and targeting capabilities, and integrated EW systems.'[2]

The J-20's emergence as the only widely fielded and produced fifth generation air superiority fighter was an important indicator of China's success in having achieved a strong standing in its aerial capabilities – with the lighter F-35 being designed primarily for air-to-ground missions, the F-22's production cut, and the Su-57 only seeing its first full regiment formed in 2024. As much as this was a result of Chinese advances, it was equally a consequence of the failures in the United States and Russia, the latter having delayed the Su-57 tremendously and abandoned the MiG 1.42 and the former having failed to develop the F-22 into a viable successor to fully replace the F-15 over a long production run. This provided China with a window to develop the J-20 into the world's premier fighter for air-to-air combat, which would have been unthinkable in the 1980s when the Soviet and American advantages over the rest of the world, and over China in particular, appeared insurmountable before both suffered sharp contractions to their defence sectors and industrial bases in the 1990s. The J-20's entry into service thus marked the first time since the Second World War that a fighter from outside the United States or Russia could be considered a serious contender for the title of the world's most formidable in an air superiority role.

While the J-20 and F-35 were in a league of their own, both as the world's only two fifth-generation fighters that were both in production and fielded at squadron level strength and in terms of the sophistication of many of their features, America and its allies' ability to rely on the F-35 in the face of peer level Chinese competition was limited. This was a result of both the tremendous issues the F-35 program faced (see Chapter 2), and to the fact that it was not optimised for air superiority roles. As observed by former USAF Chief of Staff General Mark Welsh, the F-35 'was never designed to be the next dog fighting machine. It was designed to be the multipurpose, data-integration platform that could do all kinds of things in the air-to-ground arena including dismantle enemy, integrated, air defences. It had an air-to-air capability, but it was not intended to be an air-superiority fighter. That was the F-22.'[3] USAF Combat Command Chief General Mike Hostage similarly warned: 'If I do not keep that F-22 fleet viable, the F-35 fleet frankly will be irrelevant. The F-35 is not built as an air superiority platform. It needs the F-22.'[4]

General Hostage predicted that while the F-35 was not optimally suited to an air superiority role, the F-15 and its lighter counterpart the F-16 would be obsolete by 2024. With F-22 numbers very low and shrinking, availability rates remaining by far the worst in the Air Force, and investment in their modernisation in the 2010s remaining highly modest, the Raptor fleet's viability was increasingly left in question. The result was a heavy burden on the F-35 fleet, with fast growing deployments of the aircraft to East Asia repeatedly alluded to as being a response to growing Chinese aerial warfare capabilities and to the expanding capabilities of the J-20 fleet specifically.[5]

Compounding the challenge posed by the J-20 was a significant shortfall in the size of the American fifth generation fleet compared to even Obama administration era projections. Defence Secretary Robert Gates had in 2009 stated: 'By 2020, the U.S. is projected to have nearly 2,500 manned combat aircraft of all kinds. Of those, nearly 1,100 will be the most advanced fifth generation F-35s and F-22s. China, by contrast, is projected to have no fifth generation aircraft by 2020.' He added: 'By 2025, the gap only widens. The U.S. will have approximately 1,700 of the most advanced fifth generation fighters versus a handful of comparable aircraft for the Chinese.'[6] Not only did the PLAAF receive its first J-20s four years before 2020, but the American fifth generation fleet remained well below the strength projected.

Even by January 2022, just before J-20 deliveries were accelerated, the U.S. Military had approximately 660 fifth generation fighters in service, all with very low operational readiness rates and over two thirds of which were F-35s still years away from being ready for high intensity operations and suffering major performance issues. The J-20 fleet at the time was estimated at close to 200 fighters. Approximately forty per cent of the F-35s in service, or 189 aircraft, were highly troubled early production models suffering from such widespread issues that they were not expected to ever be made viable for actual combat. Many of these were expected to fly for small fractions of their intended service lives due to structural defects, which made the discrepancy in numbers significantly narrower still.[7]

The numerical balance was set to be far less favourable for the U.S. by 2025, with significant expansion of the scale of J-20 production set to allow the PLAAF to receive the aircraft at a close to twice the rate of F-35 deliveries to the U.S. Air Force, Navy and Marine Corps combined. Deep cuts to F-35 deliveries for 2023, and further cuts in the next two years, only exacerbated this. The expected deliveries of FC-31s to the Navy by then would further expand the Chinese fifth generation fleet's numerical advantage in a potential East Asian war. The first indications that the FC-31 program may have put a fighter into production came in April 2022, a month after confirmation of USAF plans to imminently begin retiring F-22s from service.[8]

American expectations for the J-20 program, what its success could signify, and how it would influence the balance of power in North-East Asia and beyond, changed significantly as the program evolved. Following the publication of the first images of the first technology demonstrator, China military scholar and author Richard Fisher stated when speaking to CNN that the release of images was likely intentional. He highlighted the significant possibility that the J-20 would be able to outperform the F-22, particularly in thrust and non–afterburner speed, stressing that the U.S. 'should be reviving production of the F-22 and not just reviving production, we should be developing an advanced version of the F-22' to respond to the challenge. Noting the significant issues affecting the F-35 program, Fisher further warned: 'The F-35 needs another rework. It needs to be made competitive with this fighter [J-20].' 'Since World War II, the American military has never gone into battle without the assurance of air superiority. China is a rising power, and it is determined to challenge the American position globally. This fighter will allow them to do that on a military level … and from my perspective, that's simply unacceptable,' he concluded.[9]

Before the J-20 entered service, and at a time of prevailing uncertainty regarding its role, the Pentagon believed that the PLAAF sought to use stealth technology as a core component to transform 'a predominantly territorial air force to one capable of conducting both offensive and defensive operations.'[10] In 2014 the U.S.-China Economic and Security Review Commission described the J-20 in its report to Congress as 'more advanced than any other fighter currently deployed by Asia Pacific countries.'[11] A U.S. Naval War College report highlighted that year that upon entering service, the J-20 would 'immediately become the most advanced aircraft deployed by any East Asian Power.'[12] These assessments mirrored those made in China itself, a notable early example being PLAAF Senior Colonel Shen Jinke's statement just weeks after the first J-20s were delivered that the new fighter class was 'developed to meet the needs of the future battleground' and would 'further enhance the overall combat capability of the Air Force.'[13]

Training to Fight the J-20

China's challenge to American air superiority epitomised by the J-20 was responded to not only with decisions regarding research and development and other acquisitions related investments, but also in how the U.S. Armed Forces and a number of its allies trained for future air wars. The beginnings of this could be observed shortly after the fighter began to enter service in the PLAAF. In the first week of December 2018 a full-scale J-20 mock-up, funded by the U.S. Marine Corps, was seen at the USAF Air Dominance Centre in Savannah, Georgia, and according to the *Marine Corps Times* had been built for visual and sensor training.[14] The attempted replica outwardly differed markedly from the original, with control surfaces, exhaust nozzles and landing gear being the most noticeable inaccuracies.[15] Perhaps more importantly than the mock-up's military significance was its indication, perhaps intentionally, as a signal to China, that the

J-20 was increasingly being factored into American training and war plans as the 'threat of tomorrow' as the program matured.

In May 2019 the USAF announced plans to reactivate its 65th Aggressor Squadron – a unit intended to simulate the capabilities of enemy fighters to provide dissimilar 'red on blue' air combat training. The announcement followed scathing reports, including a post-audit report in April from the Department of Defence Inspector General, on the state of pilot training and in particular its lack of relevance to facing twenty-first century challenges.[16] The aggressor unit was activated in June 2022 and based at Nellis Air Force Base in Nevada, which was the USAF's leading facility for test training. The decision to equip the unit with F-35As provided a clear indication from the outset that provision of training against stealth fighters would be a primary role for the 65th, and with the J-20 being the world's only active non-American stealth fighter there was little doubt that it was the primary target. Allocation of F-35s to an aggressor unit was thus widely seen to signify that the USAF increasingly saw the Chinese program as a source of concern.

The fighters flown by the 65th had provided an indicator of which fighter classes the USAF saw as the most pressing challenge. It thus flew F-15s from 2005 to simulate the capabilities of the Su-27 Flanker and its derivatives, and previously the F-5E Tiger II to simulate advanced variants of the Soviet MiG-21. Had there been no Chinese fifth generation fighter programs, it is likely that the 65th would not have transitioned to field F-35s. Nellis spokesman Major Chris Sukach stated regarding the decision to induct F-35s: 'This added capability will enhance the already robust adversary replication provided to U.S. and partner-nation air forces through multiple training and exercise scenarios.'[17]

The commander of the 65th Aggressor Squadron, Lieutenant Colonel Brandon Nauta would later reveal that 'F-35s have been flying as red air since the inception of the program' – red air being a reference to simulating adversary capabilities in 'red on blue' engagements – but that forming a dedicated aggressor squadron with the stealth fighters still had important benefits. 'The 65th AGRS [Aggressor Squadron] now allows us to do this professionally and in a more organized manner. We will be able to provide the combat air forces (Joint and Coalition), a standardized replication template so we are all training at the same level,' he stated a month after the squadron's official reactivation. His unit aimed to reach an Initial Operating Capability around January 2023.[18]

Thirteen months after the announcement of the reactivation of the 65th Aggressor Squadron, on 22 June 2020 Head of Air Combat Command Air Force General Mike Holmes stated that F-22s coded for training could be replaced by modern trainers such as the T-7 and T-50, allowing approximately sixty Raptors to be coded for combat and reallocated. An upending of pilot training to reduce its duration from forty months to just twenty-two, freeing more aircraft for other purposes under what the general referred to as Project Reforge, was also announced to be under consideration. Holmes suggested these F-22s could be used in aggressor training – with the F-35's suitability to simulate the J-20's capabilities having been questioned on the basis that one was a much lighter single engine fighter designed primarily for strike missions while the latter was a heavyweight twin engine air superiority fighter. This discrepancy only became more pronounced as the J-20's flight performance improved significantly with the integration of new engines. The F-22 by contrast could come much closer to matching the J-20's flight performance, but could not match its advanced avionics and lacked key features such as distributed aperture systems and helmet mounted sights.

Two months later in August 2020 further reports emerged of the U.S. Armed Forces' preparations for the possibility of air-to-air combat with Chinese stealth fighters, with the Air Force and Navy increasingly seeking to mimic the J-20's stealth capabilities in training. The USAF began to use F-117 stealth jets to refine counter-stealth tactics, with the fighters having been retired from service in

2006 and flown by private contractors making them more readily available for training than F-35s or F-22s. F-117s flew with F-16s from the USAF 64th Aggressor Squadron in December 2019, and in May 2020 flew Red Air Missions in the Pacific against a Navy carrier group which was carrying out its most complex and deeply integrated phase of training prior to deployment. Only fifty-nine F-117 airframes had ever entered USAF service, and although far inferior to the J-20 and even the F-35 in terms of flight performance the aircraft had the potential to acquaint personnel with the challenges of targeting stealth aircraft. The USAF formally cleared its KC-135 Stratotankers to execute aerial refuelling operations with the F-117 in January 2021, which was widely interpreted as a sign of further plans to make use of the retired aircraft for additional counter-stealth training.

In November 2020 the USAF began to use a training program developed by firms Red 6 and EpiSci that projected seemingly real AI-flown J-20 fighters onto pilots' augmented reality helmet-mounted displays.[19] This gave a degree of preparation in engaging fifth generation targets before pilots faced USAF F-35s in their first aggressor training missions simulating 'red' enemy stealth fighters. Organised to train 'blue' units in countering stealth aircraft, these missions began in August 2021 as part of Red Flag 2021 exercises at Nellis Air Force Base – the leading dissimilar air combat training event for aggressor squadrons which had first started in 1975. Commander of the 64th Aggressor Squadron at Nellis Lieutenant Colonel Chris Finkenstadt stated regarding the exercises: 'Based on our focus toward great-power competition, we need to make sure that those [blue air] guys are ready, and we do that by presenting the best possible atmosphere we can.' An Air Force press release indicated that 'red' units won 'a lot of red air victories' in early simulated clashes – which was expected to change as counter-stealth tactics and techniques improved.[20]

F-22s were notably included on 'blue' team tasked with tackling 'red' F-35s, with Captain Patrick Bowlds, who flew Raptors at Red Flag stating: 'Having them [F-35s] on red air adds a level of complexity' to an already 'complex scenario.' 'When you have a stealth platform on red air, it makes our job a lot more difficult in terms of knowing where they are, how we are going to protect allied forces or protect points on the ground or whatever the mission set is at that point in time,' he elaborated, adding that, 'it is challenging, even flying the Raptor, to have good [situational awareness] on where the F-35s are.'[21]

In June 2022 as the 65th Aggressor Squadron was reactivated, its F-35s were shown in a colour scheme closely resembling one used on the J-20, mirroring the squadron's F-15s' prior use of a colour scheme derived from that of Russian Su-27 units. This again signified the J-20's position and that of China as the new perceived primary challenger to American air superiority. The Russians and Soviets and their MiGs and Sukhois had held the position for over sixty years, before post-Soviet decline and the extreme slowdown in progress in the Russian aviation industry allowed China to comfortably overtake it. Nevertheless, the high demand for F-35s elsewhere in the Air Force meant only eleven fighters were allocated to the aggressor squadron, with these coming from deeply flawed early production blocks which were not expected to ever be viable for frontline operations.

To provide further training and facilitate weapons testing optimised against fifth generation targets, the USAF from 2022 sought to acquire a stealth target drone to replace an unmanned modification of the F-16. Designated QF-16, the aircraft had previously been used to test anti-aircraft weapons, but were no longer considered sufficient in an era where adversaries now fielded stealth aircraft. Beyond a significant degree of autonomy, primary requirements for the new drone were as followed: 'The fifth generation representative target suite should be able to provide a remotely-controlled, destructible asset with threat representative

RF [radio frequency] Emissions, EA [electronic attack] Emissions, Radar Cross Section (RCS) signature, Infrared (IR) signature, and internally carried expendables.'[22]

While the U.S. Air Force made significant investments to adapt its training to respond to China's emergence as a leader in fifth generation fighter aviation, these efforts were undermined by the significant pressure on the fighter fleet that resulted primarily from issues with America's own fifth generation programs. In particular, the tremendous delays and cost overruns affecting the F-22 and F-35, and acquisition rates of both at just fractions of planned levels, forced the Air Force to keep fourth generation airframes in service for far longer than intended. As these aged their operational costs and maintenance needs rose steeply. By 2023, with F-22s and F-35s fielded at a fraction of numbers previously projected, the fleet's F-15s and F-16s had long outlived their planned service lives averaging thirty-eight and thirty-two years old, with their ages only set to continue to increase unless the older airframes were simply retired without replacement.[23]

Lieutenant General Joseph Guastella was among several figures in the Air Force leadership to highlight that the fleet's rising age was taking a serious toll on crews' flying hours[24] – while for those units which had transitioned to fifth generation fighters their much lower availability rates and higher maintenance needs meant their situations were often little better.[25] 'We're on a collision course,' he stressed, warning that fighter force readiness could 'fall off a cliff.' At the time of the publication of a Mitchell Institute policy paper addressing the issue, which was co-authored by Guastella in June 2023, former PACAF Vice Commander Lieutenant General (ret.) David Deptula was among figures to highlight that Chinese pilots, flying fighters which were on average several decades newer, were getting more flying hours than their USAF counterparts. Additional training 'makes a difference,' he stressed, with this giving the PLAAF an important edge in better preparing itself for warfare at a fifth generation level.[26]

The J-20 and America's NGAD Sixth Generation Fighter Program

Beyond stimulating investment in training to counter fifth generation aircraft, the J-20 program and its implications regarding the state of China's defence sector added considerable urgency to the American Next Generation Air Dominance (NGAD) sixth generation fighter program. This mirrored how the Flanker had in the 1980s added urgency to NGAD's predecessor the Advanced Tactical Fighter program which produced the F-22. In September 2020 USAF head of acquisitions Will Roper revealed that a technology demonstrator for NGAD 'has come so far that the full-scale flight demonstrator has already flown in the physical world,' and had 'broken a lot of records in the doing.'[27] Air Force Secretary Frank Kendall later referred to it as 'an X-plane program, which was designed to reduce the risk in some of the key technologies that we would need for a production program,' confirming that the first contracts for the demonstrator were issued around 2015.[28]

While the USAF and naval aviation had for three decades increasingly emphasized air defence suppression rather than air superiority, based largely on the assumption that with the Soviet defence sector no longer in existence peer level challengers in the air would only further diminish with time, the J-20 program was the primary program that simulated a partial reversal of this trend. In 2015 Chief of Naval Operations Jonathan Greenert had indicated that an American sixth generation fighter would be focused largely on electronic warfare and air defence suppression, stating: 'You know that stealth may be overrated. I don't want to necessarily say that it's over but let's face it, if something moves fast through the air and disrupts molecules in the air and puts out heat – I don't care how cool the engine can be – it's going to be detectable ... It has to have an ability to carry a payload such that it can deploy a spectrum of weapons. It has to be able to acquire access probably by suppressing enemy air defences.' 'I don't think it's going to be super-duper fast, because you can't outrun missiles,' he added.[29] This changed as the J-20 program matured and began to produce fighters for frontline service, and references to sixth generation fighters as being focused on air defence suppression and de-emphasizing stealth notably diminished sharply. NGAD was increasingly seen as an aircraft designed specifically to counter Chinese fifth and sixth generation fighters specifically.

Development of NGAD's direct predecessor the F-22 under the Advanced Tactical Fighter program notably suffered in the 1990s due to the sharp deterioration in Russia's defence sector and armed forces. Russian decline had made the MiG 1.42 program, which could have potentially produced fighters earlier than and outperforming the F-22, unviable, and without any serious challengers the F-22 suffered cuts and delays that largely appeared to stem from complacency. Technologies removed to cut costs ranged from infrared tracking systems to secondary radars. The USAF had to restructure the program several times after 1991 as Congress continued to cut funding – what *Air Force Magazine* referred to as 'programmatic turmoil'.[30] Indeed, the Cold War's end was widely speculated to be a reason why Lockheed Martin's more conservative F-22 design was chosen over the proposed 'F-23' designed by Northrop Grumman, which was a more expensive, stealthier, faster and more ambitious option.

Where the F-22's development suffered from lack of competition, the NGAD program is expected to be stimulated by Chinese advances in tactical combat aviation which have been demonstrated primarily by the J-20 program. This could mirror how the American F-15 program, the F-22's direct predecessor, saw its capability requirements revised and made more ambitious and its development accelerated in response to the demonstrated performance of the Soviet third generation MiG-25, which was considered the top fighter/interceptor of the early 1970s and which no prior USAF aircraft was capable of reliably engaging.[31] Experts on the F-15's development described the program as 'energized by the appearance of the prototype MiG-25 Foxbat ... the MiG-25 was built for sustained Mach 3 performance, smashed a number of world performance records between 1965 and 1977 ... the MiG-25's extraordinary performance was an unpleasant surprise to the West, as the MiG-15 had been in 1950. The effect of the MiG-25 revelation was to increase the emphasis on air superiority in the F-X specification.'[32] Thus while the F-22 program's results were in many ways underwhelming, the F-15 by contrast had truly revolutionary advantages over its predecessors and was considered a leading achievement of American Cold War military aviation – allowing it to become the fighter with the longest production run in history. The J-20 and its successor well under development in China would similarly 'energize' the American NGAD program fifty years later.

The J-20's key advantages over the F-22 and F-35 were primarily a result not of a greater state of Chinese technological advancement, but rather the Chinese defence sector's much greater ability to apply its latest technologies quickly and efficiently onto new platforms. This closely mirrored the advantages China's civilian industrial base and tech sector similarly enjoyed which had allowed them to become the world's largest. As a result, perhaps the greatest factor which would determine the NGAD's success in restoring an American air superiority advantage would be whether it could break out of the trends that had affected all the country's leading post-Cold War clean sheet weapons programs, particularly in aviation, to apply technologies without the numerous and severe performance bugs, delays and cost overruns which had plagued the B-2, F-22 and F-35. The J-20's successes, and what the precedent it set meant for China's future programs, including its sixth generation fighter, raised the stakes considerably and meant, unlike for the F-22 and F-35 which had faced no anticipated peer competition during development, there was far less room for the NGAD to similarly underperform.

The House Armed Services Committee was accordingly among multiple bodies to repeatedly raise concerns in the early 2020s that it was imperative for sixth generation programs to avoid key issues that had seriously affected the three major prior post-Cold War programs for manned combat jets the F-22, F-35, and the B-2 – namely 'unexpected cost growth' and 'run[ning] into problematic issues when they field the capabilities.' This went so far as the issuing of threats to cut off up to eighty-five per cent of funding to ensure sixth generation programs did not follow similar paths.[33] The House Appropriations Committee indicated that NGAD would likely be no less problematic than the F-35, and that investment in the older aircraft should be sustained accordingly. It highlighted the precedent of the F-35's delays and shortcomings which had forced the Navy to invest much more heavily than expected in continued acquisitions of its fourth generation predecessor the F-18, indicating that the F-35 would be heavily relied on as America's prime fighter well into the 2030s.[34]

As analysts at *The Drive* were among many to note in 2020 regarding the need for a very different approach to developing NGAD compared to the F-22 due to peer level challenges from Chinese fighter programs: 'The reality is that the sustainability of American air superiority over its peers has become so dire that there really isn't a choice. It's literally become a factor of change or die.'[35] They later observed in 2022 that any confidence the Pentagon had regarding its ability to tackle the J-20 appeared to have 'less to do with the jet's actual capabilities or how it might be employed,' and instead was based on its confidence in the capabilities which American sixth generation fighters were expected to bring to the field.[36] Similarly singling out the J-20 alone for mention, the monthly journal of the Air & Space Forces Association stressed that a sixth generation fighter was needed specifically to counter two threats – China's J-20 and new generations of ground-based air defences.[37] Discussing the J-20 specifically, Air Force Chief of Staff Charles Brown emphasized that the fighter could force the USAF to 'lose sleep' if the service failed to quickly field sixth generation capabilities, stressing that this was critical to 'maintain our advantage' in the face of Chinese advances.[38]

Commander of the Air Combat Command General Mark Kelly in October 2021 went as far as to compare NGAD to the Manhattan Project in its urgency and importance, stressing: 'I would like to have more of a sense of urgency and a whole-of-nation effort towards it.' The extent to which the U.S. Armed Forces relied on presumed air superiority to operate meant this was hardly an exaggeration. Due to the imminent nature of challenges to American air superiority, failing to do so would leave the USAF 'on the other side of coming in second in air superiority.'[39] Having warned nine months prior that the Chinese sixth generation fighter could be ready first,[40] Kelly reiterated that there remained uncertainty as to whether the U.S. would be the first to field a sixth generation fighter.[41] The complacency characteristic of the 1990s and 2000s had dissipated largely due to the J-20 program's successes not only in its performance, but in how quickly and cost effectively it had been developed, the rate at which the design had been enhanced post-service entry, and the rapid advances in Chinese industry and high tech which had supported it and were set to make future fighters far more formidable still.

On 1 June 2022 it was announced that the NGAD program had entered its engineering, manufacturing, and development (EMD) phase, with Air Force Secretary Frank Kendall announcing that the aircraft could be operational before 2030 and strongly emphasizing the need to induct it into service quickly.* The prime contractor for the NGAD program, or whether there would be one at all, was

---

* Regarding NGAD's accompanying 'wingman' UAVs Kendall pointed to the Ace Combat Evolution program developing artificial intelligence pilots for American fighters, and the Australian Airpower Teaming System program to develop a dedicated 'wingman' drone for future fighters, as examples of important developments underway.

not revealed,[42] although, fourteen months later it would emerge that Northrop Grumman had dropped out of the competition making it almost certain that Lockheed Martin would gain the position.[43] Analysts at the time highlighted that USAF plans to cut the number of planned operational squadrons, and begin very early retirements of the F-22, left 'a lot riding on' the NGAD program.[44] This made the potential fallout far greater should the program face even half the delays, defects and other performance issues that the F-35 had, leaving the U.S. at risk of ceding a significant air superiority advantage to China. With the Air Force having given up on plans to expand its fighter fleet, conceded to repeated failure in its effort to raise operational rates,[45] deeply cut the F-22 program, and produced F-35 at a fraction of initially planned rates, the NGAD may well have represented its last chance to reverse the trend towards relative decline in its position.

Four months after his announcement on the NGAD's progress to EMD, Secretary Kendall conceded that the program had only entered the EMD phase 'in my colloquial sense,' and that it was not in fact that far along in development.[46] Even had the program reached the next phase, this was far from a guarantee that it was on schedule. The F-35, a simpler fighter which could derive many of its most complex technologies from the already tried and tested F-22, had still taken fifteen years between the beginning of EMD, and its attaining of a limited initial operating capability in the Air Force. This precedent, and that of the similarly stalled F-22, indicated that the NGAD would not be operational until closer to 2040. Kendall's admission came just days after the head of the U.S. Air Combat Command General Mark Kelly warned that China was well positioned to begin fielding sixth generation fighters before the United States could, stating: 'I cannot tell you today what's going on in China except they're planning for their 20th National Party Congress [in October]. But I can tell you what's not happening. They're not having a debate over the relevance of six-gen air dominance. And I can also tell you they're on track.' Providing a sense of how close the race for a next generation fighter had become, he stated that the Air Force needed to 'make sure we get to six-gen air dominance at least a month prior to our competitors.'[47] The J-20's consistent far exceeding of expectations for its development and induction did much to explain American projections of how work on its successor would proceed.

In late June Secretary Kendall announced that NGAD would follow a more traditional course of development, and that highly ambitious plans to leverage new technologies to allow new air superiority fighter designs to enter service every few years, citing the precedent of the Century Series in the 1950s, had been dropped. 'The NGAD that we're working on now ... is going to take longer ... It's not a simple design ... [but a] long, hard job to build,' he elaborated.[48] The fighter was projected to cost several hundred million dollars per airframe, making it by far the most expensive in world history, which fuelled expectations that its induction would force further sharp contractions in the overall American manned combat fleet.[49] With major retirements of existing combat aircraft classes announced earlier that year largely from the higher operational cost F-22 and F-15 classes, and more following the next year which would help further reduce the USAF's annual operational expenses, Kendall stressed that this was part of a 'transformation that we're trying to achieve' that was primarily focused on preparing to potentially engage the Chinese PLA.[50] Such cuts, and major increases to the Air Force budget, were speculated to be seen as necessary to finance cutting edge programs such as the NGAD.

Weapons Programs to Counter the J-20

Beyond America's investments in sixth generation fighter development, the growing challenge posed by China's fast growth fifth generation capabilities and the J-20 in particular was a key factor influencing a number of further acquisitions decisions which could potentially bolster the U.S. Armed Forces' ability to counter adversary stealth fleets much sooner. In 2017 the U.S. Navy was reported to be considering integrating an infrared search and tracking system onto its F-18E/F Super Hornet fourth generation fighters to allow them to better engage low RCS targets. This was widely interpreted as a response to the J-20's entry into service earlier that year.[51] Severe delays integrating the F-35C into American carrier groups, and even greater delays bringing it up to a fully operational status, were other contributing factors.

In January 2022 it was announced that the U.S. Air Force would commission by far the most comprehensive set of upgrades ever applied to a portion of its F-22 fleet including belated integration of an infrared search and tracking system and upgrading of avionics to facilitate better sensor fusion, among other changes.[52] Addressing the F-22's very limited ability to network and share data with other assets, which was a major handicap in the era of network centric operations, was highlighted by USAF officers as central to planned upgrades. Options for addressing the F-22's lack of helmet-mounted sights, which was totally unique among modern fighters and left it at a tremendous disadvantage in visual range engagements, were by late 2022 still under consideration.[53] New software would also facilitate integration of the new AIM-260 air-to-air missile which was expected to bridge the performance gap with the J-20's PL-15.[54]

The J-20's primary combat advantages over the F-22 stemmed from its avionics and armaments – namely its much newer radar, distributed aperture system, helmet mounted sights and modern data links – which were technologies where the J-20 and F-35 were considered broadly on par. As noted in 2021 by F-22 pilot Captain Patrick Bowlds, who flew at simulated combat against F-35s, the F-35s 'have better detection capabilities kind of against everybody just because of their new radar and the avionics they have.' 'It definitely adds a level of complexity,' he observed.[55] While unmodernised Raptors were expected to face similar disadvantages against the J-20, bringing the F-22's avionics up to a similar level as the F-35 had the potential to restore the Raptor's position as America's most capable fighter for air superiority missions. Sensor fusion and IRSTs in particular were expected to address leading shortcomings that had long limited its ability to engage stealth targets – with helmet mounted sights also being particularly important due to the much higher chance of visual range engagements in clashes between opposing stealth aircraft. As the shortest ranged heavyweight fighter in the world, which long undermined its viability in the vast Pacific Theatre, reports of development of stealthy external pylons for fuel tanks were another welcome addition for the F-22.

The F-22's evolution differed greatly from projections made even in the late 2000s, with USAF Brigadier General Major Paul Moga, then an F-22 pilot, having stated in 2008: 'I would say based on all of the things I've read and all of the things I've heard, we are at least a couple of decades away from having to really face a significant or viable fifth generation threat. When that technology finally catches up to where the United States is today, guess what, the Raptor is going to evolve. The Raptor two decades from now that some kid's going to be flying, and I'm going to be sitting at my desk, is going to be nothing like the Raptor that's flying right now. It would kick the snot out of it.'[56] Projections at the time, one year before orders were given for termination of production, were that distributed aperture systems and helmet mounted sights would be among the upgrades the aircraft would receive. Had the F-22 followed the paths of the F-15 and the F-4 with a long production run ensuring updates to both the airframe and avionics, the J-20 would have had a far more formidable competitor. Where upgrades to the F-22 had long been seen as a guard against development of fifth generation fighters by adversaries, belated and semi-conservative upgrades to the fighter's avionics, were seen as an answer to the J-20.

With the F-22's maintenance requirements and other issues meaning it was still slated to be retired in the mid-2030s, the extent to which the USAF would be willing to invest heavily in modernising a large number of airframes from the mid-2020s remained in question. With an optimistic estimate being that close to 100 F-22s would be modernised to the new standard, by which time a fleet of over 500 J-20s with similarly advanced avionics would be operational, the USAF would not be able to back qualitative parity with quantity. The F-22's estimated much lower availability rates would only exacerbate this numerical disadvantage.

Beyond the F-22, efforts with much wider reaching implications were made to quickly improve the capabilities of the F-35 – a more straightforward task since the fighter was still in production. One of the most notable landmarks in this process was the confirmation in January 2023 that the fighter would receive a new radar, the AN/APG-85, which would cut the planned production of 3,000 preceding AN/APG-81 radars to a fraction of the number. With the J-20's Type 1475 radar thought to have significant advantages over the F-35's original radar, due its comparable sophistication, much larger size and estimated 25-37.5 per cent more transmitting/receiving modules, a new radar for the F-35 could go a long way towards bridging the gap. Delays in the F-35 program had allowed many new technologies to come of age since its radar was designed, with the AN/APG-85 expected to operationalise several of these which could significantly improve reliability, electronic warfare performance and situational awareness. Operationalising a Gallium Nitride based system provided one option to significantly ease conflict between signal strength and power usage. The new radar's developer Northrop Grumman described it as one which would 'help ensure air superiority,' providing some indication as to what primary arguments had been made to justify the program.[57]

Alongside a new radar, in the early 2020s a new engine for the F-35 was actively being considered to replace the troubled F135. The existing engine provided only half the energy that cooling the fighter required, had little hope of meeting projected near future electrical power requirements, and wore out quickly, which contributed to the fighter's low availability rates and high lifetime costs.[58] A new engine was expected to improve the fighter's flight performance and its range significantly while addressing these issues, thus bridging many of the performance gaps with the J-20. Nearer term enhancements to the F-35 focused both on increasing its firepower with 'sidekick' missile racks,[59] and on further enhancing its already world leading electronic warfare capabilities,[60] with the aircraft receiving enhancements at a much greater rate and with much more meaningful impacts on its performance than any other Western fighter class. The J-20's existence as a very potent rival fifth generation fighter provided perhaps the best argument for investments in major upgrades – an argument advocates of upgrading the F-22 during its production run had notably lacked resulting in relatively few changes throughout that period. This was particularly true for the AN/APG-85, since the already very capable AN/APG-81 was still relatively new and a fraction of the way through its planned production run.

With both U.S. and Chinese fifth generation fighter units consistently operating with support from AEW&C platforms, the J-20 was speculated to have also spurred investment in acquiring a new generation of these aircraft to increase situational awareness and provide a superior detection capability against the Chinese stealth aircraft. PACAF Commander General Kenneth Wilsbach notably stated in March 2022 regarding the first encounter between F-35s and J-20s that E-3 Sentry AEW&Cs in the region were suffering significant obsolescence issues, strongly implying that as a result during the encounter 'our early warning aircraft could not see the J-20.' 'Those sensors that we rely on the E-3 aren't really capable in the twenty-first-century, especially against a [stealth] platform like the J-20 or something similar to that. It just can't see those platforms far enough out to be able to provide an advantage to the shooters,'

Wilsbach elaborated, stressing that 'that's why I would like to have the E-7.' This was aside from maintenance issues which he emphasized seriously affected availability rates and often meant PACAF had no AEW&C capability at all.[61] The E-7 Wedgetail, boasting far superior electronics and sensors, was selected as the successor within a year of Wilsbach's statement. Funding for the aircraft was an unexpected new addition to the USAF's budget, with cuts to other programs expected to be made to fund the acquisition. The relatively sudden nature of the decision potentially indicated that it was made as a response to a new perceived threat.[62]

The J-20 program and the fighter's primary armament the PL-15 missile were also widely reported to be the primary factor stimulating investment in developing new radar guided air-to-air missiles in the United States, which could not only bridge the gap in range but also have more powerful sensors better able to lock on to stealth aircraft. The PL-15's apparent superiority was met with alarm by U.S. officials, with the head of the Air Force's Air Combat Command Herbert Carlisle remarking in September 2017: 'Look at our adversaries and what they're developing, things like the PL-15 and the range of that weapon ... How do we counter that and what are we going to do to continue to meet that threat?' He emphasised in an interview the following day: 'The PL-15 and the range of that missile, we've got to be able to out-stick that missile.'[63] Experts at *Aviation Week* described the PL-15 as having 'quickly provoked the U.S. Air Force to launch a new air-to-air missile program for the first time since the 1970s' – in reference to the AIM-260 missile program which officials directly referred to as a response to the PL-15.[64] With development initiated secretly in 2017 and announced in 2019, the American missile was expected to integrate an AESA radar for inertial guidance much as the PL-15 had done from 2015. As a less costly counterpart which could complete development more quickly, an improved AIM-120D variant, the AIM-120D3, was also prioritised for rapid development largely in response to the superiority the PL-15 had achieved over prior variants. This fitted in with official Air Force statements that the AIM-260, which was 'needed to remain ahead of adversary air threat investments,' was intended to complement, not replace, the AIM-120, likely due to the unaffordability of acquisitions in comparable numbers.[65] The AIM-120D3 was not considered on a par with the PL-15, but its disadvantages were less pronounced than previous AIM-120 models.

Responses Beyond the United States

Beyond the United States, the J-20 program and the very significant expansion in Chinese aerial warfare capabilities which it heralded provoked responses by many of the militaries which operated in East Asia. The Republic of China (RoC) Armed Forces, the official name of the armed forces of Taiwan which remain technically at war with the PLA and Chinese mainland, made multiple attempts to purchase F-35 fighters from the United States in the 2000s,[66] with these only accelerating the following decade as the J-20 program progressed faster. In September 2011, eight months after the J-20 made its first flight, RoC Deputy Minister of National Defence Andrew Yang visited the United States and reiterated that Taipei sought to acquire F-35s while continuing to upgrade its previously acquired F-16s.[67] As the J-20 program progressed far faster than anticipated, efforts by Taipei to acquire an aircraft of the same generation intensified. This mirrored renewed Taiwanese efforts in the 1990s to acquire American fourth generation fighters in response to the PLAAF's acquisition of its first Su-27s in 1991, which had brought the mainland fleet two generations forwards in sophistication.

Acquiring sophisticated armaments from America had since the 1970s been a far from straightforward process for Taipei, with the government based there having a status close to that of a non-state actor with its territory recognised by the United Nations and all UN member states including the United States as part of

China. With the Republic of China's own constitution asserting Taipei's jurisdiction over all Chinese territory, rather than over a separate state, this alongside Taipei's lack of any UN recognition only made arms sales more controversial. Under both the George W. Bush and the Barak Obama administrations the RoC was thus denied access to more modern variants of the F-16 – with even those approved for sale under George H.W. Bush in 1992 having been downgraded to Block 20 models with shorter ranges. Taipei renewed efforts to acquire F-35s almost immediately after the Donald Trump administration's inauguration, which oversaw an escalation in tensions with Beijing from late 2017.[68] A sale gained growing support in Washington as rhetoric against Beijing continued to escalate, with senators in early 2018 referring to it as a step to 'retain a democracy in the face of threats from China.'[69] The J-20 was frequently mentioned in both American and RoC arguments for supporting an F-35 sale.

By April 2018 it was evident that a Taiwanese F-35 acquisition would not materialise, with the significant possibility of the fighter's technologies being compromised to the PLA in particular leading Washington to refrain from granting approval. Republic of China Air Force (RoCAF) pilots had on multiple occasions defected to the Chinese mainland in Western aircraft, while strong pro-mainland sentiments among much of the population raised the possibility that any information the service had on the fighter would quickly be forwarded to Beijing.[70] The RoCAF subsequently moved to acquire modernised variants of the F-16, the F-16 Block 70/72, with an $8.2 billion contract for sixty-six aircraft signed in December 2019. By the time the last of the aircraft were expected to be delivered around 2030 the F-16 would have been operational in the USAF for fifty-two years, with the design increasingly described by U.S. and allied officials even in the 2010s as fast verging on obsolete.[71] The USAF had itself ceased acquisitions in 2005, and began drawing down its F-16 fleet in 2010.[72] This was only worsened by the significant delays the U.S. faced in producing the aircraft, with the terms of the contract ensuring that it would not face penalties for a late delivery.[73]

Taipei was by some estimates paying more per F-16s than the estimated flyaway cost of the J-20 despite the aircraft being well under half the size and a generation behind. The acquisition was generally seen by analysts in both Taiwan and the U.S. as far from cost effective for Taipei's defence needs, and was widely criticised as a politically motivated purchase since, unlike the F-35B the RoCAF had favoured, the F-16 could do relatively little in a Taiwan Strait war.[74] The purchase was highly beneficial to the United States, however, avoiding the risks of an F-35 sale while providing key funding for the opening of a new F-16 production line in Greenville, South Carolina, despite relatively limited demand for the old fighter elsewhere in the world. For the RoCAF the F-16 purchase would allow it to phase out its troubled French Mirage 2000 fighters, the newest and most expensive in its fleet, after over ten per cent of those delivered had crashed. France did not offer an upgrade package comparable to what the U.S. offered for the F-16, meaning there were few options to meaningfully improve the Mirage fleet even if there had been no such reliability issues, while poor production quality causing engine turbine blade cracks among other issues raised the Mirages' operational costs to around four times those of the F-16. The enhanced new F-16s, although falling far short of addressing the overwhelming disadvantages the RoCAF's top fighter units faced, would provide greater situational awareness against stealth targets and greater immunity to jamming by the PLAAF's own AESA radar-equipped fighters. They were also far more reliable and had far smaller logistical footprints and maintenance needs than the F-35A would have – let alone the particularly maintenance intensive F-35B.[75]

Despite the F-16 purchase, there were strong indications that the Taipei would continue to pursue an F-35 acquisition. At the hearing of the legislature's Foreign Affairs and National Defence Committee on 23 September, Republic of China Minister of National Defence

Yen De-fa stated regarding RoCAF modernisation plans: 'According to the military's projected threat assessment, we will need F-35s in the future.'[76] Questions regarding the J-20 and its capabilities largely dominated discussions. With advanced F-16 variants having been promoted as providing a 'path to the F-35,' namely by lowering resistance to an F-35 sale in Washington, there was considerable speculation that this had been an important motivation for Taipei to pursue the F-16 deal first.[77] The J-20 program's requirements had notably been partially premised on the need to comfortably outperform the F-35 in the expectation in the 1990s and early 2000s that these could potentially be fielded by the RoCAF from around 2015. The F-35 was at the time scheduled to enter USAF service in the late 2000s. The absence of these fighters at least until the 2030s effectively ensured the PLAAF's strong technological advantage in the air would only continue to grow.

Beyond Taiwan, eleven months after the J-20's first flight the Japanese government announced its intention to acquire forty-two F-35s in December 2011, with the PLAAF's move towards a fifth generation capability seen to have been a major factor in the decision. In 2018 Japan expanded its order to 147 F-35s, meaning they would form the backbone of the country's fighter fleet for decades to come. In the two preceding generations Japan had relied on the F-4 and F-15 heavyweight twin engine fighters to form the majority of its combat fleet, but after being prevented from acquiring their natural successor the F-22 by a congressional export ban, the lighter single engine F-35 emerged as effectively the country's only option to avoid falling a generation behind. Where the heavyweight F-4 and F-15 had each been leaders in their respective eras in flight performance, altitude ceiling, endurance, missile payload and radar size, the F-35's status as a lower end single engine aircraft within its own generation led many analysts to equate the shift towards it with a relative decline in the standing of Japanese air power.

To field a fully peer level aircraft to the J-20 that was similarly well optimised to air-to-air engagements, Japan moved in the 2010s towards developing its own twin engine stealth fighter, and flew a technology demonstrator between April 2016 and March 2018. Named the Mitsubishi Shinshin X2, the aircraft notably used indigenous engines. After indigenous derivatives of the Eurofighter, F-15 and F-22 were all considered but rejected, the Mitsubishi F-X was pursued as a clean sheet stealth fighter program. The J-20 was widely credited with having accelerated this process and shaped program requirements towards a fully fifth generation fighter optimised for air superiority.[78] Limited means and experience, however, resulted in Japan merging the F-X with the British-Swedish-Italian Tempest program in 2022 – a decision again widely seen as likely to have been heavily influenced by the J-20 program's success and what it signified regarding the future potential of China's military aviation sector.[†]

For two of China's other neighbours, India and Vietnam, which had significant territorial disputes with Beijing, the J-20 program was expected to influence their decisions regarding fifth generation fighter acquisitions. Vietnamese media outlets reported on multiple occasions, beginning in 2017, that the country was planning to acquire Russian Su-57 fighters in the late 2020s or early 2030s,

---

[†] Alongside the United States, European NATO members would increasingly deploy their F-35s for exercises in the Pacific, including on Japanese territory – a notable example being Italy's first F-35 deployment to Japan in August 2023. Japan would also provide Germany with information on F-35 operations as the country prepared to begin receiving the fighters from the United States in 2026, with Berlin expected to deploy its F-35s to the Pacific after having begun to do so with older fighters from 2022. As the United States perceived growing challenges to its military dominance in the Pacific from China, European states would make increasing contributions to attempting to sustain a Western-favouring balance of power in the region of which F-35 deployments were one of the most significant examples.

although the J-20 was seldom mentioned as the specific reason for this. India meanwhile, despite withdrawing in 2018 from a complex program to develop a new Su-57 variant and purchase joint ownership of its constituent technologies, was still considered likely to acquire the fighters either from Russian production lines or for license production domestically as it had with the Su-30 and multiple Cold War era fighter classes beforehand.[79] The J-20 program's rapid progress was cited by Indian analysts and foreign experts on Indian defence as an impetus to accelerate plans for such acquisitions.[80] The Chinese fighter's development was also thought to have influenced India's decision to sign a $5.3 billion contract for Russian S-400 air defence systems in 2018, which were designed specifically to be able to counter stealth aircraft such as F-22s.

The J-20's Challenge to Western Perceptions of Chinese High Tech

The J-20 was widely disparaged in Western commentaries after its unveiling, and following a longstanding trend in Western coverage of and attitudes towards Chinese weapons programs analysts and commentators widely claimed the fighter was a copy of or heavily based on the technologies of various other aircraft. These included, among others, the F-22, F-35, MiG 1.42, the pre-fifth generation F-117 and MiG-31, and perhaps most impossibly the French Rafale and pan-European Eurofighter.[81] With the F-22 being a longstanding symbol of American and Western primacy, and the Western world very widely described by experts as being in denial regarding China's emerging technological and economic parity,[82] the J-20's emergence as a direct Chinese equivalent to the Raptor was rationalised by claims that it must have been based on Western designs and technologies. This closely resembled the Western responses to the fighter's predecessor the J-10, which despite having been a far less remarkable achievement for its time and having clear roots in the

1960s J-9 program was very widely claimed in the West to be a copy of the cancelled Israeli Lavi combat jet. This was despite the Israeli jet having been much smaller and designed as a ground attack jet rather than an air superiority focused multirole fighter.

The J-10's airframe was approximately forty per cent larger than that of the Lavi, with the percentage difference in size being double that between the F-15 and F-18C/D while the difference in role was significantly greater. The fact that the Chinese fighter's WS-10B engine had over 160 per cent the power of the Lavi's PW1120, a tremendous difference even for fighters of different generations, should alone have been sufficient to debunk claims that one fighter was based on the other. The Lavi's weaker engine was a result not only of its much smaller size, but also its role primarily as a ground attack and close air support aircraft with only a limited secondary air-to-air capability.[83] Where the J-10 was in broadly the same class of aircraft as the F-16, the Lavi, when considered for marketing to the U.S. Air Force, was to be pitched as a successor to the A-10 attack jet accordingly.[84] With China's military aviation sector contradicting the longstanding metanarrative in the West casting the country as uninnovative in the extreme, such explanations as the J-10 being a Lavi derivative, or the J-20 being an F-22 copy, fit in with this narrative and were accordingly widely believed and propagated despite their tenuous nature.

The J-20 was a more unique aircraft than the J-10 had been, and while as the first non-American stealth fighter its commonalities with the F-22 and F-35 were quickly used by a wide range of Western sources to claim it had to be based on illicitly obtained American technologies, this was a result of the universal scientific rules of stealth technologies. There were only so many ways to shape a fighter to benefit from a high kinematic performance while minimising its radar cross section – a very finite combination of edge alignments, chines, serrations, canted control surfaces, blended wing configurations, and intake geometry. With this being considered, the J-20's appearance was more distinct from American aircraft than the stealth fighters designed by any other country.

Entrenched but increasingly outdated perceptions in the West of Chinese high tech, which drew on decades-old stereotypes of both East Asian and communist states, appeared to strongly influence many assessments of the J-20's capabilities, resulting in the aircraft consistently being underestimated. The rapid growth in the fighter's capabilities and those of its surrounding network, and the expected capabilities of future Chinese fighters which took many of the same technologies further, may well thus come as a very nasty surprise to Chinese adversaries when tested in combat. This would not be without precedent, with Chinese high tech having claimed one 'Sputnik moment' after another from the early 2010s in areas ranging from 5G to hypersonic glide vehicles to the consistent surprise of Western analysts.

The J-20's direct and most thoroughly combat tested predecessor in the role of the PLAAF's top air superiority fighter, the MiG-15, notably set a precedent in seriously challenging, and eventually shattering, the prevailing metanarrative in the West surrounding the industry which produced it. As USAF Lieutenant Colonel Earl J. McGill observed regarding the state of affairs before MiG saw combat in Korea: 'Looking back, it seems remarkable that apparently no one in the West took the MiG-15 seriously … Although it made its world debut at the Tushino Air Show, the initial response was to largely dismiss the airplane as sub-standard. Even its NATO designation, Fagot (a worthless bundle of sticks), reflected the West's initial attitude toward the jet fighter. However, when the MiG-15 appeared in the skies over Korea, disinterest turned to shock and awe.'[85] *Aviation Age* was among the sources to highlight that the MiG-15's performance was evidence that Soviet aircraft designers were 'the exact antithesis to what most Americans would expect in a Communist state,'[86] with American journalist I.F. Stone highlighting 'growing awareness' among industry experts 'that the planes encountered in the skies over Korea were not mere models copied or stolen from the West by designers sweating it out in fear of the secret police.'[87] The extent to which the J-20 and China's defence sector were being disparaged, and the multiple indicators of a very high performance, mean the fighter could well have a similar impact should it ever see combat. The rate at which successive J-20 variants have improved relative to competing fighter programs overseas mean that the later the variant that is deployed, the greater its standing against rivals will likely be.

Much as the F-22 was seen as the most widely recognised and potent symbol of unchallenged American military primacy, entering service as it did in 2005 with no rival program even at prototype stage, the J-20 program's fast and successful evolution and position as a leading contender for the title of the world's top fighter reflected the geopolitical trends of its time. The J-20A that entered production from 2019 was the first fighter to meet all operational criteria for the fifth generation. Where the F-35 could not supercruise, the F-22 could not fire high off boresight shots, use infrared sensors or operate properly as part of a broader network, and the Su-57's stealth capabilities were relatively limited and its supercruise capabilities uncertain, the J-20A had none of these issues.

The PLAAF's fielding of a large fleet of heavyweight fifth generation fighters was expected to have a significant strategic implications for China's relations with its neighbours and particularly with the United States. A USAF presentation in 2009 stated that: 'Fifth generation fighters like the F-22A and the F-35 are key elements of our Nation's defence and ability for deterrence. As long as hostile nations recognise that U.S. airpower can strike their vital centres with impunity, all other U.S. Government efforts are enhanced, which reduces the need for military confrontation.'[88] The J-20 program not only ended this American advantage, but alongside parallel similarly rapid capability advances across the PLA it also increased China's ability to deter provocation or intervention in hotspots in Chinese claimed territories in the Taiwan Strait and South and East China seas. While Lockheed Martin Aeronautics President James A. Blackwell contended in 1997 that the firm's new fighter was so capable that 'the first thing the F-22 will kill is the enemy's appetite for war,' the J-20 could well do much the same across multiple key hotspots.[89]

The prestige of being in a league of its own with the United States in developing one of the most complex and iconic kinds of weapons platforms, with the first J-20 regiment assembled an estimated seven years before any third country's fifth generation fighter would achieve the same, was a further not inconsiderable benefit. One of the many manifestations of this was in popular media, and much like the F-22 far more than other American fighters was celebrated with considerable screen time in major pictures of the late 2000s, from *Iron Man* to *TransFormers*, so too was the J-20 made an icon in Chinese films of the late 2010s and early 2020s such as *Sky Hunter* and *Wandering Earth II*. The fighter was even made the heart of its own film in 2023, *Born to Fly*, receiving treatment widely compared to that Hollywood had given America's most prestigious Cold War era fighter the F-14 with *Top Gun* in 1986.

The development of Chinese military soft power and cultivation of the PLA's image as a world leading force had potential implications beyond China's borders, with the J-20 being its most potent and recognisable icon. Indeed, as early as 2011 Taiwanese experts predicted that the J-20's success, alongside development of an array of capable support platforms such as the KJ-500, would transform the Asia Pacific's political landscape, and that the appeal of China's military strength would significantly increase the attractiveness of partnerships with Beijing in neighbouring countries.[90] The J-20 is thus expected to continue to play a central role in transforming narratives surrounding Chinese military capabilities not only among potential adversaries, but also potential partners.

Endnotes

Chapter 1

1. Li, Xiaobing, *China's Battle for Korea: The 1951 Spring Offensive*, Bloomington, Indiana University Press, 2014 (p. 11); Hanley, Charles J., *Ghost in Flames: Life & Death in a Hidden War, Korea 1950-53*, New York, Public Affairs, 2020 (p. 31).
2. Salisbury, Harrison E., *The New Emperors: China in the Era of Mao and Deng*, New York, Avon Books, 1992 (p. 106).
3. Testimony of Dean Acheson, Hearings held in executive session before the U.S. Senate Foreign Relations Committee during 1949-1950 (p. 23); Truman, Harry S., *Memoirs, Volume Two: Years of Trial and Hope, 1946-1953*, New York, Doubleday & Company, 1956 (p. 66); Harris Smith, Richard, *OSS: The Secret History of America's First Central Intelligence Agency*, Berkley, University of California Press, 1972 (pp. 259-282); Fleming, Denna Frank, *The Cold War and its Origins, 1917-1960*, Crows Nest, Allen and Unwin, 1961 (p. 570); Tuchman, Barbra W., *Sitwell and the American Experience in China 1911–1945*, London, Macmillan, 1970 (pp. 666-677); 'Letter to Congressman Hugh de Lacy of State of Washington,' *Congressional Record*, 24 January 1946, Appendix, vol. 92, part 9 (p. A225).
4. Epstein, Israel, *My China Eye: Memoirs of a Jew and a Journalist*, San Francisco, Long River Press, 2005 (p. 251); Bodenheimer, Thomas and Gould, Robert, *Rollback!: Right-wing Power in U.S. Foreign Policy*, Boston, South End, 1989 (p. 18); Philips, Steve, *The Cold War: Conflict in Europe and Asia*, Oxford, Heinemann, 2001 (pp. 71-72); Spurr, Russel, *Enter the Dragon: China's Undeclared War Against the U.S. in Korea, 1950-1951*, New York, William Morrow, 2010 (p. 106).
5. Appleman, Roy E., *South to the Naktong, North to the Yalu: United States Army in the Korean War*, Washington DC, Department of the Army, 1998 (p. 755).
6. Hanley, Charles J., *Ghost in Flames: Life & Death in a Hidden War, Korea 1950-53*, New York, Public Affairs, 2020 (pp. 144-145).

7. Li, Xiaobeing, *China's Battle for Korea: The 1951 Spring* Offensive, Bloomington, Indiana University Press, 2014 (p. 68); Futrell, Robert F., *The United States Air Force in Korea 1950-1953*, Washington DC, Office of Air Force History, 1983 (p. 339).

8. Stokesbury, James L., *A Short History of the Korean War*, New York, William Morrow, 1998 (pp. 55-56).

9. Hanley, Charles J., *Ghost in Flames: Life & Death in a Hidden War, Korea 1950-53*, New York, Public Affairs, 2020 (p. 267).

10. *Ibid* (p. 268).

11. Li, Xiaobeing, *China's Battle for Korea: The 1951 Spring* Offensive, Bloomington, Indiana University Press, 2014 (pp. 61, 69).

12. Futrell, Robert Frank, *The United States Air Force in Korea, 1950-1953*, Washington DC, Office of Air Force History, 1983 (pp. 689-690); Williams, William J., *A Revolutionary War: Korea and the Transformation of the Postwar World*, Chicago, Imprint, 1993 (pp. 144-145); Shen, Zonghong et al., 中国人民志愿军抗美援朝战士, [*A History of the War to Resist America and Assist Korea by the Chinese People's Volunteers*], Beijing, Military Science Press, 1988 (p. 319).

13. Li, Xiaobeing, *China's Battle for Korea: The 1951 Spring* Offensive, Bloomington, Indiana University Press, 2014 (p. 121); Hanley, Charles J., *Ghost in Flames: Life & Death in a Hidden War, Korea 1950-53*, New York, Public Affairs, 2020 (pp. 269, 280).

14. *Ibid* (p. 421).

15. *Washington Post*, 14 May 1952.

16. *News and World Report*, 15 December 1950.

17. Stone, I.F., *Hidden History of the Korean War*, Boston, Little, Brown and Company, 1988 (p. 341).

18. McGill, Earl J., *Black Tuesday Over Namsi: B-29s vs MiGs – The Forgotten Air Battle of the Korean War*, Solihull, Helion & Company, 2012 (Chapter 4: The Machinery of War).

19. *Ibid* (Chapter 9: Analysis, Conclusions and Reflections).

20. Hanley, Charles J., *Ghost in Flames: Life & Death in a Hidden War, Korea 1950-53*, New York, Public Affairs, 2020 (p. 358).

21. Appleman, Roy E., *Escaping the Trap: The U.S. Army X Corps in Northeast Korea, 1950*, College Station, A&M University Press, 1990 (pp. 367-368); Hastings, Max, *Korean War*, London, Michael Joseph, 1988 (p. 170).

22. Chan, Minnie, 'China's air force turns 70 with tales of its dare-to-die Korean war pilots,' *South China Morning Post*, 10 November 2019.

23. *Ibid*.

24. McGill, Earl J., *Black Tuesday Over Namsi: B-29s vs MiGs – The Forgotten Air Battle of the Korean War*, Solihull, Helion & Company, 2012 (Chapter 9: Analysis, Conclusions and Reflections).

25. Hanley, Charles J., *Ghost in Flames: Life & Death in a Hidden War, Korea 1950-53*, New York, Public Affairs, 2020 (p. 269).

26. *Ibid* (p. 375); Zhang, Xiaoming, *Red Wings over the Yalu: China, the Soviet Union, and the Air War in Korea*, College Station, Texas A&M University Press, 2003 (p. 132).

27. Joiner, Stephen, 'The Jet that Shocked the West, How the MiG-15 grounded the U.S. bomber fleet in Korea,' *Air & Space Magazine*, December 2013.

28. Stone, I.F., *Hidden History of the Korean War*, Boston, Little, Brown and Company, 1988 (p. 339).

29. Ridgway, Matthew B., *The Korean War*, Garden City, Doubleday, 1967 (p. 186).

30. Nash, Chris, *What is Journalism? The Art and Politics of a Rupture*, London, Palgrave Macmillan, 2016 (p. 91).

31. *New York Times*, 20 January 1952.

32. *Aviation Week*, 17 December 1951; *New York Daily Compass*, 3 January 1952.

33. Stone, I.F., *Hidden History of the Korean War*, Boston, Little, Brown and Company, 1988 (p. 434).

34. Hanley, Charles J., *Ghost in Flames: Life & Death in a Hidden War, Korea 1950-53*, New York, Public Affairs, 2020 (p. 359); Associated Press, 14 February 1952.

35. Hanley, Charles J., *Ghost in Flames: Life & Death in a Hidden War, Korea 1950-53*, New York, Public Affairs, 2020 (p. 350); Associated Press, 2 February 1952.

37. *New York Times*, 20 January 1952.

38. Hanley, Charles J., *Ghost in Flames: Life & Death in a Hidden War, Korea 1950-53*, New York, Public Affairs, 2020 (p. 348).

39. Xu, Yan, 第一次较量：抗美援朝战争的历史回顾与反思 [*The First Test of Strength: A Historical Review and Evaluation of the War to Resist America and Assist Korea*], Beijing Chinese Broadcasting and Television Press, 1990 (p. 207); Qi, Dexue et al., 'Enlightenment on Defeating a Strong Enemy with Inferior Weapons and Equipment in the Korean War,' 军事历史 [*Military History*], no. 6, 1999 (p. 33).

40. Stone, I.F., *Hidden History of the Korean War*, Boston, Little, Brown and Company, 1988 (p. 343).

41. *Ibid* (p. 344).

42. *New York Times*, 9 December 1951; Stone, I.F., *Hidden History of the Korean War*, Boston, Little, Brown and Company, 1988 (p. 344).

43. *Washington Post*, 22 May 1952.

44. Bruning Jr., John R., *Crimson Sky: The Air Battle for Korea*, Dulles, Brassey's, 1999 (p. xiv); Crane, Conrad C., *American Airpower Strategy in Korea, 1950-1953*, Lawrence, University Press of Kansas, 2000 (p. 107).

45. Bruning Jr., John R., *Crimson Sky: The Air Battle for Korea*, Dulles, Brassey's, 1999 (p. xiv).

46. Zhang, Xiaoming, *Red Wings over the Yalu: China, the Soviet Union, and the Air War in Korea*, College Station, Texas A&M University Press, 2003 (p. 201).

47. Wang Dinglie et al., 当代中国空军 [*China's Current Air Force*], Beijing, China Social Science Press, 1989 (pp. 208, 209).

48. *Ibid* (p. 210).

49. *Ibid* (p. 210).

50. Zhang, Lin and Ma, Changzhi, 中国元帅徐向前 [*Chinese Marshal Xu Xiangqian*], Beijing, Communist Party of China Central Academy Press, 1995 (p. 404).

51. Hastings, Max, *Korean War*, London, Michael Joseph, 1988 (p. 170).

52. Ham, Paul, *Hiroshima Nagasaki: The Real Story of the Atomic Bombings and their Aftermath*, New York, Doubleday, 2012 (pp. 488–490).

53. Harvey, Ian, 'FBI Files Reveal Winston Churchill's Secret Bid to Nuke Russia to Win Cold War,' *War History Online*, 17 November 2014.

54. Acheson, Dean G., *Present at the Creation: My Years in the State Department*, London, W.W. Norton, 1969 (pp. 463-464); Far Eastern Air Forces HQ to MacArthur, 8 November 1950, RG 6 Far East Command, Box 1, General Files 10, Correspondence Nov-Dec 1950, MacArthur Memorial Library, Norfolk VA.

55. Jackson, Robert, *Air War Over Korea*, London, Ian Allen, 1973 (p. 61).

56. Harden, Blaine, 'The U.S. war crime North Korea won't forget,' *Washington Post*, 24 March 2015.

57. Thames Television, transcript for the fifth seminar for: *Korea: The Unknown War*, November 1986.

58. LeMay, Curtis and Cantor, MacKinley, *Mission with LeMay*, New York, Doubleday, 1965 (p. 382).

59. Wilson, Ward, 'The Bomb Didn't Beat Japan ... Stalin Did,' *Foreign Policy*, 30 May 2017.

60. Truman, Margaret, *Harry S. Truman*, New York, William Morrow & Company, 1973 (pp. 495–496); 'USE OF A-BOMB IN KOREA STUDIED BY U.S. – TRUMAN,' *Pittsburgh Press*, 30 November 1950 (p. 1); The President's New Conference, 30 November 1950, The American Presidency Project, University of California at Santa Barbara.

61. 'Thaw in the Koreas?' *Bulletin of Atomic Scientists*, vol. 48, no. 3, April 1992 (pp. 18, 19); Weintraub, Stanley, *MacArthur's War: Korea and the Undoing of an American Hero*, New York, Free Press, 2000 (p. 263); Millet, Alan R., *Their War for Korea*, Washington DC, Brassey's, 2002 (p. 169).

62. Grosscup, Beau, *Strategic Terror: The Politics and Ethics of Aerial Bombardment*, London, Zed Books, 2013 (Chapter 5: Cold War Strategic Bombing: From Korea to Vietnam, Part 4: The Bombing of Korea); Levine, Alan J., *Stalin's Last War; Korea and the Approach to World War III*, Jefferson, McFarland & Company, 2005 (pp. 278, 280)

63. Pape, Robert A., *Bombing to Win; Air Power and Coercion in War*, Ithaca, Cornell University Press, 1996 (p. 146).

64. Dingman, Roger, *Atomic Diplomacy during the Korean War*, Cambridge, The MIT Press, 1988 (pp.75-76); Adams, Sherman, *Firsthand Report: The Inside Story of the Eisenhower Administration*, London, Hutchinson, 1962 (p. 102); Eisenhower, Dwight D., *The White House Years: Mandate for Change, 1953-1956*, New York, Doubleday, 1963 (pp. 179-180).

65. Wang, Yan, 彭德怀转 [*Biography of Peng Dehuai*], Beijing, Today's China Press, 1993 (pp. 502, 506).

66. Journal of the American Intelligence Professional, unclassified articles from: *Studies in Intelligence*, vol. 57, no. 3, September 2013 (pp. 22-28).

67. 'Two CIA Prisoners in China, 1952–1973,' Website of the Central Intelligence Agency, News & Information, 5 April 2007.

68. 'Idaho Crash Reveals Secret U-2 Training of Chinese,' *New York Times*, 30 August 1964; 'Pilotless U.S. Plane Downed, China Says,' *New York Times*, 17 November 1964; Journal of the American Intelligence Professional, unclassified articles from: *Studies in Intelligence*, vol. 57, no. 3, September 2013 (pp. 22-28).

69. *Ibid* (p. 28).

70. *Ibid* (p. 28).

71. Rupprecht, Andreas, *Modern Chinese Warplanes: Chinese Air Force – Combat Aircraft and Units*, Houston, Harpia, 2018 (p. 17).

72. Kirby, William C., 'The Internationalization of China: Foreign Relations at Home and Abroad in the Republican Era,' *China Quarterly*, no. 150, June 1997 (p. 458).

73. Buttler, Tony and Gordon, Yefim, *Soviet Secret Projects: Fighters Since 1945*, Hinckley, Midland Publishing, 2005 (pp. 75-77, 80, 81, 92, 107); Mason, R.A. and Taylor, John W.R., *Aircraft, Strategy and Operations of the Soviet Air Force*, London, Jane's, 1986 (pp. 66, 134, 137); 'How Soviet Leader Nikita Khrushchev Let America Win the Race to Develop the Best Fighter Jets,' *Military Watch Magazine*, 9 February 2021; Lambeth, Benjamin S., *Russia's Air Power at the Crossroads*, Santa Monica, RAND, 1996 (pp. 33-34); Grinyuk, Dmitri and Butowski, Piotr, 'An Unusual Conversation at the Main Staff,' *Krylia Rodiny*, no. 11, November 1991.

74. Didly, Douglas C. and Thompson, Warren E., *F-86 Fabre vs MiG-15: Korea 1950-1953*, Oxford, Osprey, 2013 (p. 77).

75. Gao, Charlie, 'In 1971, Indian Mig-21's Beat Some American-Built F-104A Starfighters. Was It a Fluke?' *National Interest*, 5 August 2018.

76. 'How Soviet Leader Nikita Khrushchev Let America Win the Race to Develop the Best Fighter Jets,' *Military Watch Magazine*, 9 February 2021.

77. Lake, Jon, *Jane's How to Fly and Fight in the Mikoyan MiG-29 Fulcrum*, New York City, Harper Collins, 1998 (Introduction); Lake, Jon, *MiG-29: Soviet Superfighter*, London, Osprey, 1989 (p. 7).

78. Gordon, Yefim, *Sukhoi Su-27*, Hinckley, Midland Publishing, 2007 (p. 13); Farley, Robert, 'Why The F-15 Must Fear Russia's Su-27 Fighter,' *National Interest*, 1 February 2020; Gordon, Yefim and Komissarov, Dmitry, *Sukhoi Su-57*, Manchester, Hikoki Publications, 2021 (p. 7).

79. Gordon, Yefim, *Sukhoi Su-27*, Hinckley, Midland Publishing, 2007 (pp. 514-515).

80. *Ibid* (pp. 515-516).

81. *Ibid* (p. 514).

82. *Su-27 for DCS World*, Moscow, Eagle Dynamics, 2014 (p. 3).

83. Lake, Jon, *Su-27 Flanker: Sukhoi Superfighter*, London, Osprey, 1992 (p. 88).

84. Gordon, Yefim, *Sukhoi Su-27*, Hinckley, Midland Publishing, 2007 (pp. 6, 525); *Su-27 for DCS World*, Moscow, Eagle Dynamics, 2014 (p. 3); Lake, Jon, *Su-27 Flanker: Sukhoi Superfighter*, London, Osprey, 1992 (p. 111).

85. Gordon, Yefim, *Sukhoi Su-27*, Hinckley, Midland Publishing, 2007 (p. 25, 517).
86. *Ibid* (p. 519).
87. Gordon, Yefim and Davidson, Peter, *Sukhoi Su-27 Flanker*, North Branch, Specialty Press, 2006 (p. 18); Gordon, Yefim, *Sukhoi Su-27*, Hinckley, Midland Publishing, 2007 (pp. 517-518).
88. Lake, Jon, *Su-27 Flanker: Sukhoi Superfighter*, London, Osprey, 1992 (Introduction).
89. Gordon, Yefim and Davidson, Peter, *Sukhoi Su-27 Flanker*, North Branch, Specialty Press, 2006 (p. 22).
90. Lilley, James and Shambaugh, David L., *China's Military Faces the Future*, Abingdon, Routledge, 2015. (pp. 96-99); Lake, Jon, *Su-27 Flanker: Sukhoi Superfighter*, London, Osprey, 1992 (Introduction); Ilin, Vladimir, 'Air Bases of Russia: Lipetssk – One of the Aviation Centres of Russia,' Vestnik Vozdushnogo Flota, 14 March 1995, in: Foreign Broadcast Information Service Military Affairs 95-148-S, 14 March 1995.
91. Gordon, Yefim, *Sukhoi Su-27*, Hinckley, Midland Publishing, 2007 (p. 524).
92. *Department of Defense Appropriations for 2002: Hearings Before a Subcommittee of the Committee on Appropriations House of Representatives*, One Hundred and Seventh Congress, First Session, Subcommittee on Defense, Washington DC, U.S. Government Printing Office, 2004 (p. 813).
93. Lake, Jon, *Su-27 Flanker: Sukhoi Superfighter*, London, Osprey, 1992 (Introduction).
94. Gordon, Yefim, *Sukhoi Su-27*, Hinckley, Midland Publishing, 2007 (pp. 522-523).
95. *Ibid* (p. 522).
96. *Ibid* (pp. 533-534).
97. *Ibid* (pp. 531-534); Baldauf, Scott, 'Indian Air Force, in war games, gives US a run,' *Christian Science Monitor*, 28 November 2005.
98. 'Flashback: 1991 Gulf War,' *BBC News*, 20 March, 2003.
    'Sanctions Blamed for Deaths of Children,' *Lewiston Morning Tribune*, 2 December, 1995.
    Stahl, Lesley, 'Interview with Madeline Albright,' *60 Minutes*, 12 May, 1996.
99. Gons, Eric Stephen, *'Access Challenges and Implications for Airpower in the Western Pacific,'* Santa Monica, RAND, 2011 (pp. iii, 1).

100. Press, Daryl G., 'The Myth of Air Power in the Persian Gulf War and the Future of Warfare,' *International Security*, vol. 26, no. 2, October 2001 (pp. 5-44).

101. Khalilzad, Zalmay and Shapiro, Jeremy, *The United States Air and Space Power in the 21ˢᵗ Century*, Santa Monica, RAND, 2002 (Chapter Three).

102. 解放军报 (*Jiefangjun Bao*), 25 January 1991.

103. Biddle, Stephen, *Military Power: Explaining Victory and Defeat in Modern Battle*, Princeton, Princeton University Press, 2006 (p. 20); Cordesman, Anthony H., 'The Real Revolution in Military Affairs,' *Centre for Strategic and International Studies*, 5 August 2014.

104. 'Air-Sea Battle Doctrine: A Discussion with the Chief of Staff of the Air Force and Chief of Naval Operations,' *Brookings Institute*, 16 May 2012.

105. *The Mirror* (Hong Kong), 22 January 1991; Lam, Willy Wo-Lap, 'Iraq war hands lessons to China,' *CNN*, 15 April 2003.

106. Erickson, Amanda, 'The last time the U.S. was on "the brink of war" with North Korea,' *Washington Post*, 9 August 2017; Cumings, Bruce, *Korea's Place in the Sun*, New York, W.W. Norton and Company, 1997 (p. 428).

107. Schmitt, Eric, 'In a Fatal Error, C.I.A. Picked a Bombing Target Only Once: The Chinese Embassy,' *New York Times*, 23 July 1999; 'Truth behind America's raid on Belgrade,' *The Guardian*, 28 November 1999; Sweeney, John and Holsoe, Jens and Vulliamy, Ed, 'Nato bombed Chinese deliberately,' *The Guardian*, 17 October 1999.

108. 'An Economic Analysis of the Changes in China's Military Expenditure in the Last Ten Years,' *Jingji Yanjiu* [Economic Studies], no. 6, 20 June 1990 (pp. 77-81); Jencks, Harlan W., 'Chinese Evaluations of "Desert Storm": Implications for PRC Security,' *The Journal of East Asian Affairs*, vol. 6, no. 2, Summer/Fall 1992 (p. 462).

109. Foreign Broadcast Information Service Daily Report-China 90-153 (pp. 36-38); Jencks, Harlan W., 'Chinese Evaluations of "Desert Storm": Implications for PRC Security,' *The Journal of East Asian Affairs*, vol. 6, no. 2, Summer/Fall 1992 (p. 463).

110. *South China Morning Post*, 25 March 1991 (pp. 1, 11).

111. *Xinhua*, 16 March 1991; Foreign Broadcast Information Service Daily Report-China 91-054 (pp. 27-28); Jencks, Harlan W., 'Chinese Evaluations of "Desert Storm": Implications for PRC Security,' *The Journal of East Asian Affairs*, vol. 6, no. 2, Summer/Fall 1992 (p. 463).

112. *Ibid* (p. 463-465); Foreign Broadcast Information Service Daily Report-China, 91-041 (pp. 33-35); Luo Xiaobing, 'Strengthening National Defense Building Is Important Guarantee for Economic Development ...,' *Jiefangjun Bao*, 6 February 1991.
113. *Jiefangjun Bao*, 28 March 1991.
114. *Hong Kong Standard*, 16 April 1991; *Beijing Radio*, 16 April 1991; Jencks, Harlan W., 'Chinese Evaluations of "Desert Storm": Implications for PRC Security,' *The Journal of East Asian Affairs*, vol. 6, no. 2, Summer/Fall 1992 (p. 465).
115. Tyson, James L., 'Workers of the World, Compute: China Revamps Industry,' *Christian Science Monitor*, 16 July 1991 (p. 4).
116. Rupprecht, Andreas, *Modern Chinese Warplanes: Chinese Air Force – Combat Aircraft and Units*, Houston, Harpia, 2018 (pp. 37, 38).
117. International Institute for Strategic Studies, *The Military Balance*, Volume 103, 2003 (p. 115).
118. 'Aerospace Nation: Gen Kenneth S. Wilsbach,' *Mitchell Institute for Aerospace Studies* (YouTube Channel), 15 March 2022.

Chapter 2

1. Erickson, Andrew S. and Lu, Hanlu and Bryan, Kathryn and Septembre, Samuel, 'Research, Development, and Acquisition in China's Aviation Industry: The J-10 Fighter and Pterodactyl UAV,' *Study of Innovation and Technology in China: University of California Institute of Global Conflict and Cooperation*, no. 8, 2014.
2. Freedberg Jr., Sydney J., 'Chinese Air Force Tries Hard But Plays Catch-Up With US; Watch PLA Espionage,' *Breaking Defense*, 18 September 2012.
3. Pace, Steve, *F-22 Raptor: America's Next Lethal War Machine*, New York, McGraw Hill, 1999 (p. 7).
4. [See for cost cutting cancellation of F-22's IRST and side facing radars] Rogoway, Tyler, 'No, The Su-57 Isn't "Junk": Six Features We like On Russia's New Fighter,' *The Drive*, 20 April 2018.
5. Davies, Peter E. and Thornborough, Tony, *McDonnell Douglas F-15 Eagle*, Ramsbury, Crowood Press, 2001 (p. 164).
6. Younossi, Obaid et al., *Lessons Learned from the F/A-22 and F/A-18E/F Development Programs*, Santa Monica, RAND, 2005 (p. 4); Niemi, Christopher J., 'The F-22 Acquisition Program: Consequences for the US Air Force's Fighter Fleet,' *Air & Space Power Journal*, vol. 26, no. 6, November-December 2012 (pp. 53-82).

7. Vartabedian, Ralph and Hennigan, W.J., 'F-22 program produces few planes, soaring costs,' *Los Angeles Times*, 16 June 2013.

8. *Ibid.*

9. *F-22 Pilot Physiological Issues: Hearing Before the Subcommittee on Tactical Air and Land Forces of the Committee on Armed Services House of Representatives*, One Hundred and Twelfth Congress, Second Session, Hearing on 13 September 2012, Washington DC, U.S. Government Printing Office, 2013 (p. 63).

10. O'Hanlon, Michael E., 'The Plane Truth: Fewer F-22s Mean a Stronger National Defense,' *Brookings Institute*, 1 September 1999; Battle Stations, Season 1, Episode 39, F-22 Raptor.

11. Wheeler, Winslow, 'What does an F-22 Cost?' *Project on Government Oversight*, 30 March 2009.

12. Hollings, Alex, 'From High Operating Costs to Low Production Run: all the Shortfalls that Killed the F-22 Raptor Programme,' *The Aviation Geek Club*, 17 March 2021; 'How much cheaper is the F-15EX compared to the F-35?' *Sandboxx*, 7 February 2022.

13. Axe, David, 'Hangar Queens! The U.S. Air Force's Old F-15s Keep Flying While Newer F-22s Sit Idle,' *Forbes*, 19 May 2020; Everstine, Brian W., 'Breaking Down USAF's 70-Percent Overall Mission Capable Rate,' *Air Force Magazine*, 19 May 2020.

14. Niemi, Christopher J., 'The F-22 Acquisition Program: Consequences for the US Air Force's Fighter Fleet,' *Air & Space Power Journal*, vol. 26, no. 6, November-December 2012 (p. 65).

15. 'Documents show Air Force neglected concerns about F-22 pilot safety,' *Public Integrity*, 27 September 2012; Axe, David, 'US Stealth Jets Choking Pilots at Record Rates,' *Wired*, 14 June 2012; Axe, David, 'Air Force to Stealth Fighter Pilots: Get Used to Coughing Fits,' *Wired*, 25 February 2013; Fabey, Michael, 'USAF Deciphers "Mosaic" Of F-22 Oxygen Supply Problems,' *Aviation Week*, 1 August 2012; 'Air force pilots describe health problems from flying F-22 jet,' *CBS News* (YouTube Channel), 7 May 2012.

16. 'F-22 avionics designers rely on obsolescent electronics, but plan for future upgrades,' *Military Aerospace*, 1 May 2001; Everstine, Brian W., 'The F-22 and the F-35 Are Struggling to Talk to Each Other … And to the Rest of USAF,' *Air Force Magazine*, 29 January 2018.

17. Vartabedian, Ralph and Hennigan, W.J., 'F-22 program produces few planes, soaring costs,' *Chicago Tribune*, 16 June 2013.

18. Gertler, Jeremiah, *Air Force F-22 Fighter Program*, Washington D.C., Congressional Research Service Report for Congress, 11 July 2013.

19. 'Air Force Chief Hints at Retiring the F-22 Raptor in Fighter Downsize,' *Military.com*, 12 May 2021; Newdick, Thomas, 'Yes, It's True, The F-22 Isn't In The Air Force Chief's Future Fighter Plans,' *The Drive*, 13 May 2021.

20. 'USAF: F-22 to Be Phased-Out Within Next Decade,' *The Defense Post*, 21 May 2021.

21. Gertler, Jeremiah, *Air Force F-22 Fighter Program*, Washington D.C., Congressional Research Service Report for Congress, 11 July 2013; Tirpak, John A., 'Most USAF Fighter Mission Capable Rates Rise in Fiscal 2020, Led by F-35,' *Air Force Magazine*, 24 May 2021; Rogoway, Tyler, 'F-22 Being Used To Test Next Generation Air Dominance "Fighter" Tech,' *The Drive*, 26 April 2022.

22. 'Why the F-35's Low Altitude Ceiling is a Major Drawback: Adversaries Will Almost Always Strike From Above,' *Military Watch Magazine*, 4 August 2023.

23. Tirpak, John A., 'USAF to Cut F-35 Buy in Future Years Defense Plan,' *Air Force Magazine*, 14 May 2021; 'Major Cuts to F-35 Orders Under Consideration: Air Force Chief Wants a Simpler "4+ Generation" Fighter to Replace It,' *Military Watch Magazine*, 19 February 2021.

24. Venable, John, 'Air Force's math on the F-15EX and F-35 doesn't add up,' *Breaking Defense*, 19 April 2022; Emmott, Robin, 'Belgium picks Lockheed's F-35 over Eurofighter on price,' *Reuters*, 25 October 2018; 'American Products More Cost Effective: Kuwaiti Parliament Protests Eurofighter's Exorbitant Price,' *Military Watch Magazine*, 29 June 2020; 'F-35 vs. Rafale: Does America or France Have the Better Production Fighter?' *Military Watch Magazine*, 5 March 2022; Roblin, Sebastien, 'F-35A Jet Price To Rise, But It's Sustainment Costs That Could Bleed Air Force Budget Dry,' *Forbes*, 31 July 2021.

25. Tirpak, John A., 'All For One and All for All,' *Air Force Magazine*, 14 March 2016; Axe, David, 'The F-35 Stealth Fighter's Dirty Little Secret Is Now Out in the Open,' *National Interest*, 15 May 2016.

26. Drusch, Andrea, 'Fighter plane cost overruns detailed,' *Politico*, 16 February 2014.

27. Grazier, Dan, 'Why the F-35 Isn't Ready for War,' *National Interest*, 20 March 2019.

28. Reim, Garrett, 'Lockheed Martin F-35 has 873 deficiencies,' *Flight Global*, 31 January 2020.

29. Grazier, Dan, 'F-35 Design Flaws Mounting, New Document Shows,' *Project on Government Oversight*, 11 March 2020.

30. Guertin, Nickolas H., 2022 Office of the Director, Operational Test and Evaluation Annual Report, January 2023 (p. 62).

31. Grazier, Dan, 'Deceptive Pentagon Math Tries to Obscure $100 Million+ Price Tag for F-35s,' *Project on Government Oversight*, 1 November 2019.

32. Vartabedian, Ralph and Hennigan, W.J., 'F-22 program produces few planes, soaring costs,' *Los Angeles Times*, 16 June 2013.

33. Thomson, Laura, 'The ten most expensive military aircraft ever built,' *Air Force Technology*, 30 May 2019; Liu, Zhen, 'J-20 vs F-22: how China's Chengdu J-20 "Powerful Dragon" compares with US' Lockheed Martin F-22 Raptor,' *South China Morning Post*, 28 July 2018; 'PLA's J-20 fighters years away from mass production,' *Asia Times*, 31 July 2018.

34. Gould, Joe and Insinna, Valerie, 'Ripping F-35 costs, House Armed Services chairman looks to "cut our losses",' *Defense News*, 5 March 2021.

35. 'Technical Challenges Delay Mass Production of F-35 Stealth Fighter Yet Again,' *Military Watch Magazine*, 3 January 2021; 'America's F-35 Stealth Fighter Delayed From Full-scale Production Again,' *Military Watch Magazine*, 30 October 2020; 'Full-scale F-35 Production Further Delayed: Fighter Suffers More Breakdowns Than Expected – Pentagon,' *Military Watch Magazine*, 15 November 2019.

36. Capaccio, Anthony, 'Pentagon Cuts Its Request for Lockheed's F-35s by 35%,' *Bloomberg*, 17 March 2022.

37. Tirpak, John A., 'F-35 Production Challenged to Keep Up with Demand,' *Air & Space Forces*, 3 July 2023.

38. 'Thunder Without Lightning, The High Costs and Limited Benefits of the F-35 Program,' *National Security Network*, August 2015.

39. Axe, David, 'Pentagon's big budget F-35 fighter "can't turn, can't climb, can't run",' *Reuters*, 14 July 2014.

40. Grazier, Dan, 'F-35 Continues to Stumble,' *Project on Government Oversight*, 30 March 2017.

41. Roy, Ananya, 'F-35 jets have over 200 deficiencies, unlikely to be combat ready by 2018-2019, Pentagon report says,' *International Business Times*, 17 January 2017; 'F-35 "scarcely" fit to fly: Pentagon's chief tester,' *Press TV*, 3 April 2017.

42. Grazier, Dan, 'F-35 Far from Ready to Face Current or Future Threats, Testing Data Shows,' *Project on Government Oversight*, 19 March 2019.

43. McCain, John, 'U.S. Senator, Arizona, Opening statement by SASC Chairman John McCain on the F-35 Joint Strike Fighter Program,' 26 April 2016.

44. Britzky, Haley, 'Acting SecDef Shanahan thinks the F-35 program is "f–ked up" just like everyone else,' *Task and Purpose*, 25 April 2019.

45. *Ibid*.

46. 'F-35's Troubled F135 Engine is Causing Unavailability Rates at 600% of Standard Levels,' *Military Watch Magazine*, 11 September 2022.

47. Parsons, Dan, 'Blistering Highlights From The Latest F-35 Sustainment Hearing,' *The Drive*, 9 May 2022.

48. Finnerty, Ryan, 'Overtaxed F-35 engines rack up $38 billion in extra maintenance costs,' *Flight Global*, 2 June 2023.

49. 'F-35 Sustainment: DOD Needs to Cut Billions in Estimated Costs to Achieve Affordability,' *Government Accountability Office*, 7 July 2021; Roblin, Sebastien, 'The Air Force admits the F-35 fighter jet costs too much. So it wants to spend even more.,' *NBC News*, 7 March 2021; Mehta, Aaron, 'Pentagon "can't afford the sustainment costs" on F-35, Lord says,' *Defense News*, 2 February 2018; 'Lawmakers Are Skeptical About The Services' Focus On Next Generation Fighters Over Existing Designs,' *The Drive*, 29 July 2021.

50. Hadley, Greg, 'New NDAA Takes Aim at F-35 Sustainment Costs, Joint Program Office,' *Air Force Magazine*, 10 December 2021.

51. Newdick, Thomas and Rogoway, Tyler, 'The Air Force Has Abandoned Its 386 Squadron Goal,' *The Drive*, 4 May 2022.

52. 'Why the U.S. Air Force Plans to Buy a 50 Year Old Fighter Jet: F-16 Orders Scheduled for 2023,' *Military Watch Magazine*, 23 January 2021; Axe, David, 'The U.S. Air Force Just Admitted The F-35 Stealth Fighter Has Failed,' *Forbes*, 23 February 2021; Gould, Joe and Insinna, Valerie, 'Ripping F-35 costs, House Armed Services chairman looks to "cut our losses",' *Defense News*, 5 March 2021; Newdick, Thomas, 'Air Force Boss Wants Clean-Sheet Fighter That's Less Advanced Than F-35 To Replace F-16,' *The Drive*, 18 February 2021.

53. Bath, Alison, 'Will the F-35 ever become the primary fighter jet it was supposed to be?' *Stars and Stripes*, 1 March 2023.

54. Gordon, Yefim and Komissarov, Dmitry, *Sukhoi Su-57*, Manchester, Hikoki Publications, 2021 (p. 96).

55. International Institute for Strategic Studies, *The Military Balance*, Volume 111, 2011 (Chapter Five: Russia).

56. *Ibid* (Chapter Five: Russia).

57. Kots, Andrey, "'Они бы все изменили". Боевые самолеты, без которых оставили Россию' ("'They would have changed everything." Combat aircraft Russia was left without'), *RIA Novosti*, 2 April 2021; 'Схватка за русское небо: Су-57 подрезал крылья "Беркуту"' ('Fight for the Russian sky: Su-57 clipped the wings of the "Berkut"'), *нвивнг* (Accessed 28 November 2021); Roblin, Sebastien, 'Why Russia's Super-Maneuverable Su-47 "Golden Eagle" Fighter Jet Failed,' *National Interest*, 27 April 2019; Gordon, Yefim, *Sukhoi S-37 and Mikoyan MFI: Russian Fifth-Generation Fighter Technology Demonstrators*, Hinckley, Midland Publishing, 2001 (p. 4).

58. Buttler, Tony and Gordon, Yefim, *Soviet Secret Projects: Fighters Since 1945*, Hinckley, Midland Publishing, 2005 (p. 160).

59. *Ibid* (p. 160).

60. 'Mikoyan reveals first glimpse of 1.42 multifunction fighter,' *Flight Global*, 6 January 1999; 'Russia's New Su-57 Fighters Cost Just $35 Million Each; Are Fifth Generation Jets Really Cheaper than the Su-35?,' *Military Watch Magazine*, 19 May 2019; 'В США рассказали о предшественнике Су-57' ('In the US, they talked about the predecessor of the Su-57'), *Lenta*, 21 March 2023.

61. Leone, Dario, 'Did you know the Su-57 Felon is the only Fighter Jet Equipped with DIRCM?,' *The Aviation Geek Club*, 6 February 2020; Rogoway, Tyler, 'No, The Su-57 Isn't "Junk:" Six Features We like On Russia's New Fighter,' *The Drive*, 30 April 2018; Gordon, Yefim and Komissarov, Dmitry, *Sukhoi Su-57*, Manchester, Hikoki Publications, 2021 (pp. 106, 324).

62. "'Фантом" не догоняет' ("'Phantom" is not catching up'), *Rossiyskaya Gazeta*, 16 November 2018; 'Видимые невидимки: самые известные самолеты-"стелс"' ('Visible invisibles: the most famous stealth aircraft'), *TASS*, 22 November 2017; Gordon, Yefim and Komissarov, Dmitry, *Sukhoi Su-57*, Manchester, Hikoki Publications, 2021 (pp. 110, 324).

63. Allison, George, 'Russia using new Su-57 jets against Ukraine,' *UK Defence Journal*, 9 January 2023; 'British Sources Indicate Russian Su-57 Fighters Using Extreme Range R-37M Missiles to Shoot Down Ukrainian Aircraft,' *Military Watch Magazine*, 28 February 2023; 'Russian Su-57 Stealth Fighters Deployed to Suppress Ukrainian Air Defences – Reports,' *Military Watch Magazine*, 15 June 2022.

64. Gordon, Yefim, *Sukhoi S-37 and Mikoyan MFI: Russian Fifth-Generation Fighter Technology Demonstrators*, Hinckley, Midland

Publishing, 2001 (pp. 12, 13); Buttler, Tony and Gordon, Yefim, *Soviet Secret Projects: Fighters Since 1945*, Hinckley, Midland Publishing, 2005 (pp. 153-155).

65. 'Air Combat with "Ghosts",' *Aviatsiia i kosmonavtika,* no. 7, July 1991 (pp. 4, 5); Lambeth, Benjamin S., *Russian Air Power at the Crossroads*, Santa Monica, Rand, 1996 (p.240).

66. Gordon, Yefim, *Sukhoi S-37 and Mikoyan MFI: Russian Fifth-Generation Fighter Technology Demonstrators*, Hinckley, Midland Publishing, 2001 (pp. 21, 22).

67. *Ibid* (pp. 12, 13, 21, 22, 34).

68. Butowski, Piotr, Su-57 Felon, Stamford, Key Publishing, 2022 (Chapter 1: The First Approach: MiG MFI).

69. Gordon, Yefim, *Sukhoi S-37 and Mikoyan MFI: Russian Fifth-Generation Fighter Technology Demonstrators*, Hinckley, Midland Publishing, 2001 (pp. 12-13, 15, 31).

70. *Ibid* (p. 22).

71. Gordon, Yefim and Komissarov, Dmitry, *Sukhoi Su-57*, Manchester, Hikoki Publications, 2021 (p. 25).

72. *Ibid* (p. 42); Buttler, Tony and Gordon, Yefim, *Soviet Secret Projects: Fighters Since 1945*, Hinckley, Midland Publishing, 2005 (pp. 153-155); Gordon, Yefim, *Sukhoi S-37 and Mikoyan MFI: Russian Fifth-Generation Fighter Technology Demonstrators*, Hinckley, Midland Publishing, 2001 (p. 35).

73. Kots, Andrey, '"Они бы все изменили". Боевые самолеты, без которых оставили Россию' ('"They would have changed everything." Combat aircraft Russia was left without'), *RIA Novosti*, 2 April 2021; Gordon, Yefim, *Sukhoi S-37 and Mikoyan MFI: Russian Fifth-Generation Fighter Technology Demonstrators*, Hinckley, Midland Publishing, 2001 (pp. 19-20, 35).

74. Gordon, Yefim and Komissarov, Dmitry, *Sukhoi Su-57*, Manchester, Hikoki Publications, 2021 (p. 44).

75. *Ibid* (p. 10).

76. Nine, Thomas W., The Future of USAF Airborne Warning & Control: A Conceptual Approach, Maxwell Air Force Base, Air Command and Staff College, Air University, April 1999; 'Mikoyan reveals first glimpse of 1.42 multifunction fighter,' *Flight Global*, 6 January 1999.

77. 'China's J-20: future rival for air dominance?' *Strategic Comments*, vol. 17, issue 1, 2011 (pp. 1-3); 'Видимые невидимки: самые известные самолеты-"стелс"' ('Visible invisibles: the most famous stealth aircraft'), *TASS*, 22 November 2017.

78. Lukin, Alexander, *China and Russia: The New Rapprochement*, Cambridge, Polity Press, 2018 (p. 154).
79. Johnson, Reuben F., 'Sukhoi Su-57: Will India Join the Program?' *AIN Online*, 7 February 2018; 'India, Russia to make 5th generation fighter jets,' *Times of India*, 24 January 2007; Shukla, Ajal, 'India to develop 25% of fifth generation fighter,' *Business Standard*, 21 January 2013; Gordon, Yefim and Komissarov, Dmitry, *Sukhoi Su-57*, Manchester, Hikoki Publications, 2021 (pp. 363, 364).

Chapter 3

1. Wezeman, Siemon T., 'China, Russia and the shifting landscape of arms sales,' *Stockholm International Peace Research Institute*, 5 July 2017; Menshikov, Stanislav, 'Russian Capitalism Today,' *Monthly Review*, vol. 51. no. 3, 1999 (pp. 82–86); Millar, James R., 'Can Putin Jump-Start Russia's Stalled Economy?' *Current History*, vol. 99, no. 639, October 2000 (pp. 329-333).
2. Wezeman, Siemon T., 'China, Russia and the shifting landscape of arms sales,' *Stockholm International Peace Research Institute*, 5 July 2017; Cooper, Julian, *The Future of the Russian Defense Industry* in: Allison, Roy and Bluth, Christopher, *Security Dilemmas in Russia and Eurasia*, London, Royal Institute for International Affairs, 1998 (p. 96).
3. 'SIPRI Military Expenditure Database,' *Stockholm International Peace Research Institute* (https://milex.sipri.org/sipri).
4. Mañé Estrada, Aurèlia and de la Cámara Arilla, Carmen, 'Is Russia Drifting toward an Oil-Rentier Economy?' *Eastern European Economics*, vol. 43, no. 5, September-October 2005 (pp. 46-73); Wagstyl, Stefan, 'Russia: riding with the rentiers,' *Financial Times*, 8 July 2011.
5. 'China's J-20: future rival for air dominance?' *Strategic Comments*, vol. 17, issue 1, 2011 (pp. 1-3).
6. Gordon, Yefim, *Sukhoi Su-27*, Hinckley, Midland Publishing, 2007 (pp. 253-255); Gordon, Yefim and Komissarov, Dmitriy, *Mikoyan MiG-31: Interceptor*, Barnsley, Pen and Sword, 2015 (pp. 124-126); Gordon, Yefim, *Mikoyan MiG-31*, Hinckley, Midland Publishing, 2005 (p. 134); International Institute for Strategic Studies, *The Military Balance*, Volume 93, 1993 (p. 148); Kim, Young Jeh, *The New Pacific Community in the 1990s*, Armonk, M.E., Sharpe, 1996 (p. 118); Blank, Stephen, *The Dynamics of Russian Weapon Sales to China*, Carlisle, US Army War College, Strategic Studies Institute, 4 March 1997 (p. 30).

7. 'China's J-20: future rival for air dominance?' *Strategic Comments*, vol. 17, issue 1, 2011 (pp. 1-3).

8. *Ibid* (pp. 1-3).

9. '最新: 中国空军选定下一代战机由611所方案胜出'('Latest: The Chinese Air Force selected the next generation of fighter jets by the 611 program to win'), 亚东军事网, 5 November 2010.

10. Chang, Yihong, 'China Launches New Stealth Fighter Project,' *Jane's Defence Weekly*, December 2002.

11. Knight, Will, 'Chinese Stealth Fighter Plans Revealed,' *New Scientist*, December 2002.

12. Rupprecht, Andreas, 'The PLA Air Force's "Silver-Bullet" Bomber Force,' *Jamestown Foundation China Brief*, Volume 17, Issue 10, 21 July 2017; Rupprecht, Andreas, *Modern Chinese Warplanes: Chinese Air Force – Combat Aircraft and Units*, Houston, Harpia, 2018 (p. 40).

13. Lim, Louisa, 'China Uncloaks Stealth Fighter Prototype,' *NPR*, 5 January 2011; Rizzo, Jennifer and Keyes, Charley, 'Is China closer than thought to matching U.S. fighter jet prowess?' *CNN*, 6 January 2011.

14. *Ibid*.

15. 'China stealth plane still "years away", says Pentagon,' *BBC News*, 6 January 2011.

16. Bodeen, Christopher, 'China's stealth fighter photos cause an international stir,' *NBC News*, 6 January 2011.

17. 'Gates Comments on Chinese J-20,' *Air Force Magazine*, 10 January 2011.

18. Purnell, Danielle, 'Lockheed Martin rolls-out final F-22 Raptor,' *Air Force Reserve Command Official Website*, 15 December 2011; Wolf, Jim, 'U.S. to mothball gear to build top F-22 fighter,' *Reuters*, 13 December 2011; Gertler, Jeremiah, Air Force F-22 Fighter Program, Congressional Research Service Report for Congress, 11 July 2013.

19. Bumiller, Elisabeth and Wines, Michael, 'Test of Stealth Fighter Clouds Gates Visit to China,' *New York Times*, 11 January 2011.

20. *Ibid*; Gates, Robert M., *Duty: Memoirs of a Secretary at War*, New York, Alfred A. Knopf, 2014 (Chapter 14: At War to the Last Day).

21. *Ibid* (Chapter 14: At War to the Last Day).

22. Wines, Michael and Bumiller, Elisabeth, 'Test Unrelated to Gates Visit, China Says,' *New York Times*, 12 January 2011.

23. Levine, Adam, 'Gates: Chinese further along than thought on stealth fighter,' *CNN*, 10 January 2011.

24. 'China's J-20: future rival for air dominance?' *Strategic Comments*, vol. 17, issue 1, 2011 (pp. 1-3).

25. *Ibid* (pp. 1-3).

26. Donald, David, 'Improved Chinese Stealth Fighter Nears First Flight,' *AIN Online*, 27 February 2014.

27. Gertler, Jeremiah, Air Force F-22 Fighter Program, Congressional Research Service Report for Congress, 11 July 2013.

28. Rogoway, Tyler, 'China's Own "Catfish" Flying Avionics Testbed For The J-20 Fighter Emerges,' *The Drive*, 3 February 2017.

29. Lin, Jeffrey and Singer Peter W., 'Chinese Stealth Fighter J-20 Starts Production,' *Popular Science*, 28 December 2015.

30. Rupprecht, Andreas, *Modern Chinese Warplanes: Chinese Air Force – Combat Aircraft and Units*, Houston, Harpia, 2018 (p. 40); Joe, Rick, 'China's J-20 Stealth Fighter Today and Into the 2020s,' *The Diplomat*, 16 August 2019.

31. Insinna, Valerie, 'Air Force Declares F-35A Ready for Combat,' *Defense News*, 2 August 2016.

32. 'China's first stealth fighter J-20 enters service with Air Force,' *The State Council Information Office of the People's Republic of China Official Website*, 13 March 2017.

33. '杨伟代表：歼20将进行系列化发展　不断提升作战能力' ('Representative Yang Wei: The J-20 will undergo serial development to continuously improve its combat capabilities'), *People's Daily Online*, 20 March, 2018.

34. '新一代隐身战斗机歼-20列装空军作战部队' ('The J-20 stealth fighter of the new generation is integrated into the air force's combat fleet'), *Ministry of National Defense of the People's Republic of China Official Website*, 9 February, 2018.

35. Hohmann, James, 'The Daily 202: U.S. came "much closer" to war with North Korea in 2017 than the public knew, Trump told Woodward,' *Washington Post*, 16 September 2020; 'Yes, The United States Did Draw Up A Plan To Drop 80 Nuclear Weapons On North Korea,' *The Drive*, 27 November 2020.

36. Blanchard, Ben and Oliphant, James, 'Chinese State Media Says China Should be Neutral if North Korea Attacks the U.S.,' *Time*, 11 August 2017.

37. Lo, Kinling, 'China "shoots down incoming missiles" during exercise over waters close to North Korea,' *South China Morning Post*, 5 September 2017; Gao, Charolette, 'China's Air Force Tests Missile

Defense Near North Korea Border,' *The Diplomat*, 7 September 2017; Wang, Christine, 'China reportedly boosts defense preparations along North Korean border,' *CNBC*, 24 July 2017; Berlinger, Joshua, 'China closes off big chunk of Yellow Sea for military drills,' *CNN*, 26 July 2017; 'How China Has Joined Russia in Drawing a Red Line to Prevent U.S. Military Intervention on the Korean Peninsula,' *Military Watch Magazine*, 12 September 2017.

38. 'China's stealth jet may have done flyover of S Korea,' *Asia Times*, 7 December 2017; 'China Allegedly Sends Cutting-Edge Jet to Eye US-S Korea Joint Air Drill,' *Sputnik News*, 10 December 2017.

39. Global Times on Twitter, 'Former #PLA Air Force commander, General Wang Hai, passed away on Sunday morning in Beijing, aged 94, Chinese media reported. Wang shot down 9 enemy aircraft during the Korean War, with his team engaging the US Air Force on over 80 occasions and downing 29 enemy aircraft.,' 2 August 2020.

40. Ng, Teddy, 'China deploys J-20 stealth fighter "to keep tabs on Taiwan",' *South China Morning Post*, 27 July 2019.

41. '震懾台獨分子? 中國最新戰機殲-20部署浙江 15分鐘抵台' ('To deter Taiwan independence elements? China's latest fighter J-20 deployed in Zhejiang and arrived in Taiwan in 15 minutes'), *CNews*, 28 November 2021.

42. Solen, Derek, 'Second Combat Brigade of PRC Air Force Likely Receives Stealth Fighter,' *China Aerospace Studies Institute*, May 2021.

43. Chan, Minnie, 'China deploys J-20 stealth fighter jets to units monitoring Taiwan Strait,' *South China Morning Post*, 26 June 2021.

44. Liu, Xuanzun, 'J-20 stealth fighter in service for 2nd PLA ace force with home developed engines,' *Global Times*, 18 June 2021.

45. '南部战区第5航空旅开始换装歼-20' ['The 5th Aviation Brigade of the Southern Theatre Command Began to Refit with the J-20'], *YouWuQiong*, 11 December 2021.

46. 'All Chinese Theatre Commands Now Deploy J-20 Fighters: New Stealth Air Brigade Confirmed as Fleet Growth Accelerates,' *Military Watch Magazine*, 20 April 2022.

47. Clark, Colin, 'B-21 Bomber Estimate By CAPE: $511M A Copy,' *Breaking Defense*, 19 September 2016; 'China Building Two New Fields With 230 Nuclear ICBM Silos Able to Strike America – Reports,' *Military Watch Magazine*, 28 July 2021.

48. 'J-20A Mighty Dragon production progress,' *Scramble*, 28 December 2023.

49. 'Embedded Refueling Probe Seen on China's J20 Stealth Fighter Jet,' *Defense World*, 15 November 2018; 'J-20 now capable of aerial refueling,' *China Military*, 15 November 2018.

50. Li, Jiayao, 'China confirms use of mature stealth testing technology,' *Global Times*, 22 May 2018.

51. Cenciotti, David, 'China's new stealth fighter's missile launch rails prove Beijing can improve U.S. technology,' *The Aviationist*, 26 March 2013.

52. '杨伟代表：歼20将进行系列化发展　不断提升作战能力' ('Representative Yang Wei: The J-20 will undergo serial development and continuously improve its combat capabilities'), *People's Daily Online*, 20 March, 2018.

53. Hodge, Nathan, 'China's J-20 Fighter: Stealthy or Just Stealthy-Looking?' *Wall Street Journal*, 19 January 2011; Interview with Justin Bronk: 'Why the US Military Worries About Chinese Air Power,' *Military Aviation History*, 9 September 2021.

54. Guo, Zhanzhi and Chen, Yingwen and Ma, Lianfeng, '鸭翼的雷达散射截面影响研究 ('Research on the Radar Cross Section Effect of Canards'), *Chengdu Aircraft Design Institute*, 10 September 2019.

55. Bevilaqua, Paul, 'Inventing the F-35 Joint Strike Fighter,' 2009 Wright Brothers Lectureship in Aeronautics, Aerospace Research Central, 15 June 2012 (https://arc.aiaa.org/doi/10.2514/6.2009-1650); Joe, Rick, 'J-20: The Stealth Fighter That Changed PLA Watching Forever,' *The Diplomat*, 11 January 2021.

56. '深度：歼20雷达获突破功率比F22高50% 探测范围更远' ('Depth: The breakthrough power of the J-20 radar is 50% higher than that of the F22, and the detection range is farther'), 新浪军事, 31 March 2016.

57. 'PAK-FA's New Engines Make It "Easily the Best 5th Gen Fighter in the World",' *Sputnik News*, 25 July 2017.

58. Gu, Songfen, 'Strategic Study of China's Fighter Aircraft Development,' *Fighter Aircraft Development Validation Group*, March 2003.

59. Panda, Ankit, 'China's Fifth-Generation Stealth Fighter Is in Combat Service – But With Improved Fourth-Generation Engines,' *The Diplomat*, 13 February 2018; Donald, Davis, 'Paris 2011: Chinese Chengdu J-20 Fighter Still Shrouded in Mystery,' *AIN Online*, 23 June 2011; 'WS-10 engine has 7 variants equipped in 5 fighters including J-20,' *China Arms*, 11 September 2019.

60. 'After the burn,' *Key Aero*, 10 September 2021.

61. Trade Registers, Stockholm International Peace Research Institute Arms Transfer Database (https://armstrade.sipri.org/armstrade/page/trade_register.php).

62. Donald, David, 'Chengdu's J-20 Enters Production,' *AIN Online*, 14 February 2016; Hunter, Jamie, 'China's Enhanced J-20B Stealth Fighter May Arrive Soon, Here's What It Could Include,' *The Drive*, 20 July 2020; 'Rise of the Mighty Dragon,' *Key Aero*, 7 December 2017.

63. 'Stealth fighter soon powered by local engines,' *China Daily*, 13 March 2017.

64. 'Does China's J-20 Rival Other Stealth Fighters?' *China Power: Centre for Strategic and International Studies*, January 2018; Yeung, Jessie and Lendon, Brad, 'China is sending its most advanced fighter jet to patrol disputed seas,' *CNN*, 15 April 2022.

65. Liu, Xuanzun, 'Chinese engine-equipped J-20 fighter proves plateau ability,' *Global Times*, 19 January 2022.

66. Yeung, Jessie and Lendon, Brad, 'China is sending its most advanced fighter jet to patrol disputed seas,' *CNN*, 15 April 2022.

67. Waldron, Greg, 'China's enigmatic J-20 powers up for its second decade,' *Flight Global*, 28 December 2020.

68. 'PAK-FA's New Engines Make It "Easily the Best 5th Gen Fighter in the World",' *Sputnik News*, 25 July 2017.

69. Yeo, Mike and Pocock, Chris, 'More J-20 Stealth Fighters Built in China,' *AIN Online*, 19 July 2016; Roblin, Sebastien, 'Is China About to Give Its Best Fighters Powerful New Jet Engines?' *National Interest*, 5 March 2020.

70. Gordon, Yefim, *Sukhoi S-37 and Mikoyan MFI: Russian Fifth-Generation Fighter Technology Demonstrators*, Hinckley, Midland Publishing, 2001 (p. 20); Gordon, Yefim and Komissarov, Dmitry, *Sukhoi Su-57*, Manchester, Hikoki Publications, 2021 (pp. 16-17).

71. 'J-20 stealth fighter's capabilities to be enhanced,' *China Daily*, 13 March 2018.

72. 'J-20 Begins Flying With Groundbreaking WS-15 Engine: Will China's Stealth Fighter be the World Leader in Thrust?' *Military Watch Magazine*, 15 January 2022.

73. Liu, Xuanzun, 'China's WS-15 turbofan engine undergoes tests, shows improved performance,' *Global Times*, 14 March 2022.

74. 'China: J-20's WS-15 engine undergoes multiple rounds of testing,' *China Arms*, 15 March 2022.

75. Liu, Xuanzun, 'China fully capable of jet engine development, narrowing technology gaps,' *Global Times*, 9 March 2022.

76. Liu, Xuanzun, 'China's WS-15 turbofan engine undergoes tests, shows improved performance,' *Global Times*, 14 March 2022.

77. Chan, Minnie, 'Is China's W-15 engine to power J-20 stealth fighter jet nearing completion?' *South China Morning Post*, 19 December 2022.

78. Waldron, Greg, 'Chinese executive hints at progress with J-20's new WS-15 engine,' *Flight Global*, 27 March 2023.

79. Chen, Chuanren, 'China May Have Flown J-20 With Domestic WS-15 Engines,' *Aviation Week*, 30 June 2023.

80. Liu, Xuanzun, 'China's WS-15 turbofan engine undergoes tests, shows improved performance,' *Global Times*, 14 March 2022.

81. Episkopos, Mark, 'Out of Range: Why China's J-20 Might Have the Tools to Kill an F-35,' *National Interest*, 20 June 2019; '霹雳15在200公里外直取预警机，歼20的优势太大了' ('The Thunderbolt 15 took the early warning aircraft 200 kilometres away, and the advantage of the J-20 is too great'), *Sina*, 16 January 2021; '让美国顾忌的歼20"御用武器"竟然也要出口了' ('The J-20's "Crown Weapon" that Raises American Doubts is About To Be Exported'), *Xinhua*, 28 September 2021.

82. International Institute for Strategic Studies, *The Military Balance*, Volume 119, 2019 (p. 8).

83. Lee, Tae-Woo, *Military Technologies of the World: Volume 1 and 2*, Westport, Praeger, 2009 (p. 82); Trimble, Stephen, 'New long-range missile project emerges in US budget,' *Flight Global*, 2 November 2017.

84. Chopra, Anil, 'Air Defence of India: Evolving Options,' *Indian Defence Review*, vol. 34.3, July-September 2019.

85. International Institute for Strategic Studies, *The Military Balance*, Volume 119, 2019 (p. 237).

86. *Ibid* (p. 237); Fisher, Jr., Richard D., *China's Military Modernization: Building for Regional and Global Reach*, Westport, Praeger, 2008 (p. 232); Chan, DM, 'China's military can't underestimate AIM-260,' *Asia Times*, 27 June 2019.

87. Drew, James, 'USAF seeks "interim" CHAMP, longer-range air-to-air missiles,' *Flight Global*, 17 September 2015; 'Military Strategy Forum: General Herbert "Hawk" Carlisle on Air Combat Command: Today's Conflicts and Tomorrow's Threats,' *Center for Strategic & International Studies*, 18 September 2015.

88. 'Lockheed Developing AIM-260 To Counter China's PL-15,' *Aviation Week*, 29 June 2019; Barrie, Douglas, 'AIM-260 missile: the US Air Force and beyond-visual-range lethality,' *International Institute for Strategic Studies Military Balance Blog*, 24 October 2019.

89. Newdick, Thomas, 'A Guide To China's Increasingly Impressive Air-To-Air Missile Inventory,' *The Drive*, 1 September 2022.

90. International Institute for Strategic Studies, *The Military Balance*, Volume 119, 2019 (p. 237).

91. Newdick, Thomas, 'A Guide To China's Increasingly Impressive Air-To-Air Missile Inventory,' *The Drive*, 1 September 2022.

92. Bronk, Justin, 'Russian and Chinese Combat Air Trends: Current Capabilities and Future Threat Outlook,' Royal United Services Institute, October 2020.

93. Rupprecht, Andreas, *Modern Chinese Warplanes: Chinese Air Force – Combat Aircraft and Units*, Houston, Harpia, 2018 (p. 37).

94. 'Stealth Fighter or Bomber?' *The Diplomat*, 26 July 2011.

95. Waldron, Greg, 'China's enigmatic J-20 powers up for its second decade,' *Flight Global*, 28 December 2020.

96. Sawant, Magnesh, 'Why China Cannot Challenge the US Military Primacy,' *Journal of Indo-Pacific Affairs*, Air University Press, 13 December, 2021.

97. Axe, David, 'China's Over-Hyped Stealth Jet,' *The Diplomat*, 7 January 2011; Kopp, Carlo and Goon, Peter, 'Chengdu J-XX [J-20] Stealth Fighter Prototype: A Preliminary Assessment,' *AusAirpower, Technical Report APA-TR-2011-0101*, 3 January 2011; 'J-20 Design,' *Global Security* (https://www.globalsecurity.org/military/world/china/j-20-design.htm).

98. 'Stealth Fighter or Bomber?' *The Diplomat*, 26 July 2011.

99. Joe, Rick, 'J-20: The Stealth Fighter That Changed PLA Watching Forever,' *The Diplomat*, 11 January 2021.

100. 'J-20 stealth fighter's capabilities to be enhanced,' *China Daily*, 13 March 2018.

101. '杨伟代表：我的一个梦想，未来战机由中国来制定标准' ('Representative Yang Wei: One of my dreams is that China will set the standards for future fighter jets'), State-Owned Assets Supervision and Administration Commission of the State Council, 20 March 2018.

102. 'Embedded Refueling Probe Seen on China's J20 Stealth Fighter Jet,' *Defense World*, 15 November 2018.

103. Waldron, Greg, 'China's enigmatic J-20 powers up for its second decade,' *Flight Global*, 28 December 2020.

104. Lei, Zhao, 'J-20 fighter takes part in first combat exercises,' *China Daily*, 12 January 2018.

105. 'Air Force reveals J-20 combat formation,' *People's Daily*, 21 January 2020.

106. Liu, Xuanzun and Guo, Yuandan, 'China, Russia joint drills conclude with live-fire anti-terrorism operation featuring J-20,' *Global Times*, 13 August 2021.

107. Gouré, Daniel, 'The Air Force Needs A New High-Low Mix,' *Lexington Institute*, 9 June 2016; Isachenkov, Vladimir, 'Russia, China sign roadmap for closer military cooperation,' *AP News*, 23 November 2021.

108. Hollings, Alex, 'Why the F-117 Nighthawk Is Such a Badass Plane,' *Popular Mechanics*, 12 August 2019; 'Celebrating a quarter century of Stealth,' *Flight Global*, 19 June 2007.

109. Liu, Xuanzun, 'J-20 fighters conduct nocturnal battle drill to hone stealth advantages,' *Global Times*, 16 January 2022.

110. '英媒: 中国将研发新版歼-20隐身战机　准备启动6代机项目' ('British media: China will develop a new version of the J-20 stealth fighter and prepare to launch the 6th generation aircraft project'), *Sina Military*, 15 March, 2018.

111. '新一代隐身战斗机歼-20列装空军作战部队' ('The J-20 stealth fighter of the new generation is integrated into the air force's combat fleet'), Ministry of National Defense of the People's Republic of China Official Website, 9 February, 2018.

112. 'China Tests its Newest and Most Dangerous Fighters: J-20 and J-16 Further Integrated into the Air Force,' *Military Watch Magazine*, 12 January 2018; Dominguez, Gabriel, 'China's J-20 fighter aircraft takes part in its first combat exercise, says report,' *Jane's 360*, 15 January 2018.

113. '新一代隐身战斗机歼-20列装空军作战部队' ('The J-20 stealth fighter of the new generation is integrated into the air force's combat fleet'), *Ministry of National Defense of the People's Republic of China Official Website*, 9 February, 2018.

114. Lo, Kinling, 'New fighter jets will be used in "more regular" patrols over South China Sea,' *South China Morning Post*, 13 February 2018.

115. 'China's J-20 Fifth-Gen Fighter Successfully Completes Combat Training at Sea,' *Sputnik News*, 9 May 2018.

116. 'Experts: J-20 will surely patrol Taiwan in future,' *China Military Online*, 18 May 2018.

117. 'China Deploys YJ-12B and HQ-9B Missiles on South China Sea Islands,' *Navy Recognition*, 4 May 2018.

118. Minnick, Wendell, 'China Expands Presence With Fighters on Woody Island,' *Defence News*, 8 November 2015; 'China deploys PLANAF J-11BH/BHS fighters to Woody Island,' *Alert 5*, 31 October 2015.

119. 'China Is Threatening to Fly Its J-20 Stealth Fighter over Taiwan,' *National Interest*, 21 May 2018.

120. 'Taipei Threatened by China's New Stealth Fighters? Why the J-20 is Unlikely to See Action over the Taiwan Strait,' *Military Watch Magazine*, 29 May 2018; 'Russia Now Has "Treasure Trove" of Info About Stealthy F-22s – US General,' *Sputnik News*, 5 January 2018.

121. 'J-20 fighter takes part in night-time exercise in air superiority role,' *People's Daily*, 2 June 2018.

122. Rogoway, Tyler, 'China's J-20 Stealth Fighter Stuns By Brandishing Full Load Of Missiles At Zhuhai Air Show,' *The Drive*, 11 November 2018.

123. Liu, Zhen, 'China-India border dispute: advanced fighter jets sent to nearby airbases,' *South China Morning Post*, 19 August 2020.

124. '媒体披露歼20战机真实空战实力 以"零损伤"击落敌机17架' ('The media disclosed the real air combat strength of the J-20 fighter jets and shot down 17 enemy planes with "zero damage"'), *163*, 25 September 2020; 'Chinese Media Claims J-20 Shot Down 17 "Enemy" Fighters in Exercises – How Reliable Are These Claims?,' *Military Watch Magazine*, 16 September 2020.

125. Pickrell, Ryan, 'Air Force F-35s Wrecked Enemies During Mock Air Combat,' *Task and Purpose*, 21 February 2019.

126. Liu, Xuanzun, 'China's J-20 stealth fighter jet flies without Luneburg lens, shows combat readiness,' *Global Times*, 5 April 2021.

127. *Ibid.*

128. Liu, Xuanzun, 'J-20 shows high combat readiness in New Year combat training,' *Global Times*, 9 January 2022; Liu, Xuanzun, 'Newly commissioned J-20 stealth fighters on combat alert,' *Global Times*, 17 January 2022.

129. Liu, Xuanzun, 'J-20 fighters conduct nocturnal battle drill to hone stealth advantages,' *Global Times*, 16 January 2022.

130. Battle Stations, Season 1, Episode 39, F-22 Raptor.

131. 'Aerospace Nation: Gen Kenneth S. Wilsbach,' *Mitchell Institute for Aerospace Studies* (YouTube Channel), 15 March 2022.

132. *Ibid.*

133. Liu, Xuanzun, 'J-20 fighter jet starts routine training patrols in East, South China Seas,' *Global Times*, 13 April 2022.

134. Yeung, Jessie and Lendon, Brad, 'China is sending its most advanced fighter jet to patrol disputed seas,' *CNN*, 15 April 2022.

135. 'J-20 has ability to defend nation's airspace,' *China Daily*, 15 August 2022.

136. 'J-20 fighters to escort Y-20 aircraft for 1st time in repatriating remains of CPV martyrs from S.Korea,' *Global Times*, 14 September 2022.

137. '2架殲-20戰機為接運英雄的運-20護航'('Two J-20 fighter jets escorted the Y-20 transporting the military heroes') *People's Daily*, 24 November, 2023.

138. Liu, Xuanzun, 'China's J-20 stealth fighter jets drive away foreign aircraft in combat patrols over East China Sea,' *Global Times*, 13 October 2022.

139. Liu, Zhen, 'China outlines J-20 stealth fighter's role in intercepting foreign warplanes by releasing footage that may show rare encounter with F-35,' *South China Morning Post*, 18 January 2023.

140. Liu, Xuanzun, 'PLA Air Force's Wang Hai Air Group fully equipped with J-20 fighter jets, expels foreign aircraft by giving full play to stealth capability,' *Global Times*, 17 January 2023.

141. Huang, Kristin, 'Chinese bombers, fighter jets in new year military drills appear to have boosted combat capacity,' *South China Morning Post*, 15 January 2023.

142. Liu, Xuanzun and Guo, Yuandan, 'Chinese Air Force unit that emerged victorious from Korean War vows to be ready for combat,' *Global Times*, 27 July 2023.

143. 'China's J-20 fighter jet, YY-20 refueling plane amaze audience at Changchun Airshow,' *CGTN*, 27 July 2023; 'Highlights of Changchun Air Show,' *Xinhua*, 27 July 2023.

144. Gady, Franz-Stefan, 'China's First 5th Generation Fighter Moves Into Serial Production,' *The Diplomat*, 31 October 2017.

145. *Ibid.*

146. 'Chinese J-20 Fighter, Y-20 Transport Aircraft Designs Finalized, Ready for Mass Production: Expert,' *Defense World*, 12 November 2017; Tirpak, John A., 'China Likely Stepping Up Stealth Fighter Production,' *Air and Space Forces*, 8 October 2021; Chan, Minnie, 'World-class production lines speed up deliveries of China's J-20 stealth jet fighter,' *South China Morning Post*, 27 November 2022.

147. Liu, Xuanzun, 'China ramps up J-20 stealth fighter production after domestic engine switch,' *Global Times*, 12 December 2021.

148. *Ibid.*

149. *Ibid.*

150. Tirpak, John A., 'China Likely Stepping Up Stealth Fighter Production,' *Air Force Magazine*, 8 October 2021.

151. 'Top designers announce J-20 production capacity, Y-20 domestic engines, new carrier-based fighter at Airshow China,' *Global Times*, 29 September 2021.

152. Liu, Xuanzun, 'Newly commissioned J-20 stealth fighters on combat alert,' *Global Times*, 17 January 2022.

153. 'China to speed up research into new strategic weapons for air force: J-20 chief designer,' *Global Times*, 27 September 2021.

154. Johnson, Reuben F, 'China's J-20 fifth-gen fighter moves into series production,' *Jane's*, 26 October 2017.

155. Liu, Xuanzun, 'China ramps up J-20 stealth fighter production after domestic engine switch,' *Global Times*, 12 December 2021.

156. Gertler, Jeremiah, Air Force F-22 Fighter Program, Congressional Research Service Report for Congress, 11 July 2013; 'Lockheed Martin Begins Assembly Of U.S. Air Force's First Operational F-22 Raptor,' *Lockheed Martin*, 19 March 2001.

157. 'U.S. Sources Estimate China Likely Already Fields Over 200 J-20 Stealth Fighters: Just How Many Are There?' *Military Watch Magazine*, 17 April 2022.

158. Liu, Xuanzun, 'PLA to train pilots faster with new programs amid warplane production capacity boost,' *Global Times*, 24 July 2022.

159. Mitt Romney on Twitter, 'China matches US spending on military procurement, which is tremendously dangerous given that China doesn't believe in human rights or democracy. My #FY21NDAA amendment directs the @DeptOfDefense compare our spending with that of China and Russia to provide us with a lay of land,' 20 July 2020; 'Schieffer Series: A Conversation with Senator Mitt Romney on U.S.-China Relations and Great Power Competition,' *Centre for Strategic and International Studies*, 22 July 2020.

160. Gertler, Jeremiah, Air Force F-22 Fighter Program, Congressional Research Service Report for Congress, 11 July 2013; Battle Stations, Season 1, Episode 39, F-22 Raptor.

161. Joe, Rick, 'China's J-20 Gets Another Upgrade,' *The Diplomat*, 1 August 2023.

162. Andreas Rupprecht on Twitter: 'The J-20 production rate! I have to admit, although I've now accepted a much higher production rate of the J-20, this sounds almost too good to be true: "120 J-20 production per year. at least 500 J-20s by 2025" Both Shilao and Ayi have claimed J-20 production was in 3 digit', 18 July 2023.

163. Liu, Xuanzun, 'China ramps up J-20 stealth fighter production after domestic engine switch,' *Global Times*, 12 December 2021.

164. 'Technical Challenges Delay Mass Production of F-35 Joint Strike Fighter Aircraft (F-35), Selected Acquisition Report (SAR), United States Department of Defense, March 18, 2015 (pp. 39-41).
Tripak, John A., 'Top Lawmakers Want to Slash F-35 Production, Put Funds Toward Test Capacity,' *Air and Space Forces*, May 14, 2024.

165. Gertler, Jeremiah, Air Force F-22 Fighter Program, Congressional Research Service Report for Congress, 11 July 2013; Battle Stations, Season 1, Episode 39, F-22 Raptor.

Chapter 4

1. "'歼—２０，你不要飞得那么快 … …'" ('J-20, Don't Fly So Fast … …'), *Xinhua*, 10 November 2018.

2. Duhigg, Charles and Bradsher, Keith, 'How the U.S. Lost Out on iPhone Work,' *New York Times*, 21 January 2012.

3. 'Tim Cook Discusses Apple's Future in China,' *Fortune Magazine*, 5 December 2017; Nicas, Jack, 'A Tiny Screw Shows Why iPhones Won't Be "Assembled in U.S.A.",' *New York Times*, 28 January 2019.

4. 'Tim Cook Discusses Apple's Future in China,' *Fortune Magazine*, 5 December 2017.

5. *Ibid.*

6. Duhig, Charles and Bradsher, Keith, 'How the U.S. Lost Out on iPhone Work,' *New York Times*, 21 January 2012.

7. Gould, Joe and Losey, Stephen, 'Amid hiring boom, defense firms say labor shortage is dragging them down,' *Defense News*, 5 August 2022; Tirpak, John A., 'F-35 Production Challenged to Keep Up with Demand,' *Air and Space Forces*, 3 July 2023; 'US defence contractors squeezed by shortages of labour and parts,' *Financial Times*, 26 July 2022; 'Parts shortages dog US defence contractors as war depletes arsenals,' *Financial Times*, 27 October 2022.

8. Duhig, Charles and Bradsher, Keith, 'How the U.S. Lost Out on iPhone Work,' *New York Times*, 21 January 2012; Goldman, David, 'Why Apple will never bring manufacturing jobs back to the U.S.,' *CNN*, 17 October 2012; 'Trump can't make Apple move jobs back to America,' *Business*

Insider, 4 January 2017; 'How Much Would An iPhone Cost If Apple Were Forced To Make It In America?' *Forbes*, 17 January 2018.

9. Duhigg, Charles and Bradsher, Keith, 'How the U.S. Lost Out on iPhone Work,' *New York Times*, 21 January 2012.

10. 'Ericsson, Nokia are more Chinese than meets the eye,' *Asia Times*, 7 July 2020.

11. Stewart, Phil and Stone, Mike, 'U.S. military comes to grips with over-reliance on Chinese imports,' *Reuters*, 2 October 2018.

12. Assessing and Strengthening the Manufacturing and Defense Industrial Base and Supply Chain Resiliency of the United States, Report to President Donald J. Trump by the Interagency Task Force in Fulfilment of Executive Order 13806, September 2018; Davenport, Christian, 'White House report points to severe shortcomings in U.S. military supply chain,' *Washington Post*, 4 October 2018.

13. *Ibid.*

14. Assessing and Strengthening the Manufacturing and Defense Industrial Base and Supply Chain Resiliency of the United States, Report to President Donald J. Trump by the Interagency Task Force in Fulfilment of Executive Order 13806, September 2018.

15. Tingley, Brett, 'U.S. "Not Prepared To Defend Or Compete" With China On AI According To Commission Report,' *The Drive*, 2 March 2021.

16. Peck, Michael, 'The U.S. Military's Greatest Weakness? China "Builds" a Huge Chunk of It,' *National Interest*, 26 May 2018.

17. Office of Technology Assessment, Congress of the United States, *After the Cold War: Living With Lower Defense Spending*, Washington DC, U.S. Government Printing Office, February 1992 (OTA-ITE-524, NTIS order #PB92-152537); Corrin, Amber, 'The End of the Cold War: Military reshaped, redefined,' *Federal Times*, 2 December 2015; Sandler, Todd and George, Justin, 'Military Expenditure Trends for 1960–2014 and What They Reveal,' *Global Policy*, vol. 7, issue 2, May 2016 (pp. 174-184); Conetta, Carl and Knight, Charles, 'Post-Cold War US Military Expenditure in the Context of World Spending Trends,' Project on Defence Alternatives, Briefing Memo #10, January 1997; Chernoff, Fred, 'Ending the Cold War: The Soviet Retreat and the US Military Buildup,' *International Affairs*, vol. 67, no. 1, January 1991 (pp. 111-126); Bomwan, Tom, 'Reagan guided huge buildup in arms race,' *The Baltimore Sun*, 8 June 2004.

18. The Nixon Seminar on Conservative Realism and National Security, 6 April 2021.

19. 'Industrial Capabilities,' Office of Manufacturing and Industrial Base Policy, U.S. Department of Defense, Fiscal Year 2018; *Ibid*, Fiscal Year 2019; *Ibid*, Fiscal Year 2020; *Ibid*, Fiscal Year 2021.

20. Stewart, Phil and Stone, Mike, 'U.S. military comes to grips with over-reliance on Chinese imports,' *Reuters*, 2 October 2018.

21. 'Industrial Capabilities,' Office of Manufacturing and Industrial Base Policy, U.S. Department of Defense, Fiscal Year 2018; *Ibid*, Fiscal Year 2019; *Ibid*, Fiscal Year 2020; *Ibid*, Fiscal Year 2021.

22. *Ibid*, Fiscal Year 2018

23. Bennett, John T., 'Pentagon Acquisition Chief Says Space Industrial Base May Warrant Protection,' *Space News*, 14 September 2009.

24. Davenport, Christian, 'White House report points to severe shortcomings in U.S. military supply chain,' *Washington Post*, 4 October 2018.

25. 'Vital Signs 2021: The Health and Readiness of the Defense Industrial Base,' *National Defense Industrial Association* (https://content.ndia. org/-/media/vital-signs/2021/vital-signs_2021_digital.ashx); 'Vital Signs 2020: The Health and Readiness of the Defense Industrial Base,' *National Defense Industrial Association* (https://www.ndia. org/-/media/vital-signs/2020/vital-signs_screen_v3.ashx); Tadjdeh, Yasmin, 'Erosion of U.S. Industrial Base Is Troubling,' *National Defence Magazine*, 5 February 2020.

26. Davenport, Christian, 'White House report points to severe shortcomings in U.S. military supply chain,' *Washington Post*, 4 October 2018.

27. Paszator, Andy, 'United Technologies Studies Sale of Rocket Assets,' *Wall Street Journal*, 25 July 2011.

28. 'Sukhoi, MiG merged with United Aircraft Corporation,' *TASS*, 1 June 2022; 'Russia Reconsolidates Military Aerospace Arena,' *Net Resources International*, 27 July 2008; Kwiatkowski, Alex, 'Aviation industry locked in a tailspin,' *The Russia Journal*, 7 February 2003.

29. Carafano, James Jay, 'Obama, Gates are Gutting America's Defense Industry,' *Heritage*, 1 September 2019.

30. *Ibid*.

31. Webber, Michael, *Erosion of the Defense Industrial Support Base* in: McCormack, Richard, *Manufacturing A Better Future For America*, Washington DC, The Alliance for American Manufacturing, 2009 (pp. 245-280).

32. Whalen, Jeanne, 'To counter China, some Republicans are abandoning free-market orthodoxy,' *Washington Post*, 26 August 2020.

33. Weisgerber, Marcus, 'US May Need to Nationalize Military Aircraft Industry, USAF Says,' *Defense One*, 14 July 2020.
34. *Ibid*.
35. Harshaw, Tom, 'China Outspends the U.S. on Defense? Here's the Math,' *Bloomberg*, 3 September 2018.
36. Mitt Romney on Twitter, 'China matches US spending on military procurement, which is tremendously dangerous given that China doesn't believe in human rights or democracy. My #FY21NDAA amendment directs the @DeptOfDefense compare our spending with that of China and Russia to provide us with a lay of land,' 20 July 2020; 'Schieffer Series: A Conversation with Senator Mitt Romney on U.S.-China Relations and Great Power Competition,' *Centre for Strategic and International Studies*, 22 July 2020.
37. Allison, Graham, 'China Is Now the World's Largest Economy. We Shouldn't Be Shocked,' *National Interest*, 15 October 2020.
38. Allison, Graham, 'The Great Rivalry: China vs. the U.S. in the 21st Century,' *Belfer Centre for Science and International Affairs, Harvard Kennedy School*, 7 December 2021.
39. Gaida, Jamie et al., 'ASPI's Critical Technology Tracker: The global race for future power,' Australian Strategic Policy Institute, Policy Brief, Report No. 69, 2023.
40. 'Vital Signs 2020: The Health and Readiness of the Defense Industrial Base,' *National Defense Industrial Association*; Nebehay, Stephanie, '"Driving force" China accounts for nearly half global patent filings: U.N.,' *Reuters*, 15 October 2019.
41. 'The American AI Century: A Blueprint for Action: Transcript,' *Center for a New American Security*, 17 January 2020.
42. 'Putin: Leader in artificial intelligence will rule world,' *CNBC*, 4 September 2017.
43. Gibson, Liam, 'China develops AI to design hypersonic missiles,' *Taiwan News*, 26 March 2022; Chen, Stephen, 'Chinese researchers turn to artificial intelligence to build futuristic weapons,' *South China Morning Post*, 5 December 2021.
44. Che, Stephen, 'In China, AI warship designer did nearly a year's work in a day,' *South China Morning Post*, 10 March 2023.
45. Trevithick, Joseph, 'Putin Says Whoever Has the Best Artificial Intelligence Will Rule the World,' *The Drive*, 6 September 2017; Haga, Wes and Crosby, Courtney, 'AI's Power to Transform Command and Control,' *National Defense*, 13 November 2020.
46. Mizokami, Kyle, 'The Air Force's Secret New Fighter Jet Will Come With an R2-D2,' *Popular Mechanics*, 23 December 2020.

47. Liu, Xuanzun, 'Next gen fighter jet forthcoming in great power competition: J-20 chief designer,' *Global Times*, 27 July 2020.
48. Liu, Xuanzun, 'China's J-16 fighter jet is flawless and much superior to the Su-30: pilot,' *Global Times*, 24 March 2021; 'J-16 vs. J-10C: Chinese Pilot Reveals Which Elite Fighter is Superior,' *Military Watch Magazine*, 26 March 2021.
49. Gordon, Yefim, *Sukhoi Su-27*, Hinckley, Midland Publishing, 2007 (p. 248); Gordon, Yefim and Davidson, Peter, *Sukhoi Su-27 Flanker*, North Branch, Specialty Press Publishers, 2006 (p. 39).
50. Altman, Howard, 'Air Force's Next Generation Air Dominance 'Fighter' Program Enters New Stage,' *The Drive*, 2 June 2022.
51. Xuanzun, Liu, 'J-20 fighter could get directed-energy weapon, drone-control capability: experts,' *Global Times*, 23 January 2022.
52. Macias, Amanda, 'Elon Musk tells a room full of Air Force pilots: "The fighter jet era has passed",' *CNBC*, 28 February 2020.
53. Birkey, Douglas, 'Sorry, Elon, fighter pilots will fly and fight for a long time,' *Defense News*, 2 March 2020.
54. Allen, Gregory C., 'Understanding China's AI Strategy,' *Center for a New American Security*, 6 February 2019.
55. Trevithick, Joseph, 'AI Claims "Flawless Victory" Going Undefeated In Digital Dogfight With Human Fighter Pilot,' *The Drive*, 20 August 2020.
56. Newdick, Thomas, 'AI-Controlled F-16s Are Now Working As A Team In DARPA's Virtual Dogfights,' *The Drive*, 22 March 2021.
57. Liu, Xuanzun, 'PLA deploys AI in mock warplane battles, "trains both pilots and AIs",' *Global Times*, 14 June 2021; Trevithick, Joseph, 'Chinese Pilots Are Also Duelling With AI Opponents In Simulated Dogfights And Losing: Report,' *The Drive*, 18 June 2021.
58. Fullerton, Jamie and Farmer, Ben, 'China testing unmanned tank in latest foray into AI military technology,' *The Telegraph*, 21 March 2018; 'How China is Using AI to Turn its Massive Type 59 Tank Divisions Into an Army of Lethal Combat Robots,' *Military Watch Magazine*, 5 April 2021; 'China has developed first unmanned main battle tank MBT Type 59,' *Army Recognition*, 19 March 2018.
59. Trevithick, Joseph, 'Artificial Intelligence Takes Control Of A U-2 Spy Plane's Sensors In Historic Flight Test,' *The Drive*, 16 December 2020.
60. Judson, Jen, 'US Army taps industry for autonomous drones to resupply troops,' *Defense News*, 15 January 2021.

61. Tingley, Brett, 'U.S. "Not Prepared To Defend Or Compete" With China On AI According To Commission Report,' *The Drive*, 2 March 2021.
62. Trevithick, Joseph, 'This Is the Tech Special Operators Want for Their Light Attack Planes,' *The Drive*, 16 August 2017.
63. Trevithick, Joseph, 'Artificial Intelligence Takes Control Of A U-2 Spy Plane's Sensors In Historic Flight Test,' *The Drive*, 16 December 2020.
64. Allen, Gregory C., 'Understanding China's AI Strategy,' *Center for a New American Security*, 6 February 2019.
65. Central Military Commission Joint Staff, 'Accelerate the Construction of a Joint Operations Command System with Our Nation's Characteristics CMC Joint Operations Command Center,' *Seeking Truth*, 15 August 2016.
66. Schmidt, Eric et al., Final Report, National Security Commission on Artificial Intelligence, March 2021 (https://www.nscai.gov/wp-content/uploads/2021/03/Full-Report-Digital-1.pdf).
67. Tingley, Brett, 'U.S. "Not Prepared To Defend Or Compete" With China On AI According To Commission Report,' *The Drive*, 2 March 2021.
68. Rogoway, Tyler, 'The Alarming Case of the USAF's Mysteriously Missing Unmanned Combat Air Vehicles,' *The Drive*, 2 July 2020.
69. Duke, J. Darren, 'Illiteracy, Not Morality, Is Holding Back Military Integration of Artificial Intelligence,' *National Interest*, 15 February 2021.
70. Defense Secretary Dr. Mark T. Esper speaks at the National Security Commission on Artificial Intelligence public conference, Liaison Washington Capitol Hill Hotel, Washington DC, 5 November 2019.
71. 'US has already lost AI fight to China, says ex-Pentagon software chief,' *Financial Times*, 10 October 2021.
72. 'A Conversation with General John Hyten, Vice Chairman of the Joint Chiefs of Staff,' *Center for Strategic and International Studies* (YouTube Channel), 17 January 2020.
73. 'The American AI Century: A Blueprint for Action: Transcript,' *Center for a New American Security*, 17 January 2020.
74. 'Artificial Intelligence: How knowledge is created, transferred, and used: Trends in China, Europe, and the United States,' *Elsevier*, December 2018.

75. 'Who Is Winning the AI Race?,' *MIT Technology Review*, 27 June 2017.
76. 2021 AI Index Report, Stanford Institute for Human-Centered Artificial Intelligence, March 2021 (https://aiindex.stanford.edu/report/).
77. Shankland, Stephen and Keane, Sean, 'Trump creates American AI Initiative to boost research, train displaced workers,' *Cnet*, 11 February 2019.
78. Li, Daitian and Wang, Tony W. and Xiao, Yangao, 'Is China Emerging as the Global Leader in AI?,' *Harvard Business Review*, 18 February 2021.
79. Robles, Pablo, 'China plans to be a world leader in Artificial Intelligence by 2030,' *South China Morning Post*, 1 October 2018; Allen, Gregory C., 'Understanding China's AI Strategy,' *Center for a New American Security*, 6 February 2019.
80. 'China AI Development Report 2018,' China Institute for Science and Technology Policy, Tsinghua University, July 2018 (http://www.sppm.tsinghua.edu.cn/eWebEditor/UploadFile/China_AI_development_report_2018.pdf).
81. Hao, Karen, 'Yes, China is probably outspending the US in AI – but not on defense,' *MIT Technology Review*, 5 December 2019.
82. Schmidt, Eric et al., Final Report, National Security Commission on Artificial Intelligence, March 2021 (https://www.nscai.gov/wp-content/uploads/2021/03/Full-Report-Digital-1.pdf).
83. Vincent, James, 'China and the US are battling to become the world's first AI superpower,' *The Verge*, 3 August 2017.
84. Kia, On Wong Wilson, 'China's AI Strike Force on COVID-19,' *Asian Education and Development Studies* vol. 10, no. 2, 2021 (pp. 250-262).
85. *Ibid* (pp. 250-262).
86. Giles, Martin, 'The US and China are in a quantum arms race that will transform warfare,' *MIT Technology Review*, 3 January 2019.
87. Chen, Stephen, 'How China hopes to win the quantum technology race,' *South China Morning Post*, 29 October 2020; 'Xi stresses advancing development of quantum science and technology,' *CGTN*, 17 October 2020; 'China to include quantum technology in its 14th Five-Year Plan,' *State Council of the People's Republic of China*, 22 October 2020; Ho, Matt, 'Chinese scientists challenge Google's "quantum supremacy" claim with new algorithm,' *South China Morning Post*, 16 March 2021.

88. Kania, Elsa B. and Costello, John K., 'Quantum Hegemony: China's Ambitions and the Challenge to U.S. Innovation Leadership,' Centre for a New American Security, September 2018.

89. Kwon, Karen, 'China Reaches New Milestone in Space-Based Quantum Communications,' *Scientific American*, 25 June 2020; Yin, J. et al., 'Entanglement-based secure quantum cryptography over 1,120 kilometres,' *Nature*, vol. 582, 2020 (pp. 501–505).

90. Yu, Dawei, 'In China, Quantum Communications Comes of Age,' *Caixin*, 6 February 2015.

91. Billings, Lee, 'China Shatters "Spooky Action at a Distance" Record, Preps for Quantum Internet,' *Scientific American*, 15 June 2017.

92. Kania, Elsa B. and Costello, John K., 'Quantum Hegemony: China's Ambitions and the Challenge to U.S. Innovation Leadership,' Centre for a New American Security, September 2018.

93. Šiljak, Harun, 'China's quantum satellite enables first totally secure long-range messages,' *Down to Earth*, 18 June 2020.

94. 'A Twenty-First-Century Sputnik Moment: China's Mozi Satellite,' *Nippon.com*, 13 August 2019; Aron, Jacob, 'Why quantum satellites will make it harder for states to snoop,' *New Scientist*, 24 August 2016; Šiljak, Harun, 'China's quantum satellite enables first totally secure long-range messages,' *Down to Earth*, 18 June 2020.

95. Kwon, Karen, 'China Reaches New Milestone in Space-Based Quantum Communications,' *Scientific American*, 25 June 2020; Yin, J. et al., 'Entanglement-based secure quantum cryptography over 1,120 kilometres,' *Nature*, vol. 582, 2020 (pp. 501–505).

96. Chen, Stephen, 'China uses quantum satellite to protect world's largest power grid against attacks,' *South China Morning Post*, 10 December 2021.

97. 'China Builds the World's First Integrated Quantum Communication Network,' *Scitech Daily*, 6 January 2021; Chen, Yu-Ao et al., 'An integrated space-to-ground quantum communication network over 4,600 kilometres,' *Nature*, vol. 589, January 2021 (pp. 214–219).

98. 'The quantum internet is already being built,' *Cosmos*, 12 April 2018.

99. Ananthaswamy, Anil, 'Quantum Astronomy Could Create Telescopes Hundreds of Kilometers Wide,' *Scientific American*, 19 April 2020; Lucy, Michael, 'The quantum internet is already being built,' *Cosmos Magazine*, 12 April 2018; 'Quantum telescope could make giant mirrors obsolete,' *Physics World*, 29 April 2014.

100. Kania, Elsa and Costello, John, 'Quantum Leap (Part 2): The Strategic Implications of Quantum Technologies,' *China Brief, Jamestown Foundation*, vol. 16, issue 19, 21 December 2016.

101. Yu, Dawei, 'In China, Quantum Communications Comes of Age,' *Caixin*, 6 February 2015; An, Weiping, '量子通信引 发军事领域 变革' ('Quantum Communications Sparks Off Transformation in the Military Domain), *PLA Daily*, 27 September 2016.

102. *PLA Daily*, 27 September 2014.

103. Ball, Philip, 'Physicists in China challenge Google's "quantum advantage",' *Nature*, 3 December 2020.

104. Sparkes, Matthew, 'China beats Google to claim the world's most powerful quantum computer,' *New Scientist*, 5 July 2021; Chik, Holly, 'Chinese quantum computer "sets record" in processing test,' *South China Morning Post*, 13 July 2021.

105. 'Chinese scientists develop new quantum computer with 113 detected photons,' *China Daily*, 26 October 2021; 'China launches world's fastest programmable quantum computers,' *South China Morning Post*, 26 October 2021.

106. Ball, Philip, 'Physicists in China challenge Google's "quantum advantage",' *Nature*, 3 December 2020; Garisto, Daniel, 'Light-Based Quantum Computer Exceeds Fastest Classical Supercomputers,' *Scientific American*, 3 December 2020; Garisto, Daniel, 'Quantum Computer Made from Photons Achieves a New Record,' *Scientific American*, 6 November 2019.

107. Chen, Stephen, 'How China hopes to win the quantum technology race,' *South China Morning Post*, 29 October 2020.

108. Berendsen, René G., *The Weaponization of Quantum Mechanics: Quantum Technology in Future Warfare*, U.S. Army Command and General Staff College Fort Leavenworth, KS, School of Advanced Military Studies, 2019.

109. Chen, Stephen, 'Chinese team says quantum physics project moves radar closer to detecting stealth aircraft,' *South China Morning Post*, 3 September 2021.

110. Lin, Jeffrey and Singer, P.W., 'China's latest quantum radar could help detect stealth planes, missiles,' *Popular Science*, 11 July 2018; Huang, Kristin, 'The Chinese advanced radars taking on stealth aircraft,' *South China Morning Post*, 23 April 2021; Simonite, Tom, 'China Stakes Its Claim to Quantum Supremacy,' *Wired*, 3 December 2020; Kania, Elsa B. and Armitage, Stephen, 'Disruption Under the Radar: Chinese Advances in Quantum Sensing,' *Jamestown Foundation*, 17 August 2017.

111. Chen, Stephen, 'Chinese smart satellite tracks US aircraft carrier in real time, researchers say,' *South China Morning Post*, 10 May 2022; Honrada, Gabriel, 'China's AI makes its satellites spies in the sky,' *Asia Times*, 11 April 2022; Chen, Stephen, 'Chinese AI turns commercial satellite into a spy tracker able to follow small objects with precision: paper,' *South China Morning Post*, 7 April 2022.

112. Roblin, Sebastien, 'China's Quantum Radars Could Make Detecting U.S. Submarines a Breeze,' *National Interest*, 3 February 2021; 'No More Stealth: China's Quantum Radar Could Reveal All Submarines,' *National Interest*, 9 July 2020.

113. Zhen, Liu, 'China's latest quantum radar won't just track stealth bombers, but ballistic missiles in space too,' *South China Morning Post*, 15 June 2018.

114. Kania, Elsa and Costello, John, 'Quantum Leap (Part 2): The Strategic Implications of Quantum Technologies,' *China Brief*, *Jamestown Foundation*, vol. 16, issue 19, 21 December 2016.

Chapter 5

1. Gordon, Yefim and Davidson, Peter, *Sukhoi Su-27 Flanker*, North Branch, Specialty Press, 2006 (pp. 41, 64).

2. 'Aerospace Nation: Gen Kenneth S. Wilsbach,' *Mitchell Institute for Aerospace Studies* (YouTube Channel), 15 March 2022.

3. Tirpak, John A., 'Divestitures and Purchases: USAF's 2023 Aircraft Plans,' *Air Force Magazine*, 29 April 2022.

4. Fisher Jr, Richard D., China's Global Military Power Projection Challenge to the United States, Testimony Before the House Permanent Select Committee on Intelligence, United States House of Representatives, 17 May 2018.

5. Andreas Rupprecht on Twitter: 'The J-20 production rate! I have to admit, although I've now accepted a much higher production rate of the J-20, this sounds almost too good to be true: "120 J-20 production per year. at least 500 J-20s by 2025." Both Shilao and Ayi have claimed J-20 production was in 3 digits', 18 July 2023.

6. *Ibid.*

7. Gertler, Jeremiah, Air Force F-22 Fighter Program, Congressional Research Service Report for Congress, 11 July 2013.

8. Losey, Stephen, 'F-35 delivery delays to cost Lockheed hundreds of millions in 2023,' *Defense News*, 20 July 2023.

9. Tripak, John A., 'Top Lawmakers Want to Slash F-35 Production, Put Funds Toward Test Capacity,' *Air and Space Forces*, May 14, 2024.

10. Liu, Xuanzun, 'Chinese engine-equipped J-20 fighter proves plateau ability,' *Global Times*, 19 January 2022.

11. Liu, Xuanzun, 'Innovation of twin-seat J-20 stealth fighter to lead world, military experts say after reported maiden flight,' *Global Times*, 7 November 2021.

12. *Ibid*; Tate, Andrew, 'China may be developing first two-seat stealth combat aircraft,' *Jane's*, 18 January 2019; 'J-16 vs. J-10C: Chinese Pilot Reveals Which Elite Fighter is Superior,' *Military Watch Magazine*, 26 March 2021.

13. Huang, Kristin, 'China's air force unveils new twin-seat J-20 stealth fighter jet in video,' *South China Morning Post*, 12 January 2021.

14. Gordon, Yefim and Davidson, Peter, *Sukhoi Su-27 Flanker*, North Branch, Specialty Press, 2006 (Chapter 4).

15. *Ordnance Industry Science Technology*, August 2022.

16. Chan, Minnie, 'China's stealth fighter goes into mass production after thrust upgrade,' *South China Morning Post*, 12 July 2020.

17. 'J-20 stealth fighter's capabilities to be enhanced,' *China Daily*, 13 March 2018.

18. *Ibid*.

19. Grier, Peter, 'A Quarter Century of AWACS,' *Air Force Magazine*, 1 March 2002; Veronico, Nic and Dunn, Jim, *21st Century U.S. Air Power*, Grand Rapids, MI, Zenith Imprint, 2004 (p. 83); LaFayette, Ken, 'The E-3 Sentry Airborne Warning and Control System,' *Warfare History Network*.

20. Gordon, Yefim, *Sukhoi Su-27*, Hinckley, Midland Publishing, 2007 (p. 182).

21. Gordon, Yefim and Komissarov, Dmitriy, *Mikoyan MiG-31: Interceptor*, Barnsley, Pen and Sword, 2015 (pp. 124-126); Halloran, Richard, 'Iran Set to Use F-14s to Spot Targets,' *New York Times*, 7 June 1984.

22. Gordon, Yefim, *Sukhoi Su-27*, Hinckley, Midland Publishing, 2007 (pp. 253-255).

23. Rogoway, Tyler, 'Israel Is Treating America's Throwaway F-15D Eagles As New Found Treasure,' *The Drive*, 20 December 2017.

24. Xuanzun, Liu, 'J-20 fighter could get directed-energy weapon, drone-control capability: experts,' *Global Times*, 23 January 2022.

25. Trevithick, Joseph, 'Boeing Unveils New Two-Stage Long-Range Air-To-Air Missile Concept,' *The Drive*, 21 September 2021; Trevithick, Joseph, 'Boeing's Modular Air-To-Air Missile Concept Gets Air Force Funding,' *The Drive*, 30 September 2022.

26. Heath, Timothy R. and Gunness, Kristen and Cooper III, Cortez A., 'The PLA and China's Rejuvenation: National Security and Military

Strategies, Deterrence Concepts, and Combat Capabilities,' Santa Monica, RAND, 2016 (pp. 38-39).

27. Chan, DM, 'Stealth wars: China's J-20 vs USAF's F-35,' *Asia Times*, 30 July 2019.

28. *China Military Power: Modernising a Force to Fight and Win*, Washington DC, Defence Intelligence Agency, 2019 (p. 85).

29. Roblin, Sebastien, 'Meet The FB-22 Stealth Bomber: It Would Have Been Russia's Worst Nightmare,' *1945*, 29 March, 2022.

30. *Ibid.*

31. Tirpak, John, 'Long Arm of the Air Force,' *Air Force Magazine*, October 2002; Cortes, Lorenzo, 'Roche Looking to Next Year for Near-Term Proposals on Strike Concepts,' *Defense Daily*, 18 March 2004; Vago Muradian, 'F-22 May be Modified as Speedy New Medium Bomber to Strike Moving Targets,' *Defense Daily International*, 18 January 2002.

32. Cortes, Lorenzo, 'Air Force Issues Clarification on FB-22, FY'11 Delivery Date Possible,' *Defense Daily*, 10 March 2003.

33. Sweetman, Bill, 'Smarter Bomber,' *Popular Science*, 25 June 2002.

34. Gordon, Yefim and Davidson, Peter, *Sukhoi Su-27 Flanker*, North Branch, Specialty Press, 2006 (pp. 75, 76, 80, 81); 'Meet the Su-34, Russia's Supersonic Strike Aircraft NATO Fears,' *National Interest*, 4 June 2018; Cy-34 (Su-34), *Sukhoi Official Website* (https://www.sukhoi.org/products/samolety/254/).

35. Huang, Kristin, 'Why two heads would be better than one for China's "Mighty Dragon" fighter jet,' *South China Morning Post*, 27 April 2021.

36. Xuanzun, Liu, 'J-20 fighter could get directed-energy weapon, drone-control capability: experts,' *Global Times*, 23 January 2022.

37. Chan, Minnie, 'Drones to become "loyal wingmen" for China's advanced J-20 stealth fighter jets, state media reports,' *South China Morning Post*, 20 October 2022.

38. Chan, Minnie, 'China's J-20 stealth fighter joins the People's Liberation Army air force,' *South China Morning Post*, 10 March 2017.

39. Military and Security Developments Involving the People's Republic of China 2020, Annual Report to Congress, United States Department of Defence (p. 51); Military and Security Developments Involving the People's Republic of China 2021, Annual Report to Congress, United States Department of Defence (p. 56).

40. Rogoway, Tyler, 'China's J-20 Stealth Fighter Stuns By Brandishing Full Load Of Missiles At Zhuhai Air Show,' *The Drive*, 11 November 2018.

41. Cone, Allen, 'Lockheed's Sidekick adds increased firepower to F-35 fighters,' *Lockheed Martin*, 3 May 2019.

42. Military and Security Developments Involving the People's Republic of China 2021, Annual Report to Congress, United States Department of Defence (p. 144).

43. Liu, Xuanzun, 'Military developing airborne laser attack pod, says report,' *Global Times*, 7 January 2020.

44. Xuanzun, Liu, 'J-20 fighter could get directed-energy weapon, drone-control capability: experts,' *Global Times*, 23 January 2022.

45. Keller, Jared, 'Another Dead End for Airborne Lasers: Air Force Scraps Effort to Mount Directed-Energy Weapon on Fighter Jet,' *Military.com*, 17 May, 2024.

46. Liu, Xuanzun, 'J-20 fighter pilot calls for improved military communications network development,' *Global Times*, 9 March 2023.

47. 'Mitchell Institute's Deptula on China's J-20 Stealth Fighter,' *Defense and Aerospace Report* (YouTube Channel), 11 November 2016.

48. Liu, Xuanzun, 'J-20 fighter pilot calls for improved military communications network development,' *Global Times*, 9 March 2023.

49. Liu, Xuanzun, 'Test pilot sees China's J-20 to get 2D thrust vectoring nozzles,' *Global Times*, 19 April 2021.

50. *Ibid*.

51. 开了眼了 on Twitter: 'Let's enjoy it together. (with video attachment),' 27 August 2022 (https://twitter.com/RupprechtDeino/status/1563407148260151297).

52. 乐子壬1号机 on Twitter: 'WS-15? (with video attachment),' 20 September 2022 (https://mobile.twitter.com/kt396/status/1572175436783976450?fbclid=IwAR2dJMySeZzzNSLJVFaKZPaHGlu7fhEN3077AemtHmXPn_PzeuGBiITIxHw&fs=e&s=cl).

53. '在见到J20之前我没想过一架飞机还能这样飞' ('before seeing the J-20 I never conceived that an aircraft could fly like this'), 大卫坑 (Billibilli Account), 14 November 2022.

54. Koryakin, Oleg, 'Первый и последний: чем был уникален истребитель Су-37' ('First and last: what made the Su-37 fighter unique'), *Rossiyskaya Gazeta*, 2 April 2020.

55. Chen, Stephen, 'Chinese scientists hail "incredible" stealth breakthrough that may blind military radar systems,' *South China Morning Post*, 19 July 2019.

56. *Ibid*.

57. Chen, Stephen, 'Chinese scientists create a "plasma shower" to improve stealth bomber performance,' *South China Morning Post*, 26 August 2022.

58. Gordon, Yefim, *Sukhoi S-37 and Mikoyan MFI: Russian Fifth-Generation Fighter Technology Demonstrators*, Hinckley, Midland Publishing, 2001 (pp. 21-22).

59. 'Here's How A-12 Oxcart Created Plasma Stealth By Burning Cesium-Laced Fuel,' *Fighter Jets World*, 10 March 2021.

60. 'Vladimir Putin said Tsirkon hypersonic missile to be deployed in January,' *Navy Recognition*, 22 December 2022.

61. Freedberg Jr., Sydney J., 'F-35 Ready For Missile Defense By 2025: MDA Chief,' *Breaking Defense*, 11 April 2018.

62. LaGrone, Sam, 'Video: Successful F-35, SM-6 Live Fire Test Points to Expansion in Networked Naval Warfare,' *United States Naval Institute*, 13 September 2016; Abbott, Rich, 'New Demonstration Shows F-35's Data Sharing Capability,' *Aviation Today*, 8 August 2019.

63. Osborn, Kris, 'The F-35 Strengthens Its Role in Missile Defense,' *National Interest*, 30 November 2021.

64. Rogoway, Tyler, 'The Airborne Laser May Rise Again But It Will Look Very Different,' *Jalopnik*, 18 August 2015.

65. Chen, Stephen, 'China's heat-seeking radar with 300km range boosts anti-stealth tech, say defence scientists,' *South China Morning Post*, 23 August 2022.

66. Mizokami, Kyle, 'China Is Already Planning Its Next-Generation Fighter Jet,' *Popular Mechanics*, 15 March 2018.

67. Tirpak, John A., 'Kelly Worries F-35 Flying Costs Won't Hit Target, and That China May Get NGAD First,' *Air Force Magazine*, 26 February 2021.

68. Insinna, Valierie, 'China "on track" for 6th-gen fighter, US Air Force needs to get there first: ACC chief,' *Breaking Defense*, 26 September 2022.

69. Kadidal, Akhil, 'China shows concept of tailless future fighter jet,' *Jane's*, 7 February 2023; 'Will China Develop a Sixth Generation Tailless Derivative of its J-20 Stealth Fighter? New Images Give Hints,' *Military Watch Magazine*, 9 February 2023.

70. Liu, Xuanzun, 'Next gen fighter jet forthcoming in great power competition: J-20 chief designer,' *Global Times*, 27 July 2020.

71. Tirpak, John A., 'Saving Air Superiority,' *Air and Space Forces*, 27 February 2017; 'Air Force Next-Generation Air Dominance Program,' *Congressional Research Service*, 23 June 2022.

72. Losey, Stephen, 'T-7 Red Hawk trainer makes its debut,' *Defense News*, 30 April 2022.

73. Cohen, Rachel S., 'Air Force Introduces e-Planes for the Digital Era,' *Air Force Magazine*, 14 September 2020.

74. Tirpak, John A., 'How Boeing Won the T-X,' *Air Force Magazine*, 1 July 2019.

75. Tirpak, John A., 'Roper's NGAD Bombshell,' *Air Force Magazine*, 1 October 2020.

76. Tirpak, John A., 'Kendall: Digital Engineering Was "Over-Hyped," But Can Save 20 Percent on Time and Cost,' *Air and Space Forces*, 23 May 2023.

77. Marrow, Michael, 'Over two years late: Air Force now expects first T-7As in 2025, IOC in 2027,' *Breaking Defense*, 21 April 2023; 'Advanced Pilot Trainer: Program Success Hinges on Better Managing Its Schedule and Providing Oversight,' *Government Accountability Office*, 18 May 2023.

78. '杨伟代表：歼20将进行系列化发展　不断提升作战能力' ('Representative Yang Wei: The J-20 will undergo serial development and continuously improve its combat capabilities'), People's Daily Online, 20 March, 2018.

79. 'Top designers announce J-20 production capacity, Y-20 domestic engines, new carrier-based fighter at Airshow China,' *Global Times*, 29 September 2021.

80. '3D打印助军事变革: 研制新战机从20年缩短到3年' ('3D printing helps military revolution: the development of new fighters is shortened from 20 years to 3 years'), *China Aviation News*, 29 January 2015.

81. *Ibid.*

82. 'Large titanium wing spar made by Additive Manufacturing,' *Powder Metallurgy Review*, 2 December 2013.

83. 'J-20 stealth fighter's capabilities to be enhanced,' *China Daily*, 13 March 2018.

84. 'Russia may upgrade advanced Su-57 aircraft to 6th-generation fighter jet,' *TASS*, 1 November 2017; 'Russia's Su-57 plane tests onboard systems for 6th-generation fighter jet – source,' *TASS*, 16 July 2018; 'Russian Fifth-Gen Stealth Fighter to Get Artificial Intelligence,' *Sputnik News*, 25 August 2018; 'Russia testing remotely piloted mode in Su-57 fifth-generation fighter's trials,' *TASS*, 24 August 2020; 'How Russia's Upcoming "EMP Gun" Directed Energy Weapon Could Improve Its Su-57 Fighters and MiG-41 Interceptors,' *Military Watch Magazine*, 1 March 2021.

85. Rogoway, Tyler, 'F-22 Being Used To Test Next Generation Air Dominance "Fighter" Tech,' *The Drive*, 26 April 2022; Larson, Caleb, 'Technological Testbed: Next Generation Stealth Fighter Tech to Be Trialed in the F-22,' *National Interest*, 25 April 2022.

86. Suciu, Peter, 'NGAD 6th Generation Stealth Fighter: Completely Unaffordable?' *1945*, 2 May 2022.

87. Grazier, Dan, 'Deceptive Pentagon Math Tries to Obscure $100 Million+ Price Tag for F-35s,' *Project on Government Oversight*, 1 November 2019; Thomson, Laura, 'The ten most expensive military aircraft ever built,' *Air Force Technology*, 30 May 2019; Liu, Zhen, 'J-20 vs F-22: how China's Chengdu J-20 "Powerful Dragon" compares with US' Lockheed Martin F-22 Raptor,' *South China Morning Post*, 28 July 2018.

88. Eckstein, Megan, 'F-35 Program Facing Delays in Full-Rate Production, As DoD Struggles to Integrate Into Simulators,' *United States Naval Institute News*, 18 October 2019; Newdick, Thomas, 'It's Official: Pentagon Puts F-35 Full-Rate Production Decision On Hold,' *The Drive*, 31 December 2020.

89. Newdick, Thomas, 'China Acquiring New Weapons Five Times Faster Than U.S. Warns Top Official,' *The Drive*, 6 July 2022.

90. '170920_Hyten Speaks at AFA Conference,' *stratcompa* (Youtube Channel), 21 September 2017.

91. World Intellectual Property Indicators 2018, Geneva, World Intellectual Property Organization, 2018; World Intellectual Property Indicators 2023, Geneva, World Intellectual Property Organization, 2023.

92. Charpentreau, Clement, 'No FCAS before 2050, says Dassault CEO,' *Aerotime*, 9 June 2022.

93. 'J-20 stealth fighter's capabilities to be enhanced,' *China Daily*, 13 March 2018.

94. Cirincione, Joseph, *Repairing the Regime: Preventing the Spread of Weapons of Mass Destruction*, London, Routledge, 2000 (p. 192); Khripunov, Igor, 'Russia's Weapons Trade: Domestic Competition and Foreign Markets,' *Problems of Post-Communism*, vol. 46, no. 2, March/April 1999 (p. 41).

95. 'Is the U.S. Training to Fight Algeria? Major Drills Simulate Attack on North African S-400 Air Defences,' *Military Watch Magazine*, 18 June 2021.

96. 'Pakistan's Interior Minister Who Announced J-10C Purchase Says J-20 Stealth Fighter Deal Likely: Is it Possible?' *Military Watch Magazine*, 7 March 2022.

97. *Ibid.*

98. 'Why India needs to fast track the PAK-FA,' *Russia Beyond*, 10 June 2018.

99. DGPR (AIR FORCE) on X: 'INDUCTION AND OPERATIONALIZATION CEREMONY HELD AT AN OPERATIONAL AIR BASE OF PAKISTAN AIR FORCE' (Video Attached), 3 January, 2024.
100. 'Stealth Fighter or Bomber?' *The Diplomat*, 26 July 2011.
101. Liu, Xuanzun, 'J-20 fighter jets highlight China-Russia joint strategic drills opening,' *Global Times*, 9 August 2021.
102. 'Stealth Fight: Why We Could Soon See China's J-20 and Russia's Su-57 in Mock Air Battles,' *Military Watch Magazine*, 30 January 2022.

Chapter 6

1. Trevithick, Joseph and Rogoway, Tyler, 'F-22 And F-35 Datalinks Finally Talk Freely With Each Other Thanks To A U-2 Flying Translator,' *The Drive*, 30 April 2021; Insinna, Valerie, 'Here's why the Valkyrie drone couldn't translate between F-35 and F-22 jets during a recent test,' *C4ISRN*, 19 December 2020; Tirpak, John A., 'Skyborg Drone Translates Between F-35 and F-22 in Test,' *Air Force Magazine*, 16 December 2020.
2. 'Mitchell Institute's Deptula on China's J-20 Stealth Fighter,' *Defense and Aerospace Report* (YouTube Channel), 11 November 2016.
3. Harper, Jon, 'Kendall: Air Force's next-gen fighter will be "better than anything" China can produce,' *Defense Scoop*, 29 September 2022.
4. 'Department of Defense Press Briefing by Secretary James and Gen. Goldfein on the State of the Air Force in the Pentagon Briefing Room,' *Department of Defense Official Website*, 10 August 2016.
5. Liu, Zhen, 'China military's landmark J-20 stealth fighter started a decade of modernisation,' *South China Morning Post*, 31 January 2021.
6. International Institute for Strategic Studies, *The Military Balance*, Volume 120, 2020 (p. 236); Rogoway, Tyler, 'China's Type 055 Super Destroyer Is A Reality Check For The US And Its Allies,' *The Drive*, 28 June 2017.
7. 'Aerospace Nation: Gen Kenneth S. Wilsbach,' *Mitchell Institute for Aerospace Studies* (YouTube Channel), 15 March 2022.
8. *Ibid.*
9. Liu, Xuanzun, 'China's J-20 stealth fighter jets drive away foreign aircraft in combat patrols over East China Sea,' *Global Times*, 13 October 2022.

10. Grier, Peter, 'A Quarter Century of AWACS,' *Air Force Magazine*, 1 March 2002; Veronico, Nic and Dunn, Jim, *21st Century U.S. Air Power*, Grand Rapids, Zenith Imprint, 2004 (p. 83); LaFayette, Ken, 'The E-3 Sentry Airborne Warning and Control System,' *Warfare History Network*.

11. Li, Junsheng and Chen, Bo and Hou, Na, *Cooperation for a Peaceful and Sustainable World: Part 2*, Bingley, Emerald, 2013 (pp. 18-19).

12. Yeo, Mike, 'China ramps up production of new airborne early warning aircraft,' *Defense News*, 5 February 2018.

13. 'Aerospace Nation: Gen Kenneth S. Wilsbach,' *Mitchell Institute for Aerospace Studies* (YouTube Channel), 15 March 2022; Tirpak, John A., 'USAF Selects Boeing's E-7A Wedgetail as Successor to AWACS,' *Air & Space Forces*, 28 February 2023.

14. Newdick, Thomas, 'The Air Force Has Abandoned Its 386 Squadron Goal,' *The Drive*, 4 May 2022.

15. International Institute for Strategic Studies, *The Military Balance*, Volume 122, 2022 (Chapter Three: North America; Chapter Six: Asia).

16. Rupprecht, Andreas, 'Images confirm Y-20U aerial tanker is in PLAAF service,' *Jane's*, 30 November 2021.

17. Douhet, Giulio, *The Command of the Air*, Maxwell AFB, Air University Press, 2019 (p. 22).

18. Slessor, John C., *Air Power and Armies (1936)*, Tuscaloosa, The University of Alabama, 2009 (p. 11).

19. 'Air Force reveals J-20 combat formation,' *People's Daily*, 21 January 2020.

20. Liu, Xuanzun, 'China's J-16D electronic warfare aircraft starts combat training, "to team up with J-20 stealth fighter",' *Global Times*, 6 November 2021.

21. 'PLA retrofits old bombers as electronic warfare aircraft,' *Asia Times*, 22 January 2018.

22. 'China Modifies H-6G Bomber into Electronic Warfare Aircraft,' *Defense Mirror*, 22 January 2018.

23. Erickson, Andrew S. and Lu, Hanlu and Bryan, Kathryn and Septembre, Samuel, 'Research, Development, and Acquisition in China's Aviation Industry: The J-10 Fighter and Pterodactyl UAV,' *Study of Innovation and Technology in China: University of California Institute of Global Conflict and Cooperation*, no. 8, 2014.

24. Military and Security Developments Involving the People's Republic of China 2020, Annual Report to Congress, United States Department of Defence (p. 76).

25. Liu, Xuanzun, 'JF-17 fighter jet gets J-20's combat missile: reports,' *Global Times,* 29 April 2021.
26. 'China decided to compare Su-35 and J-10C fighters in training aerial combat,' *Top War,* 16 June 2020.
27. 'J-10C beats J-16 and Su-35, winning the most "Golden Helmets",' *China-Arms,* 15 December 2021.
28. 'China's J-16 Fighters Entering Service in Larger Numbers: Form Lethal Triad Alongside New J-10C and Stealthy J-20,' *Military Watch Magazine,* 19 August 2018.
29. Interview with Justin Bronk: 'Why the US Military Worries About Chinese Air Power,' *Military Aviation History,* 9 September 2021.
30. Stillion, John and Perdue, Scott, 'Air Combat Past, Present and Future,' Project Air Force briefing, August 2008, Unclassified/FOUO/Sensitive, Slide 29; Watts, Barry, 'The F-22 Program in Retrospect,' Center for Strategic and Budgetary Assessments, August 2009.
31. 'Does China's J-20 Rival Other Stealth Fighters,' *Centre for Strategic and International Studies* (https://chinapower.csis.org/china-chengdu-j-20/).
32. 'Double Vision: Making Sense of China's Second "Stealth" Fighter Prototype,' *Wall Street Journal,* 18 September 2022.
33. Cenciotti, David, 'China's New Carrier-Based Stealth Fighter Makes First Flight,' *The Aviationist,* 29 October 2021.
34. Liu, Xuanzun, 'China establishes office to promote exports of the FC-31 stealth fighter,' *Global Times,* 18 February 2022.

Chapter 7

1. 'Aerospace Nation: Gen Kenneth S. Wilsbach,' *Mitchell Institute for Aerospace Studies* (YouTube Channel), 15 March 2022.
2. Military and Security Developments Involving the People's Republic of China 2020, Annual Report to Congress, United States Department of Defence, 2020 (p. 75).
3. Mehta, Aaron, 'Boeing Positions F-15 as F-22 Supplement,' *Breaking Defense,* 15 September 2015.
4. Cenciotti, David, '"If we don't keep F-22 Raptor viable, the F-35 fleet will be irrelevant" Air Combat Command says,' *The Aviationist,* 4 February 2014.
5. 'China's stealth jet may be ready this year, US commander says,' *Straits Times,* 2 May 2018.
6. Johnson, Reuben F., 'Myths Of The Raptor,' *CBS News,* 28 June 2009.

7. Grazier, Dan, '108 U.S. F-35s Won't Be Combat-Capable,' *National Interest*, 16 October 2017; Trevithick, Joseph, 'USMC's Older F-35Bs May Only Be Able To Fly Around A Quarter Of Their Expected Service Life (Updated),' *The Drive*, 1 February 2019.

8. Chan, Minnie, 'Is China ready for aircraft carrier No 4? Talk swirls over stealth fighter jets at PLA naval base,' *South China Morning Post*, 1 May 2022.

9. Rizzo, Jennifer and Keyes, Charley, 'Is China closer than thought to matching U.S. fighter jet prowess?' *CNN*, 6 January 2011.

10. Cordesman, Anthony H. and Colley, Steve and Wang, Michael, *Chinese Strategy and Military Modernization in 2015: A Comparative Analysis*, Washington DC, Centre for Strategic and International Studies, 2015 (p. 285).

11. 2014 Report to Congress of the U.S.-China Economic and Security Review Commission, One Hundred Thirteenth Congress, Second Session, November 2014 (p. 311).

12. Dutton, Peter and Erickson Andrew S. and Martinson, Ryan, *China's Near Seas Combat Capabilities*, Newport, Naval War College, China Maritime Studies Institute, 2014.

13. Lendon, Brad, 'China's new J-20 stealth fighter screams on to scene,' *CNN*, 1 November 2016.

14. Snow, Shawn, 'Don't expect the Corps' new Chinese J-20 stealth fighter to be dogfighting with Marine jets,' *Marine Corps Times*, 21 December 2018.

15. Demerly, Tom, 'USAF Confirms: The Chinese J-20 Spotted In Georgia Is a Mock-Up Used For Training by the U.S. Marine Corps,' *The Aviationist*, 9 December 2018.

16. Audit of Training Ranges Supporting Aviation Units in the U.S. Indo-Pacific Command, Department of Defense, Office of the Inspector General, 17 April 2019.

17. 'American Pilots Training to Hunt Stealth Fighters; F-35s to Mimic J-20 and Su-57 In New Aggressor Squadron,' *Military Watch Magazine*, 15 May 2019.

18. Hunter, Jamie, 'F-35 Stealth Fighters Are Revolutionizing The USAF's Aggressor Force,' *The Drive*, 12 August 2022.

19. Hollings, Alex, 'Stealth Death Match: China's J-20 Vs. F-22 Raptor (Who Wins?),' *1945*, 24 April 2022.

20. Vanover, Christie, 'Nellis AFB aggressors, F-35 pilots "punish" blue air to develop unstoppable force,' *United States Air Force Official Website*, 4 August 2021; Newdick, Thomas, 'F-35s Have Flown Their

First "Red Air" Missions As Dedicated Stealth Aggressor,' *The Drive*, 4 August 2021.

21. Pickrell, Ryan, 'A US F-22 Raptor pilot describes the challenge of going up against F-35 red air aggressors,' *Business Insider*, 30 August 2021.

22. Trevithick, Joseph, 'Stealthy Target Drones Sought As QF-16 Program Winds Down,' *The Drive*, 23 August 2022.

23. Tirpak, John A., 'New Study: USAF Needs Big Cash Infusion to Overcome Aging Fighter Fleet,' *Air & Space Forces Magazine*, 29 June 2023; Guastella, Joseph and Birkey, Douglas and Gunzinger, Eric and Poling, Aidan, 'Accelerating 5th Generation Airpower: Bringing Capability and Capacity to the Merge,' *Mitchell Institute*, vol. 43, 29 June 2023.

24. Tirpak, John A., 'New Study: USAF Needs Big Cash Infusion to Overcome Aging Fighter Fleet,' *Air & Space Forces Magazine*, 29 June 2023; Guastella, Joseph and Birkey, Douglas and Gunzinger, Eric and Poling, Aidan, 'Accelerating 5th Generation Airpower: Bringing Capability and Capacity to the Merge,' *Mitchell Institute*, vol. 43, 29 June 2023.

25. 'Only 30% of American F-35s Are Fully Mission Capable: Program Chief Slams "Unacceptable" Fleet Performance,' *Military Watch Magazine*, 3 April 2023; Abrams, A.B., 'South Korean Defense Sources Express Concerns About Unreliable F-35 Fighters,' *The Diplomat*, 7 October 2022; Freedberg Jr., Sydney J., 'F-35 readiness and flight hours fell in 2022, says CBO,' *Breaking Defense*, 13 February 2023.

26. Tirpak, John A., 'New Study: USAF Needs Big Cash Infusion to Overcome Aging Fighter Fleet,' *Air & Space Forces Magazine*, 29 June 2023; Guastella, Joseph and Birkey, Douglas and Gunzinger, Eric and Poling, Aidan, 'Accelerating 5th Generation Airpower: Bringing Capability and Capacity to the Merge,' *Mitchell Institute*, vol. 43, 29 June 2023.

27. Tirpak, John A., 'Roper's NGAD Bombshell,' *Air Force Magazine*, 1 October 2020.

28. Altman, Howard, 'Air Force's Next Generation Air Dominance "Fighter" Program Enters New Stage,' *The Drive*, 2 June 2022.

29. LaGrone, Sam, 'CNO Greenert: Navy's Next Fighter Might Not Need Stealth, High Speed,' *United States Naval Institute*, 4 February 2015.

30. Tirpak, John A., 'Raptor 01,' *Air Force Magazine*, July 1997 (p. 48).

31. Davies, Steve and Dildy, Doug, *F-15 Eagle Engaged, The World's Most Successful Jet Fighter*, Oxford, Osprey, 2007 (p. 12); Rininger, Tyson V., *F-15 Eagle At War*, Minneapolis, Zenith Press, 2009 (p. 16); Jenkins, Dennis R., *McDonnell Douglas F-15 Eagle: Supreme Heavy-Weight Fighter*, Leicester, Midland Publishing, 1998 (pp. 7-8); Gordon, Yefim, *Mikoyan MiG-25 Foxbat: Guardian of the Soviet Borders*, Hersham, Ian Allen Publishing, 2007 (pp. 98-101).

32. Davies, Peter E. and Thornborough, Tony, *McDonell Douglas F-15 Eagle*, Ramsbury, Crowood Press, 2001 (p. 8).

33. 'U.S. Congress Could Restrict Funding for Ambitious Sixth Generation Fighter Programs,' *Military Watch Magazine*, 25 June 2020.

34. Shelbourne, Mallory, 'Navy Questions Future Viability of Super Hornets; Recommends Against New Buy,' *United States Naval Institute News*, 3 August 2021.

35. Rogoway, Tyler, 'The Air Force's Secret Next Gen Air Dominance Demonstrator Isn't What You Think It Is,' *The Drive*, 21 September 2020.

36. Trevithick, Joseph, 'Air Force Generals Aren't "Losing Sleep" Over China's J-20 Stealth Fighter,' *The Drive*, 23 September 2022.

37. Tirpak, John A., 'Piecing Together the NGAD Puzzle,' *Air and Space Forces*, 29 April 2022.

38. Trevithick, Joseph, 'Air Force Generals Aren't "Losing Sleep" Over China's J-20 Stealth Fighter,' *The Drive*, 23 September 2022.

39. 'NGAD: USAF's sixth generation fighter is on schedule, acquisition official says,' *Aerospace Manufacturing*, 11 October 2021.

40. Tirpak, John A., 'Kelly Worries F-35 Flying Costs Won't Hit Target, and That China May Get NGAD First,' *Air Force Magazine*, 26 February 2021.

41. 'NGAD: USAF's sixth generation fighter is on schedule, acquisition official says,' *Aerospace Manufacturing*, 11 October 2021.

42. Altman, Howard, 'Air Force's Next Generation Air Dominance "Fighter" Program Enters New Stage,' *The Drive*, 2 June 2022.

43. Dubois, Gaston, 'Northrop Grumman drops out of USAF sixth-generation fighter competition,' *Aviacionline*, 27 July 2023.

44. Altman, Howard, 'Air Force's Next Generation Air Dominance "Fighter" Program Enters New Stage,' *The Drive*, 2 June 2022.

45. Insinna, Valerie and Losey, Stephen, 'US Air Force bails on Mattis-era fighter jet readiness goal,' *Defense News*, 8 May 2020.

46. Insinna, Valierie, 'Pentagon inspector general has questions about the Air Force's sixth-gen fighter,' *Breaking Defense*, 27 September 2022.

47. Insinna, Valierie, 'China "on track" for 6th-gen fighter, US Air Force needs to get there first: ACC chief,' *Breaking Defense*, 26 September 2022.

48. Tirpak, John A., 'Kendall Dispenses with Roper's Quick NGAD Rhythm; System is Too Complex,' *Air and Space Forces*, 24 June 2022.

49. 'NGAD To Cost "Multiple Hundreds of Millions" Each,' *Aviation Week*, 27 April 2022.

50. Losey, Stephen, 'Air Force would cut 150 aircraft, including A-10s, buy fewer F-35s in 2023 budget,' *Defense News*, 28 March 2022; Trevithick, Joseph, 'F-15E Strike Eagle Fleet To Be Slashed By Over Half: Report,' *The Drive*, 16 March 2023.

51. 'Here's How the F/A-18 Super Hornet Will Be Able to Fight Against J-20 and Su-57 Stealth Fighters,' *The Aviation Geek Club*, 26 October 2017.

52. Newdick, Thomas and Rogoway, Tyler, 'The F-22 Raptor Could Finally Get the Infrared Sensor It Was Originally Promised,' *The Drive*, 13 January 2022; Hunter, Jamie, 'F-22 Raptor Being Readied For AIM-260 Missile By "Green Bats" Testers,' *The Drive*, 11 August 2022.

53. *Ibid.*

54. *Ibid.*

55. Pickrell, Ryan, 'A US F-22 Raptor pilot describes the challenge of going up against F-35 red air aggressors,' *Business Insider*, 30 August 2021.

56. 'Dogfights of the Future,' IMDB, Dogfights, Season 2, Episode 18, 22 May 2008.

57. Helfrich, Emma, 'F-35 Will Get New Radar Under Massive Upgrade Initiative,' *The Drive*, 3 January 2023.

58. Venable, John, '9 reasons why the F-35 needs a new engine,' *Breaking Defense*, 1 November 2022.

59. Cone, Allen, 'Lockheed's Sidekick adds increased firepower to F-35 fighters,' *Lockheed Martin*, 3 May 2019.

60. Helfrich, Emma, 'New Electronic Warfare Suite Top Feature Of F-35 Block 4, Air Combat Boss Says,' *The Drive*, 9 March 2023.

61. 'Aerospace Nation: Gen Kenneth S. Wilsbach,' *Mitchell Institute for Aerospace Studies* (YouTube Channel), 15 March 2022; Waldron, Greg, 'E-3 insufficient for timely detection of J-20: Pacific Air Forces chief,' *Flight Global*, 17 March 2022.

62. Tirpak, John A., 'USAF Selects Boeing's E-7A Wedgetail as Successor to AWACS,' *Air & Space Forces*, 28 February 2023.

63. Axe, David, 'New Chinese Missile has USAF Spooked,' *Real Clear Defense*, 24 September 2015.

64. Trimble, Steve, 'The Weekly Debrief: Does Raytheon's New AIM-120D3 Beat China's Best Missile?' *Aviation Week*, 25 July 2022; Tirpak, John A., 'Piecing Together the NGAD Puzzle,' *Air and Space Forces*, 29 April 2022.

65. Trimble, Steve, 'The Weekly Debrief: Does Raytheon's New AIM-120D3 Beat China's Best Missile?' *Aviation Week*, 25 July 2022; 'US Air Force, Raytheon Missiles & Defense execute first live-fire test of AMRAAM F3R,' *Raytheon Missiles and Defense*, 18 July 2022.

66. 'Taiwan seeks advanced U.S. jet fighters,' *RIAN*, 26 March 2009.

67. 'Taiwan plans to request F-35s from US,' *Taipei Times*, 20 September 2011.

68. Gady, Franz-Stefan, 'Taiwan Pushes for Sale of F-35 Fighter Jets,' *The Diplomat*, 3 May 2017.

69. Gould, Joe, 'Give Taiwan the F-35 to deter China, top senators tell Trump,' *Defense News*, 26 March 2018.

70. 'Taiwan told to boost training for pilots amid F-35 sale doubt,' *Asia Times*, 17 April 2018; 'How Taiwanese Veteran Pilots Defected to China With Their American Jets,' *Military Watch Magazine*, 8 May 2021.

71. 'Decision on F-16 fighter jet replacement likely in next few months: Ng Eng Hen,' *Straits Times*, 30 June 2018; Cenciotti, David, 'AIR FORCE: "If We Don't Keep The F-22 Raptor Viable, The F-35 Fleet Will Be Irrelevant",' *Business Insider*, 4 February 2014.

72. 'U.S Air Force struggles with aging fleet,' *USA Today*, 4 November 2012.

73. 'Taiwan's $124 Million F-16s to Arrive a Year Late: U.S. Faces No Penalties,' *Military Watch Magazine*, 6 May 2023.

74. Thompson, Drew, 'Hope on the Horizon: Taiwan's Radical New Defense Concept,' *War on the Rocks*, 2 October 2018; Axe, David, 'Taiwan Might Experience Buyers Remorse Over the F-16 Fighter,' *National Interest*, 29 January 2022.

75. Ait, Abraham, 'F-16延遲交貨 戰力受質疑' ('Delivery of F-16s Delayed, Combat Capacity Questioned'), *China Times*, 6 May 2023.

76. 'F-16V funding bill passes initial review,' *Taipei Times*, 24 September 2019.

77. Suciu, Peter, 'Could India Get F-35s and F-21 Fighters? Not if China and Russia Have Their Way,' *National Interest*, 15 April 2021; Trevithick, Joseph, 'Lockheed Martin Deletes Claim That Its Rebranded F-21 Could Be A Path To Indian F-35s,' *The Drive*, 20 February 2019.

78. 'Japan to build stealth fighter jets by 2014,' *Air Force Times*, 10 December 2007.
79. 'Russia and India Discussing License Production of Fifth Generation Fighters at Aero India 2023: Su-57 to Follow Su-30MKI's Path?' *Military Watch Magazine*, 16 February 2023.
80. Simha, Rakesh Krishnan, 'Why India needs to fast track the PAK-FA,' *Russia Beyond*, 10 June 2016.
81. 'China stealth fighter copied parts from downed US jet",' *BBC News*, 24 January 2011; Cenciotti, David, 'Is the Chengdu J-20 an F-22/YF-23/Mig-31 hybrid?' *The Aviationist*, 5 January 2011; 'Did The J-20 Come From This MiG?' *Military.com*, 19 August 2011; Eaton, Kit, 'China's Stealth Fighter Flies, But Does it Work By Ripping Off U.S. Tech?' *Fast Company*, 11 January 2011.
82. Allison, Graham, 'America second? Yes, and China's lead is only growing,' *Boston Globe*, 22 May 2017.
83. Golan, John W., *Lavi: The United States, Israel, and a Controversial Fighter Jet*, Sterling, Potomac Books, 2016 (pp. 33-43).
84. *Ibid* (pp. 134, 191-192).
87. McGill, Earl J., *Black Tuesday Over Namsi: B-29s vs MiGs – The Forgotten Air Battle of the Korean War*, Solihull, Helion & Company, 2012 (Chapter 4: The Machinery of War).
85. Stone, I.F., *Hidden History of the Korean War*, Boston, Little, Brown and Company, 1988 (p. 342).
86. *Ibid* (p. 342).
87. Department of the Air Force Presentation to the House Armed Services Committee Subcommittee on Air and Land Forces, United States House of Representatives, Subject: Air Force Programs, Combined Statement of: Lieutenant General Daniel J. Darnell, Air Force Deputy Chief Of Staff For Air, Space and Information Operations, Plans And Requirements (AF/A3/5), Lieutenant General Mark D. Shackelford, Military Deputy, Office of the Assistant Secretary of the Air Force for Acquisition (SAF/AQ), [and] Lieutenant General Raymond E. Johns, Jr., Air Force Deputy Chief of Staff for Strategic Plans And Programs (AF/A8), 20 May 2009 (pp. 7, 8).
88. Tirpak, John A., 'Raptor 01,' *Air Force Magazine*, July 1997 (p. 48).
89. Axe, David, 'China's Over-Hyped Stealth Jet,' *The Diplomat*, 7 January 2011.

Index